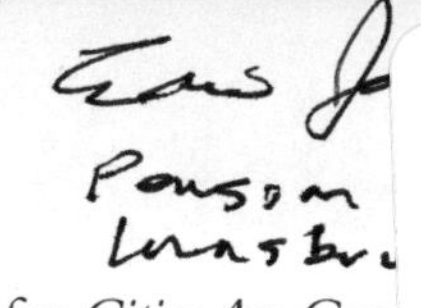

Praise for *Cities Are Good*

'A beautifully written and highly readable declaration of the potential for human salvation through the city' Danny Dorling, author of *All That Is Solid*

'A dizzying global tour of the modern metropolis . . . there's a persuasive energy to this optimistic celebration' *Metro*

'A surprisingly positive perspective on urban living' *Traveller*

'Hollis aims to set the record straight on the places where more than half the world's population now lives. He does so with gusto . . . An intriguing book' *The Times*

'To describe such a meticulously researched work as a 'labour of love' seems inadequate. The author presents a compelling case for the benefits of city living' *Port*

'A good read, popular without being condescending, for students of the modern city and the metropolises of the future' *Kirkus Reviews*

'Hollis reminds us that it is not gadgetry, nor design, that really makes a city . . . That's a thought about our urban environs profound enough to keep the mental gears turning for the rest of the summer and far beyond' *NPR.org*

'Hollis has done his reading . . . The research he cites teems with quirky surprises' *Toronto Star*

'Combining a wealth of info on cities the world over with anecdote and experience, Hollis's fascinating book touts the theory that our path to salvation is the city itself' *Fabric*

'A tour de force of the 21st century metropolis . . . A persuasive defence of the city and, as there is no escape from it, a call to make it good for us' *Deccan Herald*

'Beautifully written and absorbing . . . This is an inspiring, richly illustrated, and thoroughly enjoyable read' *Good Book Guide*

'A useful counterpoint to those who would argue that the big bad city is to be escaped at all costs' *Observer*

BY THE SAME AUTHOR

The Phoenix: The Men Who Made Modern London
The Stones of London: A History in Twelve Buildings

CITIES ARE GOOD FOR YOU

The Genius of the Metropolis

LEO HOLLIS

B L O O M S B U R Y

LONDON • NEW DELHI • NEW YORK • SYDNEY

First published in Great Britain 2013
This paperback edition published 2014

Bloomsbury Publishing, London, New Delhi, New York and Sydney
50 Bedford Square, London WC1B 3DP

www.bloomsbury.com

Bloomsbury is a trademark of Bloomsbury Publishing Plc

A CIP catalogue record for this book is available from the British Library

ISBN 978 1 4088 4348 2

10 9 8 7 6 5 4 3 2 1

Typeset by Hewer Text UK Ltd, Edinburgh

Printed and bound in Great Britain by CPI Group (UK) Ltd, Croydon, CR0 4YY

To Louis and Theadora

CONTENTS

Preface

ON THE HIGH LINE

I start at street level and the elevator raises me at a steady pace into the air. I begin to see the city from a new perspective as the pavement recedes below me. There is something thrilling about being able to look down on the city, no longer part of the throng, above the bustle and fug of the traffic, even if only from this height. Manhattan is a place that has been transformed by verticality; one feels it even going the small distance from the ground at West 14th Street up to the High Line, 25 feet above the Meatpacking District. As the elevator door opens, one leaves the underworld of the everyday city and enters another urban realm.

The High Line Park was first imagined in 1999 when two local residents, Joshua David and Robert Hammond, dreamed of transforming the derelict elevated railway line that ran through their neighbourhood in west-side Manhattan. By this time, the old industrial wasteland had turned into a wilderness of grasses and weeds, a blight on the landscape resulting in the local landlords calling for its destruction. The two set up Friends of the High Line despite Mayor Giuliani signing demolition papers for the rusting ruin. By 2002, the city had changed its mind; three years later, the line was handed over to City Hall and architects started to think about how to transform it into a living part of the community.

The landscape architects James Corner Field Operations became the lead team in devising the plans, with designs to turn a mile of the old rail line into a linear garden 25 feet above pavement level. The work was begun in April 2006 and continued until 9 June 2009 when the first section running along the Hudson River from Gansevoort Street to West 20th Street was opened to the public. Section Two, which runs from 20th Street through West Chelsea to 30th Street, was finished two years later in June 2011. Plans are in place to complete the final section of the line that will end near the Javits Center close by 34th Street. Since spring 2012 a public-arts programme has been underway, with a regular series of billboard projects as well as performances.

I am not alone; there is constant movement as the High Line has become one of the most popular sites for both visitors and New Yorkers. The rail line runs south to north and clusters of pedestrians are interweaving, following the flow in both directions. The pace is slower than on the street below; this is somewhere to saunter rather than sprint, a reminder that the city is not just one thing – a place of velocity, work, stress – but has many qualities that are too often forgotten or overlooked.

The city is vast enough to offer up its own image for every user. Thus for an economist it is a money machine; for a geographer, it is a social, topographical ecosystem; for an urban planner, it is a problem that needs to be rationalised; for a politician, an intermeshed weave of power; for an architect, it is the place where flesh meets stone; for an immigrant it is the hope of home and getting one foot on the ladder; for a banker it is a node within a vast network of global trading markets; for a free runner it is an assault course to be conquered. The city is too complicated for a solitary definition,

Walking on the High Line

and perhaps it is one of our greatest mistakes to think of it as a singular, measurable quality. Rather than looking for a single explanation, or a unique function, we must consider it as the interaction of different, albeit defined, parts.

It is places like the High Line that allow us to think again about the city and how it can make us happy. Throughout history, critics have warned against the city's destructive power. The atomising effect of urban life has been a charge levelled by naysayers since the time of the very first city. Out of the ruins of ancient Babylon, an excavated tablet reveals what is perhaps the first anti-urban rebuke:

> The city dweller, though he be a prince, can never eat enough
> He is despised and slandered in the talk of his own people
> How is he to match his strength with him who takes the field?[1]

The city has long been considered the destroyer of men and, worse, their souls. Literature is littered with stories of the virtuous traveller brought low by its temptations. When Dante wrote of Hell, he had Renaissance Florence in mind. The romantic philosopher Jean-Jacques Rousseau saw the city not as a place of liberty but rather 'a pit where almost the whole nation will lose its manners, its laws, its courage and its freedom'.[2]

Later, many would agree with Henry Ford, who believed that 'we shall solve the city by leaving the city. Get the people into the countryside, get them into communities where a man knows his neighbours ... there is nothing to do but abandon the course that gives rise to them'.[3] Ford may have known something about selling cars but his view on the city, like his dictum on history, is bunk. Much is often made of what is lost as one enters the city; less is spoken of what is gained.

Sitting on a bench, taking a respite, one can see clearly how the many parts of the city come together and intermingle just as the flowers and shrubs bud and blossom in the well-tended beds that snake through the subtly designed concrete floor of the structure. The eye is drawn to many distractions, but perhaps most interesting of all is the other people who are also here. The city is a place where strangers come together, and at times like this it is possible to think that the metropolis is perhaps our greatest achievement.

Considering the genius of the metropolis is not a straightforward task. It is so easy to overlook the evidence in front of us. For centuries we have been taught that the city was bad for us, that it was the drain of our humanity, that it destroyed the old ways and traditions, split families and offered little in exchange but disorder, dirt and noise. It is this negative reading of the city that has affected policy, literature and architecture, sometimes to disastrous effect.

Today, we face a new set of challenges even more complex and pressing than ever before: climate change, unprecedented migration, the depletion of limited resources and a widely perceived decline in the civic values that hold our societies together. The consequences of a failure to acknowledge these problems are profound. Humanity stands at a tipping point between disaster and survival, and the city is the fulcrum upon which our future balances. In 2007 the UN announced that for the first time in human history 50 per cent of the world's population lived in cities: 3,303,992,253, as compared to a rural population of 3,303,866,404. This number is rising at a rate of 180,000 every day; by 2050, it is projected that 75 per cent of the world's population will live in cities.

We are now an urban species. In the developed world, we have become used to this reality, but elsewhere, in Africa, Asia, Latin America, these urban quakes are being felt for the first time. We are in the midst of the last great human migration in history: in the next five years it is predicted, for instance, that Yamoussoukro, Côte d'Ivoire, will grow 43.8 per cent; and Jinjiang in China by 25.9 per cent. By contrast London will only expand 0.7 per cent and Tokyo, currently the largest city in the world, 1 per cent. As I write, 150–200 million Chinese people are moving between the village and the city – the equivalent of twenty Londons or six Tokyos. The contemporary city is not what we have assumed and is about to change once again.

This book is a rallying call for the reclamation of the city from the grumbles of the sceptical and the stuck-in-the-mud naysayers. I believe that cities are good for us, and may just be the best means to ensure our survival. As I will show in the following chapters, we have often misread the city and this has informed the way we have designed, planned and policed it. Often the aspects of the urban personality that have most disconcerted us are actually the signals of the most vitality. As a result, the best parts of our home have been stifled and replaced by an idea of the city that has discouraged community, complexity and creativity.

By exploring the latest ideas, observations and innovations, I want to develop a new argument for urbanism, to rewrite the story of the past, and provide new hope for the future. The book will travel to a number of places around the globe to look at the many different faces of the city; it also delves into the past to search for continuities and characteristics that help us understand the contemporary. I shall show that the city has a personality that is often ignored: that the city is not a rational, ordered place but a complex space that has more in common with natural organisms such as beehives or ant colonies.

This observation has profound implications for how the city works. If the city is a complex place then it expresses certain characteristics that are commonly under-appreciated and have an impact on the ways we look at the political structure of the community. It also allows us to reassess the city as a built environment and as a creative place. Does the way we build the city have an influence on the way we behave? Can we create places that allow us to have good ideas? In particular, I will look at how building community and the question of trust are central to the idea of the happy city.

Yet, even standing on the High Line and looking along the streets that radiate outwards, one must acknowledge that the city is a place of extremes, inequality and injustice. It is a place that attracts the super-rich who want to consume the finest things the metropolis can offer, and the very poor who struggle to stay alive. In the coming decades the slums of the world are set to become the fastest-growing regions; these are often places of desperation, without resources, water and security as well as the precariousness of the informal economy. The metropolis is also the place on the front line of the climate-change debate. Cities take more than 2 per cent of the earth's surface but use at least 80 per cent of all energy. If we cannot make our cities more sustainable, they could easily become our coffin rather than our ark.

Most importantly, as I watch the people walking up and down the High Line, sitting and chatting on benches, taking off their shoes and dipping their feet into the shallow pools, young toddlers giggling as they splash about until their clothes are soaked, I am reminded how cities can affect us, individually and as a group – and perhaps even make us better people.

It is time to think again about the city, before it is too late.

1
WHAT IS A CITY?

Close your eyes and imagine a place where you feel most happy. How often is this an urban scene? When considering where it is most healthy to raise your children, do you instantly picture a rural idyll, and the pleasures of a life conducted around the village school gates? Returning, as most of us do, to the reality of city life, are the frustrations of the packed train carriage on your rushed commute to work always balanced by the proximity to art galleries, good cinemas and gourmet food shops? And what of that particular loneliness that comes from walking the city by oneself? Sometimes it feels liberating, but how far away is the threat of danger, of becoming lost, of losing one's sense of self?

I was born in London and by the age of ten I was travelling around the city by bus on my own, exploring the places beyond my neighbourhood, realising that the metropolis was far larger and more diverse than anything I could imagine. Broader than the limits of my childish comprehension, London became the definition of the world itself. And when I later moved to the countryside during my teenage years, the magnetic allure of the now far-off capital become more powerful. It was only after my university studies that I returned to the city for good and started out hoping to find a place called home.

Today, the city is the place where I live but also who I am. London is now a part of my identity, twisting through my DNA like an invisible third spiral of a helix. When I first returned to the city, I began walking around to find out more about the nearby neighbourhoods where I had now moved and then later, as my confidence grew, I ventured further afield. Walking in the city offers particular joys, and a uniquely human scale, and pace, to one's understanding of it. Crossing from east to west, I would spend the weekend uncovering the stories of the past, first weaving together the historical narratives found in the monuments and architectural wonders; then finding other stories, less well known, that offered new perspectives. Finally, I could construct my own stories as I navigated streets and quarters that were now familiar yet still able to reveal themselves in unexpected ways.

Walking in London led me to think about the people who once were there, and what they left behind. The metropolis I was exploring was an example of the greatest social experiment in human history. People had been making their homes beside the Thames for almost 2,000 years. The study of the past nonetheless forced me to look at the contemporary city in the hope of understanding how it worked, where its genius might lie. I soon found that history alone did not answer the question and that I needed to look at the city in a number of new, different ways, reaching far beyond the archives or library. In addition I found that as I looked around the city, it also changed me.

The anatomy of the city itself is one of the most misunderstood questions of our times. Over the previous centuries, thinkers, architects, scientists and politicians have come up with their own definitions of what is a city. For many, the DNA of the city can be found in its moment of creation and it is through looking at how the first cities were formed that reveals the essential urban characteristics. For others, the city is a physical place and should be measured by its size, volume or shape. Yet, beyond the traditional definitions, perhaps there is a more dynamic way of describing the metropolis. As we face the largest migration in history, in which billions from the countryside will move to the city in the next decades, as well as the innovations in technology that allow us to view and collect more data than ever about the urban world, are we about to change the way we think about the metropolis once more?

Take, for example, two cities, in many ways the opposite of each other: Barcelona in Spain and Houston, Texas. One is an ancient city that has been transformed in the last forty years after decades of neglect; the other is a new metropolis, the fastest-growing conurbation – or network of urban communities – in America. The contrast shows us how difficult it is to define what a city is today, what can make it successful, how we can learn, plan and improve the urban places around us.

In the 1970s Barcelona was in desperate straits following the end of the Franco dictatorship: the ancient city centre had been allowed to rot while suburbs ranged in all directions without planning. The new socialist mayor Pasqual Maragall, elected in 1982, was determined to restore life to the city yet he was restricted on all sides. The medieval core of Barcelona had to be preserved, while the sea to the south and the mountains to the north-east meant that there was little room for expansion; the new city had to be created out of the old, and after winning the right to hold the 1992 Olympic Games a wholesale renovation was heralded under the guidance of urban planner Joan Busquets.

Busquets believed that rather than imposing a bold new vision on the city, the plans should reinforce Barcelona's existing qualities: as a dense environment, the city should become more dense, and the city centre should become a place that people would want to come to. In effect, Barcelona was forced to shrink in order to become more vital. Much emphasis was put on to regenerating the public and cultural spaces of the city, in particular Las Ramblas, the long spinal thoroughfare that runs from the Gothic quarter to the nineteenth-century Plaça de Catalunya. For a long time this was considered a dangerous, seedy place to avoid but redesigns, pedestrianisation and regular kiosks transformed it into an area that is loved by visitors and locals alike. Barcelona today is one of the most exciting destinations in Europe; its regeneration is a model that has been adopted by many other cities as the template of how to turn a metropolis around.

Houston, Texas, on the other hand, is so successful that it is expanding outwards in all directions; in the last decade over 1 million people have migrated there and have found a new home amongst the 2,000 square miles of sprawl that surround the city. This is an example of sun-belt migration, the middle-class exodus from the north to the warmer south, that is changing America. The movement to Houston alone will represent 80 per cent of the population shift in the US between 2000 and 2030, doubling the city size from 2.1 million to 5 million. Why are so many people moving there?

As Harvard economist Ed Glaeser calculates, while the average middle-class family might earn less than in Manhattan or the Bay Area, the quality of life is much higher in Houston: house prices are cheaper, tax is lower, schools and infrastructure are good, the daily commute is not too arduous. In the end Texans are a surprising 58 per cent better off than New Yorkers, and live in quiet suburban communities with low crime rates, little interference and consistent climate. What is not to like about this scenario? For many it is the definition of a perfect life. As a result Houston will continue to grow, despite the economic downturn.

Both Barcelona and Houston raise questions about the city: will the megapolis grow so vast that it loses its centre, continue to expand without end, making it impossible to see the border between city, suburb, exurb or townscape? Will this endless expansion force us to rethink what a city is? In contrast, Barcelona, heading in the opposite direction, has gained much in return: it is a city for people, filled with inclusive spaces that attract all types of visitors. But how long can it continue with this level of density? Is growth inevitable and what is the social cost of such change?

In order to answer these questions, we need to go back to the origins of what a city is, and how it works.

Why did people ever come together in the first place? We know a surprising amount about the history of cities; it was in the city, after all, that writing and accounting were first invented. Its dimensions have been measured since *The Epic of Gilgamesh* and since the biblical moment when Joshua circled Jericho seven times in seven days carrying the Ark of the Covenant. But the origins of the first cities are less well known.

The first moment of urban creation is often shrouded in myth. In the biblical tradition, the metropolis was invented by Cain, the murderer, and as a result, according to St Augustine in *The City of God*, the city of man was for ever cursed by the mark of fratricide. Myths linger over the foundation of other cities: Rome was founded by Romulus who slew his brother Remus, mirroring the biblical story; London was discovered by Brutus, ancient ancestor of Trojan Aeneas, who was sent to Britain by the goddess Diana.

Even in more modern times, the power of the foundation myth is strong. In 2003 the British origins of Calcutta, renamed Kolkata in 2001, were challenged in court and a judge was asked to adjudicate on whether the Indian port had been founded by the East

India Company or had, as suggested by the plaintiffs, been a more ancient community as proved by the discovery of archaeological finds at Chandraketugarh nearby. Origins matter.

These legends hide the practicalities of human life. Almost every world city, however, is in fact defined not by its founding kings and mischievous gods but by geography, circumstance and convenience, either as a redoubt against enemies or an advantageous crossing point along trade routes; and in both cases close to sustaining resources. Rome was founded as a natural defence protected by seven hills; London was the most easterly point on the River Thames that could be crossed safely as the Romans arrived from the south coast; Paris, Lagos and Mexico City were all founded on islands protected by the waters surrounding them; Sana'a, the capital of the Yemen, Damascus, Xi'an, one of the four ancient cities of China, despite their inhospitable surroundings, were all born as important staging posts on prosperous caravan routes. The foundation myths also hide another truth: that the first city emerged from a sudden shocking moment in time – the first urban revolution.

Damascus is considered the oldest inhabited city, with a history that stretches to the second millennium BCE; founded by Uz, son of Aram. It has been the home to Arameans and Assyrians, conquered by Alexander the Great and then the Romans, the Caliphate, the Mongols and the Mamluks, and later assumed by the Ottoman Empire; finally to be 'liberated' by T. E. Lawrence in 1918. Today, once again, the city is on the verge of collapse or a new era. Yet 1,000 years before Damascus was even founded, Uruk, the first city, situated in the deserts of southern Iraq and home to Gilgamesh, already had a population of over 50,000, protected by walls that enclosed an area of 6 square kilometres; now those once great fortifications lie in dust. But where did such settlements come from, if not from myth?

There is no more powerful image of the city than its relationship

CORBIS

The ruins of Uruk, all that is left of the first city

with the countryside that surrounds it. This Manichean division between the rural and the urban has shadowed history from the first laments of *The Epic of Gilgamesh*. We have been taught that the metropolis grew out of the countryside parasitically – the farm became a village, then a town and finally a city. This sequence of events has haunted our impression of the city as a place that leeches blood from the surrounding countryside, draining the life from the nation. The first person to propose this sequence of events was not, however, a Sumerian chronicler, nor a classical philosopher, but the eighteenth-century economist Adam Smith, and few since have challenged his assertion.

But what if – contrary to Smith – the city invented the countryside? Evidence of subsistence farming dates back 9,000 years, long before the first cities, though this does not necessarily explain the rise of the first cities such as Uruk, Jericho, Ji (Beijing), Anatolian Çatalhöyük, Syrian Tell Brak, Mohenjo-daro in modern-day Pakistan, or Teotihuacan, Mexico. We have to rethink our assumptions about the incremental development of cities emerging slowly from smaller settlements, for the birth of the metropolis was anything but gradual. Indeed, rather than emerging out of countryside, the first cities arose despite their surroundings.

As in Uruk, and other early settlements in Mesopotamia, archaeological evidence of the first cities of the Harappan civilisation in the Indus Valley, Pakistan, reveals that a revolution occurred at some point in the third millennium BCE. Within less than 300 years a rural community was transformed into an urban power. Archaeologists chart this momentous shift by the sudden emergence of systems of writing, weights and measures; there are also signs of organised town planning and public architecture: ditches, sewers, grids, as well as the development of a distinct style of pottery that suggests a specialisation of skilled labour and a market for goods beyond the basic needs of subsistence.

From these moments of the first urban revolution, cities became something different. The city was born out of trade and developed agricultural sciences such as irrigation and crop selection to support this exchange. Astronomy was developed in order to predict the seasons and support these trading communities. It was the innovations of the city that produced a surplus to feed the citizens who did not work the soil. Urban technology transformed subsistence farming to the extent that workers could leave the fields and work in other forms of industry. 'It was not agriculture, for all its importance, that was the salient invention, or occurrence if you will, of the Neolithic Age,' observes the urban writer Jane Jacobs. 'Rather it was the fact of sustained, interdependent, creative city economies that made possible many new kinds of work, agriculture among them.'[1]

The metropolis was also defined by its walls that acted as a fortification and a trade barrier as well as, in some cases, a measure of citizenship where belonging was bestowed on those born within. During the Italian Renaissance, the walls of the city state were elaborate and forbidding, displaying both the martial power and the commercial success of the community. Fragments of these walls can still be seen in many of the major cities of the world: from Paris to Marrakech to Beijing. Elsewhere, even when the walls have been dismantled such as in London or Florence, the road scheme still traces the ghostly outline of the old city limits.

And just as the protective walls of the city started to define urban identity, so the spaces within the city itself became divided. Cities have always been places where strangers meet to trade; and storehouses were needed to house the commodities that were exchanged. In addition to the grain, herds and precious luxuries that had been foraged, mined and harvested, the first city was a place filled with workshops where an ordinary object – a bowl, horn or hide – was worked into a desirable product. So cities became places where men who worked with their hands rather than the soil were able to trade for sustenance, exchanging goods for food.

But urban life has always been about more than just survival. As well as trade and work, the first city was also a place of ideas and knowledge. The skills of the artisans gave each neighbourhood a reputation, and in time certain quarters became renowned for their crafts, from ancient pottery to fine carving. It was in the first cities that writing was formulated; initially as a means of accounting, recording property rights and the transactions between traders; then charting the night skies, reading the fortunes of the city in the constellations. Later, writing was used to remember the stories that established the first settlements in myth.

Thus the city was born from a moment of revolution that changed the way people came together and organised themselves. But what did this new social order look like?

The true identity of the city has no single explanation. The historical origins of the metropolis offer some insights into how the city was formed and why, but this does not necessarily tell us how the many parts come together, and what dynamic characteristics make the city so different from everything else. Anyone reading Marco Polo's description of Cambaluc (Beijing), the great capital of the Khan, gets a sense of the elegance and majesty of the Imperial city, the impressive dimension of the streets and the power of the wealthy who lived behind the palace walls:

> It is 24 square miles, since each side is 6 miles long. It is walled around with walls of earth, ten paces thick at bottom, and a height of more than ten paces. There are twelve gates, and over each gate there is a great and handsome palace, so that there are on each side of the square three gates and five palaces; for there is at each angle also a great and handsome palace. In the palaces there are vast halls in which are kept the arms of the city guard.
>
> The streets are so straight and wide that you can see right along them from end to end and from one gate to the other. And up and down the city there are beautiful palaces, and many great and fine inns and fine houses in great numbers. All the plots of ground on which the houses of the city are built are four-square, and laid out with straight lines; all the plots being occupied by great and spacious palaces, with courts and gardens of proportionate size. Each square plot is surrounded by handsome streets for the traffic. Thus the whole city is arranged in squares just like a chessboard.[2]

Contrast this with a more recent description of Greenwich Village by the local author Jane Jacobs who lived in Hudson Street:

> The ballet of a good city sidewalk never repeats itself from place to place, and in any one place is always replete with new improvisations ... Mr Halpert unlocking the laundry's handcart from its moorings to a cellar door, Joe Cornacchia's son-in-law stacking out the empty crates from the delicatessen, the barber bringing out his sidewalk folding chair, Mr Goldstein arranging the coils of wire which proclaim the hardware store is open, the wife of the

Hudson Street

> tenement's supervisor depositing her chunky three-year-old with a toy mandolin on the stoop.

And so it continues: the lunchtime crowd; the early-evening games of the local teenagers, 'a time of roller skates and stilts and tricycles, and games in the lee of the stoop with bottle tops and plastic cowboys'; until the end of the day when all that was left was the muffled sounds of parties, singing, the distant siren of the police car. Something is always going on, the ballet is never at a halt, but the general effect is peaceful and the general tenor is leisurely. People who know well such animate city streets will know how it is.[3]

These are two wholly different visions of what a city is. In Marco Polo's city, the space is described as grand streets and palaces; the city is its physical form. For Jane Jacobs, there is hardly a word spent on the fabric of the cityscape, which is solely the backdrop for the human drama of urban life. So where do we find the real city: in the fabric of the place or in the bustle of the people who live there?

For centuries bustle has often been the most desperate problem of the city. In the minds of thinkers, planners and politicians, the metropolis, long considered the product of the human intellect, has been seen as a reasonable, ordered and measured place. Just as classical economists have viewed us as rational, uncomplicated movers within the market, so urban planners have hoped that straight streets and building regulations would create efficient neighbourhoods and happy, uncomplicated citizens.

It is time, however, to rethink these basic assumptions. We are not as impartial, linear, self-interested and coldly logical as the equations want us to be, and neither are the places where we live.

The city street is complexity in action. It is not something that can be explained precisely, but we know it when we see it. It is perhaps for this reason that complexity itself has been so difficult to define; one recent attempt unhelpfully stated that a complex system 'was a system made up of complex systems'.[4] But the idea has an unusual origin in the research labs in America during the Second World War, when the conflict brought together many distinguished thinkers to defeat Nazi Germany. This unexpected interaction across the disciplines would have a lasting effect on the way we look at the world; in particular, the interweaving of computing, cryptography, mathematics and missile technology to become the forcing ground of a new kind of science.

In 1948, in an article in *American Scientist*, Warren Weaver, the head of the Rockefeller Foundation, one of the leading funding bodies in the US, applauded the collaborative nature of the war effort and set out to show that both this and the rise of computing could answer a new set of questions that previously had been ignored.

To this point, he wrote, scientists had focused their attention on two types of exploration: 'simple' problems, such as the relationship between the moon and the earth, how a marble rolls down a hill, the elasticity of a spring, based on a minimal set of variables; and 'disorganised complexity', problems containing so many variables that it was impossible to calculate the individual characters: the prediction of water molecules in a flowing river; the workings of a telephone exchange or the balance sheet of a life-insurance company. There was, however, a third set of problems: organised complexity. Weaver summed up this new field:

> What makes an evening primrose open when it does? Why does salt water fail to satisfy thirst? ... On what does the price of wheat depend? ... How can currency be wisely and effectively stabilised? To what extent is it safe to depend on the free interplay of such economic forces as supply and demand? ... How can one explain the behaviour

> patterns of an organised group of persons such as a labour union, or a group of manufacturers, or a racial minority? There are clearly many factors involved here, but it is equally obvious that here also something more is needed than the mathematics of averages.[5]

It needed a man of Warren's invention (and obsession) to think about life in a different way, and his 1948 paper defined a new path for finding patterns and order within the disorderly. Asking whether one could make connections between a virus, the gene, the rise and fall in the price of wheat, and the behaviour of groups, Weaver answered his own question: 'They are all problems which involve dealing simultaneously with a sizeable number of factors which are interrelated into an organic whole. They are all, in the language here proposed, problems of organised complexity.'[6]

Just as Jacobs would later observe on the Manhattan streets, Weaver proposed that under the chaotic surface, an unsighted order or pattern could be found, and that it would take a new kind of science to reduce these strange rhythms into equations. Rather than looking at individual bodies, scientists should study the connections between things, how they related and interacted. Thus he suggested that the world was made up of systems, groups of linked individuals who had a powerful impact on each other. The art of Complexity Theory, therefore, was to work out the original forms of the system and to calculate the particular dynamic that transformed them.

Weaver's work set out the template of the science of self-organised systems; in time, the ideas opened new avenues of enquiry in biology, technology, physics, cybernetics and chemistry. His fascination with systems became the language expressed in E. O. Wilson's groundbreaking study of anthills and the development of his socio-biological ideas of the super-organism. Complexity

Theory became central to the development of the packet-switch method that underpins the internet. The theory has also been the driving force behind the Black-Scholes algorithm that raised Long-Term Capital Management to the peaks of financial success in the 1990s, and its eventual collapse in 2000; as well as James Lovelock's theory of the earth as a self-organised structure, Gaia. It has even been used to study the power of social networks as well as an exciting new means to map the brain.

Jane Jacobs was one of the first people to connect the ideas of complexity and the city. She was not an academic, nor an architect, planner or public official; however, her insights into how the city worked, her almost instinctive belief in the complexity of the streets, had far-reaching effects on how cities are made today. In her most famous work, *The Death and Life of Great American Cities*, she set out her rallying cry for complex spaces:

> Under the seeming disorder of the old city, wherever the old city is working successfully, is a marvellous order for maintaining the safety of the streets and the freedom of the city. It is a complex order . . . This order is all composed of movement and change, and although it is life, not art, we may fancifully call it the art of the city and liken it to the dance.[7]

Jacobs called this dance the Ballet of Hudson Street, after her own corner of Greenwich Village. In contradiction of the traditional view of cities as grand boulevards and ordered squares, Jacobs proffers the chaotic streetscape as the genome of the metropolis. The city is a collection of complex spaces, not rational, cold places. This intricate streetscape is perhaps the most important, and forgotten, definition of what is a city, and it is here, in the interactions of the people living their ordinary lives, going about their business and enjoying the variety of the neighbourhood, that the genius of the metropolis can be found. If planners and architects were to pay more attention to the unusual ways that complexity works, and to think more about the life of the street rather than only seeing the empty spaces between buildings, our cities could be very different, perhaps even happier, places.

But the problem with complexity is that it is unpredictable; like an organism, it evolves in unexpected ways. So if we were to put a city into the laboratory what would it look like? The Dutch architect Rem Koolhaas holds many radical opinions on the city. Evolving from his time as a professor in practise of architecture and design at the Graduate School of Design, Harvard, Koolhaas and his team proposed the idea of the programmable city, called the Roman City Operating System (R/OS). As Weaver sets out in his first explorations, a complex system starts with a surprisingly simple collection of things, and thus Koolhaas strips the city to its basic components, 'standardised parts arranged on a matrix'.[8] These initial parts are based on the building blocks of Rome, the ancient city first developed beside the Tiber but which was then translated across the empire and remains today the template of the western metropolis.

Koolhaas is hoping to strip the city down to its basic essentials: the places necessary for a city to thrive. But more than that he wants to show how they transform in unexpected ways once they interact. Like all complex systems, we can define the initial elements but we cannot measure accurately or predict what will happen when they come together. Thus the elements of the city – from arches, temples and aqueducts to basic rules of the grid system and Roman town planning – are divided up and placed within the city space. Once the city has been fully programmed, Koolhaas urges you to press the start button and watch as it proliferates.

From such simple parts, a complex city is quickly born. As the separate parts start to interact, intergrate, correspond and converse, new hybrid spaces are invented, places change shape and characteristics. Some neighbourhoods find an unexpected order while other enclaves live on the edge of chaos. Like a beehive, a termite mound or the petals of a flower, the city generates its own complexity, emerging from within the connections, interactions and networks.

The city is an organism; it has its own special powers; and over time the whole becomes more powerful than the sum of its parts. The complex city cannot be defined by a catalogue of its elements.

Thus to judge a city by its physical fabric alone is a mistake; this is not the genius of the metropolis. Complexity comes from our interactions: we are constantly making connections, moving from place to place, travelling into the office in the morning, making friends and holding business meetings, queuing for a service, picking the children up from school and ferrying them to sports club, or, later that night, enjoying the pleasures that urban life offers, while others clean the office, pick up the coffee mug you left on the desk, drive the subway train that finally takes you home. These connections are important; they formulate the network of the city, they are basic units of energy in the city's metabolism. As a city grows, so does the intensity of these connections.

But some connections are more important than others, and some work differently from others. Family ties and strong friendships are essential to everyone. The evolutionary thinker Robin Dunbar roughly calculates that most people sustain a close network of up to 150 social relationships. Yet looking at most people's friends list on Facebook, we have a far larger group of acquaintances, work colleagues, friends of friends. In addition there is the other group of people who we do not often consider part of our social network:

people you used to work with but have lost touch; the ex-partner of your partner's best friend; the sales agent that you see once a year at a conference; the university acquaintance who has just sent a friend's request on LinkedIn.

These loose connections are called 'weak links' and were first formulated by the American sociologist Mark Granovetter. In his groundbreaking study he explored the power of weak ties in the pursuit of finding a new job; he discovered that one was most likely to get a recommendation or a referral from a loose acquaintance rather than a close friend. Weak links, he proposed, offered connections into a wider circle of people and places than those that one sees regularly and live and work in the same places. As he states: 'Individuals with few weak ties will be deprived of information from distant parts of the social system and will be confined to the provincial news and views of their close friends. This deprivation will not only insulate them from the latest ideas and fashions but may put them in a disadvantaged position in the labour market.'[9]

It is often assumed that coming into the city from outside one expects a cold shoulder and a resentful shrug: the city excludes outsiders. Poets from Wordsworth to Baudelaire have written of the sensation of being adrift within the city, the anonymity of being in the crowd. The urban myth of the person who was found dead in their apartment long after their passing because no one was a neighbour is an oft-repeated mantra for the inhospitable nature of the city. In addition, the city is a place of such churn and movement it is almost impossible to make meaningful relationships with those around you.

And yet, although this may be an indication that the city is an increasingly atomised space where we lose the traditional connections with family and community, these are not replaced by a meal for one, sat in front of Facebook in a studio flat. Indeed, despite the fact that more and more people are living on their own these days – in New York over a third of the population live by themselves – it is hard to be lonely in the city.

The complexity of the city offers more chances of making connections than anywhere else. In 1938 the Chicago sociologist Louis Wirth published his classic essay, 'Urbanism as a Way of Life', as a result of a study of recent Jewish immigrants into the city. He discovered that city life was a threat to culture, that it undermined traditional ties and replaced them with 'impersonal, superficial, transitory and segmental [relationships]. The reserve, the indifference and the blasé outlook which urbanists manifest in their relationships may thus be regarded as devices for immunising themselves against the personal claims and expectations of others.'

But it is precisely these 'impersonal, superficial, transitory' relationships that make the city so unique and important. It is the abundance of these weak ties that brings people to the city, for it is the intensity of these informal relationships that makes the city so special – and it is these weak ties that will hold the mega-city together. In his book *Loneliness*, evolutionary psychologist John Cacioppo proposes that we are hard-wired to be together and that a sense of loneliness is a warning sign, telling us to make more connections for improved chances of survival rather than an existential condition.

As the mega-city grows around us we are going to have to adapt our connections and relationships accordingly, finding new ways of living together that benefit us all.

The city is built on weak links; it is these moments of human contact that act like electricity for the city. As a result, the city as a whole becomes more powerful than the sum of its parts and this strange phenomenon – which complexity theorists call emergence – means that the complex city offers a unique dynamism. It is also the energy behind the Ballet of Hudson Street and is the raw material from which are developed trust and community despite the strains of urban life.

This energy has a strange power that then feeds back into the fabric of the city itself, and this power is worth examining. Geoffrey West is not your normal theoretical physicist. Educated at Cambridge, he moved to the US and held a number of posts, setting up the high-energy physics group at the Los Alamos National Laboratory. It was while he was there that he become fascinated by the question of metabolism: the relationship between an animal's size, shape and how much energy it needs to keep going.

West was inspired by the world of the Swiss botanist Max Kleiber, who in the 1930s studied the relationship of body weight, size and consumption of energy of various animals from a mouse to a cat, an elephant and even a whale. What he found was unexpected, and proved that there was a direct link, a scaling law, between the size of the beast and its energy usage. It also shows that a larger animal is likely to live longer than a small one: for while most animals die at between 1–2 billion heartbeats, a chicken heart beats 300 times a minute, an elephant's only 30 times. Kleiber found a direct relationship between size and life expectation. In his research West refined Kleiber's original laws and attempted to find out why they worked.

In 2005 West was named president of the Santa Fe Institute, the mecca of study in Complexity Theory, set up in the 1980s to explore the connections between physics, mathematics, computation and evolutionary biology (the institute is so multidisciplinary that even the novelist Cormac McCarthy has a desk in the facility). There, West turned his focus on the nature of cities, perhaps the greatest self-organising organism of all; the results would gain him the honour of being named one of *Time* magazine's '100 Most Influential People in the World'.

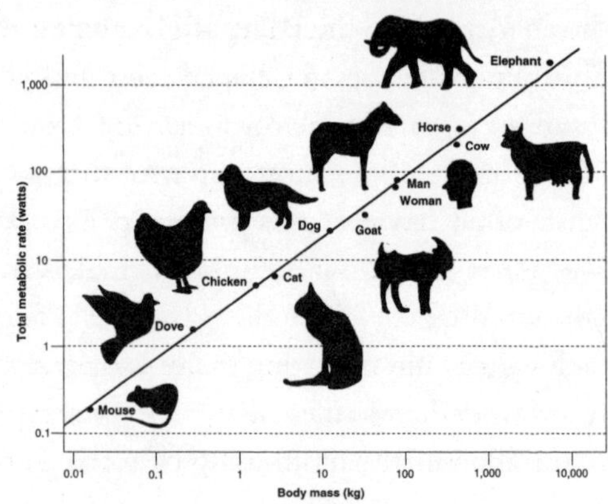

Klieber's diagram shows the relationship between size and metabolism

West studied how cities developed dynamically as they grew in size: how they changed shape and personality, how interactions intensified with increased levels of density. As he later admitted in an interview: 'We spend all this time thinking about cities in terms of their local details, their restaurants and museums and weather . . . I had this hunch that there was something more, that every city was also shaped by a set of hidden laws.'[10]

He was determined to find the rules governing the complexity of the city. Already he understood something of the nature of self-organised systems, but he gave it a twist by considering the city as an organic whole, as one might think of a beehive, or an anthill, or even an elephant.

Thus he gathered together as much data as he could – measurements of scale of urban centres in the US over 50,000 citizens; statistics on gross metropolitan product; crime figures; the amount of money made from each petrol station in all fifty-two states; patents as well as tax returns – and put them all together to find the underlying order of how the city worked. The study did not just cover American cities but also included data from the National Bureau of Statistics in China, from Eurostat, even measurements of road surfaces from across Germany. Combined, the information formed one of the most powerful data sets imagined. What West discovered, however, was even more exciting.

In a 'unified theory of urban living', West proposed, all cities are the same and all follow the same rules. Therefore, while we can see individual cities as having their own particular history and personality, underlying rules apply and prove that they have more in common with each other than not. In addition, just as the metabolism of a mouse has some connection to the metabolism of a whale, so size is the major determinant of the character of a city. In effect, tell West the population figure for any city and he can give you the basic characteristics of the place: 'I can take these laws and make precise predictions about the number of violent crimes and the surface area of roads in a city in Japan with 200,000 people. I don't know anything about this city or even where it is or its history, but I can tell you all about it.'[11]

Yet while you can calculate the urban metabolism just as you can that of an elephant, in another way cities are very different from animals. Klieber's original law of energy consumption worked on a sublinear quarter-rule, so that the metabolic rate does not correspond exactly to an increase in body size. Rather than the metabolic rate increasing by 100 per cent whenever the animal doubles in size, it follows a 'sublinear' path and increases by only 75 per cent.

The city, on the other hand, follows a similar 'superlinear' power law, so that every time it doubles in size, it increases its efficiency and energy use. West's results can be seen across the board: moving to a city that is twice the size will increase per capita income, it will also be a more creative and industrious place; as the pace of all socio-economic activity accelerates, this leads to higher productivity while economic and social activities diversify.[12] The increased complexity that comes from the agglomeration that one finds in the city, therefore, is what makes cities special.

As West said in a 2010 interview with the *New York Times*, he offers a scientific bedrock to Jane Jacobs's imaginative hunch: 'One of my favourite compliments is when people come up to me and say, "You have done what Jane Jacobs would have done, if only she could do mathematics" . . . What the data clearly shows, and what she was clever enough to anticipate, is that when people come together, they become much more productive.'[13] While Jacobs focused her attention on her own front stoop and observed life on her local street, West's superlinear power law shows how this complexity is applicable wherever people gather.

The city of the twenty-first century will not be a rational or ordered place; the world city will more likely resemble the chaotic lives of the hundreds of thousands who have just arrived and are looking for a home. It will be a dynamic place of transition and transformation, discovering for itself the underlying laws of how it works. It is perhaps only West's 'unified theory of urban living' that will survive the social, economic and political upheavals of the coming decades. This is both an exciting and disquieting possibility. Yet there are also very good reasons to be hopeful. And this hope comes from choosing to think about the people, not places, of the city: how they live, work, play and behave.

2

INSIDE THE BEEHIVE

Complexity is found on the edge of chaos and cities can be dangerous, unpredictable places. There is an odd sensation of being in a crowd, that one is no longer oneself, no longer in control, exposed to the flows and emotions of the throng around you. Throughout history there has been a fear of the mob, a word that was created in the 1680s to describe the *mobile vulgaris*: the faceless, seething mass that could rise up at any moment.

Since then, writers have revealed the madness of crowds, while others have tried to show how wise the collective can be. As Elias Canetti shows in his book *Crowds and Power*, those in charge have always looked on the mass with suspicion and fear; the crowd was something to control, break up, bring to heel by any means necessary. This sense of precariousness was brought close to home in August 2011 when riots ignited throughout London. It started like so many riots before in Britain, the US, France and elsewhere: an attack on a young black man at the hands of the authorities.

On 4 August 2011 29-year-old Mark Duggan was shot by armed police in Tottenham, north London, and the next three days were filled with rumours: that he had shot at the police first; the bullet had passed through his chest and stuck in the hand radio of the officer behind him; he had a gun down his sock; it was a replica gun; it was a real gun kept in a sock but under the passenger seat of the car. That he was a family man, a loving father of four children; that his uncle was a gangster on the Manchester drugs scene. That he was under surveillance because he was suspected of planning a revenge killing, and was acting suspiciously.

Yet no officials felt it worthwhile to tell the family that their son, husband, father had died, and on Saturday 6 August, they led a peaceful march outside Tottenham police station, hoping to obtain some answers. The protesters stood quietly outside the station all afternoon waiting for an official to explain what had happened. The riot that followed that night and for three nights afterwards was recorded, then beamed around the world.[1]

The following day, Sunday 7 August, the news began to spread, the contagion infecting the BlackBerry SMS network, Facebook and other mobile technologies. As soon as it got dark, violence erupted once more in Tottenham as well as in Brixton, Islington and even in the centre of the city at Oxford Street. On the Monday night a furniture store in Croydon was burned to the ground, the whole event captured by a hovering helicopter on BBC News24. There were stories of gangs rushing into restaurants and demanding jewellery from diners as they sat at their tables. The robbery of one foreign student was caught on webcam, giving the impression that his assailants had first approached him to see if he was all right. There was dramatic footage of metal shutters on the fronts of shops being peeled back and swarms of looters piling in.

In the aftermath of the 2011 riots, while there was much commentary on the greed and shamelessness of the young, the problems of social exclusion and unemployment, disenfranchisement and trust, there was little discussion of the role of London itself, the ways that the city works, or what happens when it doesn't.

On this occasion, not for the first time, the city turned in on itself with extraordinary violence; the complex system self-destructed. The mayor and politicians, the normal systems of control, were incapable of taking hold of the situation. Yet perhaps we should be asking why these are such uncommon scenes? If the city is as chaotic and lawless as we assume, why are there so few riots?

Consider the beehive.

Throughout history, man has been judged in contrast to the humble bee; since classical times writers, philosophers and politicians have examined the intricate goings-on of the beehive as a metaphor for human society, the intimate relationship between the metabolism of the city and the hive. In Virgil's elegy to rural life, *The Georgics*, the beehive was a model of democracy: 'all's the state's; the state provides for all'.[2] But how was the state organised? Virgil identified a hierarchy within the commune, governed by an elected male, who could be usurped if found wanting. At the lower rungs of the ladder, each individual bee was a trader, and benefited not just himself but the whole through his honest toil.

In subsequent centuries, the image of the industrious beehive was revived whenever the complexity of human interaction sought explanation. However, the metaphor was a flexible one: for Seneca, the principal bee was an unelected king. In the feudal period, the unquestioning worker bee was a paradigm for the serf or villein who had no right to improve his station in life. The English word 'bee' derives from the Dutch name for 'king' and so, in Shakespeare's *Henry V*, the bee was once more imagined as the model for a stable society, everyone happy in their place.[3]

When revolution was in the air, was the hive a kingdom or a republican commonwealth? Were the workers slaves or stakeholders? And what of the identity of the leader? It was not until improvements in scientific observation, conveniently coinciding with the reign of Elizabeth I, that writers claimed that the hive was 'an Amazonian or feminine Kingdome'.[4]

By the beginning of the eighteenth century, as the cities of the world began rapidly to expand, nurturing protean consumer markets, globalised trade and the twinkling of the Industrial Revolution, the hive became a uniquely urban metaphor. As a result, rather than stand as a symbol for a rigid, ordered hierarchy, the hive became the model for a chaotic scrum of selfishness, industry and profit. This was summed up in Bernard Mandeville's vituperative poem 'The Fable of the Bees', published in 1714.

Mandeville now portrayed the city as a swarm in which all the bees were driven by self-interest. More dangerously, he proposed that without vice – the individual pursuit of material gain – the hive collapsed. London at that time was the greatest city in the world, at the centre of an emerging empire that stretched from the cantons of Calcutta to the sugar plantations of Jamaica, with a banking culture far more advanced than any European rivals. As Mandeville walked around the city, he read the streets, dictating a scene that we recognise today – the modern capital with all its contradictions, perils and paradoxes. However, his poem celebrated the complexity: 'Thus every Part was full of Vice, / Yet the whole Mass a Paradise'.[5] The city itself was the incubator of the deadliest sins yet counterintuitively combined to create a place of virtue.

Was it trade itself that kept the city safe? Did the prospects of business regulate and pacify society? Mandeville offers a vision of the city that did not need mayors, politicians or police, for the market itself was the invisible hand that made a virtuous whole out of the self-interested parts.

Contrast this beehive with a contemporary image from the

work of the French street artist JR, who uses his large black and white flyposts to question people's assumptions about their place in society. In 2011 he was awarded the TED Prize, yet his career began when he found a camera on the Paris Métro and began to plaster around the city vast portraits of people that he knew from the *banlieus*, the forgotten estates on the periphery of Paris. The exhibition was called *Portrait of the Generation* and he was determined to use the largest gallery in the world as his canvas: the city itself.

Next, JR started a project in Israel, affixing large portraits of both Israeli and Palestinian residents upon the newly constructed concrete border wall. In 2008 he began a series of projects called *Women are Heroes* in Brazil, Kenya, India and Cambodia. In Rio de Janeiro, JR visited the oldest favela in the city: Morro da Providencia. There he photographed many of the women he met and then attached large-format portraits of their eyes to the outside of the

Morro da Providencia, Rio de Janeiro, decorated by JR's murals

slum's buildings, giving the eerie impression of the favela itself looking out over the rest of the city. For JR, this project was a reminder of the role of women at the heart of the community yet it was also a graphic manifestation of how life on the streets itself cannot be ignored.

In *The Death and Life of Great American Cities*, Jacobs shows how the street develops its own equilibrium, which she calls 'the eyes on the street': 'an intricate, almost unconscious, network of voluntary controls and standards among the people themselves, and enforced by the people themselves'.[6] On Jacobs's street these include the shopkeepers, the old woman who sometimes sits on the stoop on a warm evening and the regulars at the White Horse Bar. It is through these small meetings and contacts that an ordinary street can be transformed into a self-organising public space. Yet it often takes an artist like JR to remind us of this power, to make this invisible system that balances the everyday life of the city visible once more.

So how does the city work? Is it self-regulated like the beehive or the favela, controlled by the market or the eyes on the street? Both are examples of complexity working within the community, the power of connections as a means of ordering our everyday relationships. But the sense of precariousness never seems far away, that things will fall apart at any moment.

The city is a place of liberty, where we are free to pursue our own individual fortunes, but it is also a place that crams many different people together, threatening conflict and inequality. Today there are places in the world where the slums of the very poorest who cannot afford clean water are within yards of the palaces of the super-rich with crystal-blue swimming pools. As a result we often write the city's story in terms of the tensions between the top and the bottom, between the haves and the have-nots, the powerful and the weak. Because of this we assume that inequality is hard-wired into the city – that there has to be those who prosper and those who are desperate, that power will always be in the hands of the few who run the city from above.

This is not the way a beehive works nor is it how Jacobs's Hudson Street regulates itself, and is the result of a fundamental misunderstanding of complexity itself. Despite the importance of the queen bee, her royalty is something that we as human observers have bestowed upon her, not her followers. The beehive is in fact a completely democratic decision-making organism, as Thomas D. Seeley explains: 'The queen lies at the heart of the whole operation . . . it is also true that thousands of attentive daughters (workers) are all ultimately striving to promote her survival and reproduction. Nevertheless, a colony's queen is not the royal decider . . . indeed there is no all-knowing central planner . . . the work of a hive is instead governed collectively by the workers themselves.'[7]

Every complex system – an anthill, beehive or city – is built up from the inside: generated rather than fabricated. In other words, a complex city is created from the bottom up rather than the top down. Thus, although we assume that because the city walls were commissioned by kings and because the political power of the metropolis is enshrined in the stones of the palace, cathedral, banks and parliament, this is where power flows from, think again; it is not that simple. Power emerges and is regulated from the bottom up and can be found in the places where the most people are. The energy of Jacobs's Hudson Street is, as we have seen, the electricity that drives the city. It is this energy – the life of the street itself – that is the true measure of the vitality of the metropolis.

Yet cities have mayors who claim to have the power of the city in their hands. What is the nature of this relationship between the political muscle of the men in suits, and the quieter self-regulation of the eyes on the streets? We need mayors but we need vibrant streets as well. City hall and the street need to find a way of creating a dialogue. But where does this equilibrium lie? How much of it concerns the personality of the person in charge and his own relationship with the city? Can technology be used to negotiate the distance between parliament and community? Does the Information Age change this relationship, finding a new balance between the two ends of the city?

Part of the answer to these questions can be unearthed in an intellectual debate of the seventeenth century: in the work of Thomas Hobbes and John Locke about the nature of power itself. Hobbes was a mathematician who as a young man spent much time travelling through Europe as a tutor to various young aristocrats. On one such voyage, he was fortunate enough to meet Galileo Galilei. As England was slowly descending into civil war in the 1640s, Hobbes began to think about how to use science to understand human society. In *Leviathan*, which was published in 1651, he set out a pitiful vision of human nature: that man was driven by his desires, and was constantly at war with his fellow men. As a result:

> In such condition there is no place for industry, because the fruit thereof is uncertain: and consequently no culture of the earth; no navigation, nor use of the commodities that may be imported by sea; no commodious building; no instruments of moving and removing such things as require much force; no knowledge of the face of the earth; no account of time; no arts; no letters; no society; and which is worst of all, continual fear, and danger of violent death; and the life of man, solitary, poor, nasty, brutish, and short.[8]

Hobbes's only solution to this vicious state of nature was firm and indissolvable power. Thus in his history of human society, the first society, and the first city, was formed with an unbreakable social contract in which the supreme power was always right, and its methods could never be questioned. This sovereign could take the form of one man – a monarch; a select group – the aristocracy; or a democractic assembly of all. Of these three, only the first was incorruptible. In Hobbes's city, power came from only one place – from above – and was to be enforced in any way the sovereign saw fit. This authority was not to be questioned, as all protest threatened a return to that vicious state of nature.

John Locke experienced the same civil war as a young boy; his father fought on the side of the Parliamentarians against the Royalists and witnessed horrific atrocities. As a young philosopher in Oxford, following the wars, Locke hoped to formulate a social system that would banish the terrors of his childhood for ever. Like Hobbes, he sought to rewrite the social contract but, instead of fear, Locke thought that trust was at the heart of all relationships and he saw the state of nature as a place of equality, rather than a place of violence.

In his *Two Treatises of Government*, Locke attempted to describe a harmonious city, one that had found a balance between the people on the streets and the powers of the crown. In this new society, power was not the last redoubt against chaos but the mutual pooling of rights into sovereign hands. The contract that regulated this relationship was a dynamic document setting out the rights, obligations and limits of all signatories. Power flowed between the streets and the citadel. The people were allowed to overthrow a tyrant; the dutiful sovereign had obligations towards his subjects.

These seventeenth-century texts may seem arcane and irrelevant to the complex modern world, but they are not. Imagine two cities: Hobbestown and Lockeville. Both are vibrant, contemporary metropolises, places that people travel far to reach in the hope of making their fortune and calling them home. While each city has many qualities, each encapsulates those of the founding philosophical fathers.

The modern face of Hobbestown can be found around the world: Beijing, the glistening capital of the Republic of China, has transformed since Deng Xiaoping's economic reforms in the 1990s, yet it still remains a closely regulated city in which the party and the mayor have control over land, business and community. The city showed its best face in 2008, when it staged the most expensive Olympic Games in history, centred around the Bird's Nest stadium, partly designed by local artist Ai Wei Wei.

Similarly, the rapid rise of Dubai from a dusty Gulf town to a metropolis dedicated to finance, leisure and trade is one of the urban triumphs of the past decades. The city's initial success was founded on the discovery of oil in 1966, yet in the hands of the Al Maktoum dynasty, the city has diversified its power with ambitious state-initiated projects such as expanding the port, attracting international business, land development and tourism. Dubai is now a mecca for pleasure seekers and businessmen. This is typified by the Burj Khalifa, the largest skyscraper in the world, which rises high above the desert, symbolising the city's thrusting modernity.

However, all is not as it seems. In August 2011, while under house arrest in China, Ai Wei Wei described the true face of the city that had been hidden from the tourists: 'A city is a place that can offer maximum freedom . . . Beijing is two cities. One is of power and of money. People don't care who their neighbours are; they don't trust you. The other city is one of desperation . . . Everything is constantly changing, according to somebody else's will, somebody else's power.'[9] As he continues to be under constant surveillance and harassment from the authorities, he has been accused of economic crimes for tax evasion, as well as crimes of pornography and bigamy. He has been banned from travelling outside China.

Dubai, in theory, is a nation run by a constitutional monarchy but most of the key government roles are in the hands of family members. The city was built by thousands of workers shipped in from the subcontinent who have few rights and no chance to share in the pleasures of the state or citizenship. In both Beijing and Dubai the desires of state, in the person of the party or the Emir, supersede the individual citizen. Rapid urban change has been entirely driven from above. Without a doubt, both places are hugely successful models of what a city can be; but is this the kind of place you would want to live?

Singapore, the world's most successful city state, on the southern tip of the Malay Peninsula, is perhaps the paradigmatic Hobbestown. Despite a constitution modelled on the British parliamentary system, with frequent compulsory elections, it has had only one party in power since gaining self-governing status in 1959 and independence in 1963: Lee Kuan Yew's People's Action Party (PAP). Singapore has been called many things, from 'Disneyland with the death penalty'[10] to 'one of the cleanest, safest, richest and dullest cities in the world',[11] but there is no question that, in its first fifty years, it became one of the great global cities of our times.

This confused picture is reflected in Singapore's standing within the many rankings that now catalogue the different faces of the world's cities. In 2011 it ranked first in the Mercer Consulting Best City for Infrastructure and the Ericsson Networked Society list; *Forbes* magazine called it the 'World's Smartest City'; it came third in the ranking for the Euromonitor Top City Destination and fifth in both the Global Power City Index and the Cities of Opportunity.[12] Across the board the city had risen into the top five for business; however, in the *Economist* Liveability rankings, it came an unimpressive fifty-second, brought down by the categories of environment and freedom.

CORBIS

The Singapore waterfront: urban paradise or despotic theme park?

The island state first came to prominence as an Imperial entrepot between Britain and South-east Asia, and in the nineteenth century was developed as a multinational community of Europeans, native Malay and Chinese merchants who set up a bridgehead to the mainland, and Indians who arrived to service the empire. After a failed experiment to unify with Malaysia between 1963 and 1965, independent Singapore set out to establish a new identity alongside an economic policy of renewal, for as Lee Kuan Yew later wrote in his autobiography: 'We had to create a new kind of economy, try new methods and schemes never tried before anywhere else in the world, because there was no other country like Singapore.'[13]

The PAP were determined to make Singapore the gateway to Asia, to encourage foreign investment into the city and to make the port the transport and business hub for the region. Lee developed an idiosyncratic method to ensure Singapore's future: he had been inspired by Japan's authoritarian control of the island in 1942, as he was starting off his career as a wartime entrepreneur. After

1945 he travelled to Britain and was impressed by the Labour Government efforts to establish the welfare state. On his return, he formulated his own non-ideological pragmatic philosophy on how to get things done, a mixture of authoritarianism and welfare; as he famously told the *Strait Times*: 'We decide what is right. Never mind what the people think.'[14] This approach has proved to be remarkably successful.

From the 1960s, Lee's strong government nurtured the free market, initiated rapid state-led industrialisation and far-reaching infrastructure schemes such as housing and transport, and imposed strict social policies encouraging savings rather than consumption, as well as a cheap and compliant workforce. As Lee has noted, there was not enough time to engage with the people over a shared vision of the city: 'close engagement of the mass citizenry was not only unnecessary but would have been a nonstarter'.[15] Instead, he ensured that Singapore became the perfect environment for foreign investment. In addition to cheap labour, there was widespread promotion of education to improve the skilled workforce, so that where the average 1960s adult had only three years of schooling, today the city boasts a 95 per cent literacy rate. It was also important to stamp out corruption, so Lee raised civil-service wages while also raising the penalties for being caught.

He then courted the petrochemical industry and electronics firms as well as encouraging multinational corporations to make the island home for their local headquarters, attracted by the low costs of development, a good infrastructure and political stability. By 1980 the economy benefited from $7,072 million in foreign investment. Yet during that decade the city also suffered from its first recession. This was partly due to the rise of neighbours such as Indonesia and Malaysia who also started to offer low labour costs and basic services, forcing Singapore to rethink.

In response Singapore declared another era of redevelopment both to the fabric of the city and the people living there. There was an effort to encourage local entrepreneurship while also attracting more hi-tech and knowledge-based industries, such as Lucas Films and Biopolis, an international bio-tech research centre, to the island. Culture and tourism have also become important, accounting for $5.6 billion by 1999, and exemplified by the new Marina Bay complex, including theatres, a business hub and even more malls in a city that seems dominated by 'consumptionscapes', as well as a Formula 1 racetrack.

Singapore now sells itself as the super-charged Asian creative hub. Yet this commitment to the Information Age comes with risks and has altered the relationship between the government and the people, who are now encouraged to be innovative, independent and educated. You cannot encourage innovators and a knowledge economy and then expect them to act like dutiful servants: schools began to teach a new curriculum that encouraged critical thinking rather than learning by rote; the launch of the 'Singapore One' initiative guaranteed every citizen a high-speed internet connection while the iN2015 masterplan hopes to develop a new generation of global business leaders.[16]

This revolution within a revolution – which in time will surely come to question Singapore's Hobbesian way of life – has nonetheless been dictated from the top down. The appearance of the new regime as a 'listening government' that today encourages criticism needs to be taken with a pinch of salt, as commentator Karl Hack notes: it may no longer be 'just an authoritarian one-way street but rather a two-way street in which the lane travelling towards the government is narrower'.[17]

Singapore's Hobbestown may appear to be an unsurpassable example of how to develop a world-beating city, proving that a firm hand and strong government are the only things that can assure the metropolis. This is in extreme contrast to Lockeville, the city where the relationship between the political élite and the streets is a free and fair dialogue. Lockeville itself might never look as impressive or grandiose as Hobbestown; here, centrally planned projects do not get waved through without discussion; the infrastructure will most likely be stretched and in need of repair; the listening city is also a talking city and there are many opinions to take into consideration. One such example can be found just 12 kilometres west of Manhattan.

Having reached its zenith at the beginning of the twentieth century as an industrial powerhouse, port and centre for the insurance industry, downtown Newark still boasts elegant, early-Beaux Art skyscrapers and Art Deco apartment blocks that have only recently been renovated after decades of neglect. The decline began after the Second World War when industry moved on and real estate began to plummet; at the same time the city's population halved. As the middle classes fled for the suburbs, the inner city was flooded by the great migration of black and Latino migrants moving up from the south in search of work. In the hands of weak politicians, the city soon began to spiral. In 1967, ignited by another instance of police brutality against the black majority, riots tore through the streets. In 1981 the murder rate stood at 161 deaths a year, while a quarter of all families lived below the poverty line. In the 1990s Newark was named 'the most dangerous city in America'.

Since 2006 Cory A. Booker has been the mayor charged with Newark's revival and his administration offers fascinating insights into the workings of a hypothetical Lockeville. Booker was born in Washington, DC but grew up in the affluent neighbourhood of Harrington Park, New Jersey. He graduated from Stanford where he excelled as an American football player; he was then awarded a

Rhodes scholarship to Oxford and finally ended his studies at Yale Law School. His parents were part of the civil-rights generation and the first African-American executives at IBM; he later claimed that they raised him as an idealist, and taught him that 'we were a country that was formed in perfect ideals but a savagely imperfect reality'.[18] Before finishing at Yale he moved into a flat on the sixteenth floor of Brick Towers, central Newark, having been inspired by the story of 78-year-old Virginia Jones, who had refused to leave the building despite the murder of her son in the lobby by a local gang. Booker started to campaign for residents' rights and stayed living in Brick Tower until it was demolished in 2006.

Booker failed to win the mayorship on his first attempt in 2002, but won with a 72 per cent majority in 2006, when the incumbent Sharpe James stepped down from the race (and two years later was convicted for corruption). Booker's campaign gained media attention; Oprah Winfrey called him 'a genius' and he ran on a ticket of public safety, urban renewal and respect.

While many dismissed the new mayor as 'all talk', Booker understands the power of communication. As well as holding regular surgeries to which citizens are invited to bring their worries, Booker often spends his evenings riding alongside the patrolmen on the streets, talking to the people he finds. Following the murders of three young men he even entered the pulpit to spread his message. When Brick Towers was demolished, he moved to a new trouble spot on Hawthorne Avenue in order to keep close to his work.

As he announced in 2006, Newark was to lead the way in urban transformation, and when President Obama requested that Booker join his own team in 2008, Booker refused, preferring to run for a second mayoral term. Newark is now the fastest-growing city in north-east US, and violent crime has been drastically reduced. In

2010 Mark Zuckerberg, CEO of Facebook, donated $100 million to the city's schools and many others have started to see Newark as a place worth investing in. This re-emerging Lockeville is on the way to recovery and while it might never achieve the economic might of Singapore, it is anything but a 'machine without a soul'.

In 2010 Booker won a second term with a slightly lower percentage, on the promise of continuing the fight. It has not always run smoothly. In order to cut costs, he had to make tough decisions on budget spending; some police had to be laid off and crime rates began to rise once again. In 2011 he was forced to testify in the trial of his deputy, who was indicted for extortion. At the same time, Booker had attracted over $700 million in new building contracts, offering jobs for 2,500 locals. Yet the most startling action of his mayoralty came in April 2012, when Booker, refusing to listen to security advice, saved a woman from a burning house in his own neighbourhood of Upper Clinton Hill. In a press conference the following day, after a visit to the hospital for smoke inhalation and minor burns, he observed: 'I'm a neighbor who did what most neighbors would do.'[19]

Fortunately, most cities look more like Lockeville rather than Hobbestown, yet they unfortunately lack charismatic politicians like Booker. The image of Booker talking to kids on the street corner, living within one of the more deprived neighbourhoods of his community, is a powerful one that encourages trust amongst Newarkers. For many cities, however, it is more common to judge a mayor by his public works, and whether the trains run on time, rather than his character. Thus throughout history politicians have used architecture to manage and control the relationship between City Hall and the street. For centuries the emphasis was on grandeur, conjuring an awesome power in stone. Consider, for example, the traditional places of power: the Assemblée Nationale in Paris, the Senate House in Washington, the Houses of Parliament in Westminster. Despite being beacons of democracy, these are places where the machinations of power are firmly fixed behind closed doors, apart from seats for a handful of invited guests in the public galleries. From the streets outside one cannot see the democratic process being enacted in our name.

In recent decades, however, a number of architects have proposed that there is a relationship between the visibility of democracy and trust; this 'architecture of transparency' blows away the cobwebs of secretive government and forces a new openness. In 1992, following the collapse of the Berlin Wall, Foster + Partners were invited to renovate the historic Reichstag in Berlin; the brief was to create a symbol for the reunification of the whole nation as well as a home for the democratic future of Germany, the Bundestag. The glass dome, which rises above the original 1870s building, stands above the central debating chamber, allowing visitors to look down into the room and observe democracy in action. Foster + Partners repeated the trick in 2002 with the new City Hall in London, home for the recently created Greater London Authority and mayor (who have respectively called the building 'the glass testicle' [Ken Livingstone] and more primly 'the glass gonad' [Boris Johnson]). The ovoid building was completely created in glass, transparent from all directions.

A more recent, and more radical, experiment in transparency can be found at City Hall in Tallinn, Estonia, designed by the groundbreaking Danish architects Bjarke Ingels Group (BIG), who plan to create a vast periscope within the central council chamber, so that the politicians inside can look up and see the life upon the streets, focusing their minds on what they are supposed to be doing, and who they are supposed to be representing. In reverse, the people on the streets can also see into the chamber and survey the efforts of the people who are supposed to be working in their name. As BIG highlight in their outline: 'In a traditional tower only the king at the top gets to enjoy the great view. The periscope is a form of democratic tower, where even the average Tallinn citizen on the street gets to enjoy the overview from the top.'[20]

The Tallinn City Hall offers an image for the new relationship between the politicians and the streets in glass and steel. Yet there is no reason to believe that this will really change the way the city works, or that architecture is as dynamic or immediate as imagined. Could design ever be as effective as the experience of Mayor Booker leaving Newark City Hall and talking to his voters?

The spirit of the city does not come from the civic structures or latest architectural adventures commissioned to mediate urban relations. Instead, its personality and character emerges from the connections and relationships between the many people who come together there. And just as the density and intermeshing of connections nurtures the complexity of a place, so the city becomes a superlinear site for information.

It is information, not architecture, that constitutes the lifeblood of Lockeville. So rather than considering the relationship between City Hall and the street as one of the distance between two places, instead we should consider them as two information sources. It is not enough for City Hall to give the impression of being a listening place; it has to be a place in constant dialogue. Booker clearly understands the value of making personal contact with the people that he represents but he also appreciates the power of technology to connect with them.

Thus, as much as the power of his personality and the will to be on the front line, it is Booker's use of technology that makes him the mayor of Lockeville. For example, he set up his first blog in August 2008 and later joined Facebook, YouTube and Twitter (currently with over 1.2 million followers). Since then, new media has been at the centre of his listening government. In 2009 he launched the Newark Tech Corps to explore ways of enhancing and harnessing democracy through technology. While this is by no means a replacement for solid policy or effective implementation, it nonetheless changes the power relations within the city.

Booker understands what political blogger Josh Sternberg highlights as the four advantages of new media in the hands of a local politician: create a conversation; report a broader strategy; bring about change; put people at the centre of policy. Booker's use of inspirational quotes, 're-tweeting' positive messages, invitations to events and notes of encouragement are direct and personal, helping

CORBIS

Mayor Cory Booker digging in the Snowmaggedon

to develop a trusting conversation between city hall and street, and in January 2011 he launched the Get Moving campaign, reporting on his own fitness regime in order to get others to exercise.

This use of technology was highlighted during the blizzards of December 2010 when Newark was under a blanket of snow. As the streets ground to a standstill, Booker's Twitter account began to fill up with requests for help. 'Can u DM me his phone #?RT @ NewNewark: @corybooker rec this text Tell mayor, Mr Lou Jones 224 Richileu ter. He's disabled needs help.' The mayor began first by allocating resources and then by going out onto the street himself with a shovel to dig out stranded residents.

On 28 December he was digging until 3 am. While many critics complained that this stunt was the result of a flawed emergency plan, it had a powerful effect upon the community, encouraging other residents to help. One Tweeter, Gustin, announced: 'I think the lesson that @corybooker taught us is that we've got to take responsibility for our own block. I'm heading out.'[21]

The events of 'Snowmageddon' also attracted large media attention that promoted Booker's message, often comparing his response favourably to New York's mayor, Michael Bloomberg, as well as the fortunes of Newark itself.

While Mayor Booker has used social media to offer his constituents a very personal relationship, there are also a number of other instances that show the power of sharing information to enhance the city. In 2009 Mayor Bloomberg launched the BigApps competition, offering the relatively small prize of $5,000 to the developer who could come up with the best software to help people 'use' New York better. He also opened up to developers the NYC Data Mine, the city's online data resource for all statistics and government information. The results were astounding. Over eighty new apps were delivered within three months, and among the winners announced in January 2010 were NYC WayFinder, which helps to get you to the nearest subway station; TaxiHack, which allows users to post real-time comments on taxis; and apps that help you find a school, bullying hotspots, the nearest trees, 3D maps for the iPhone, and in which public library you can find a certain book.

A second competition was launched in autumn 2010 with an increased $40,000 prize. The winning ideas included Sportaneous, which facilitates the organisation of pick-up games and sports at public venues using real-time data from the NYC Parks and Recreation Department; Bestparking, which finds out the best places to park in the city and Brooklyn, and was quickly downloaded by over 100,000 urban drivers; and Roadify, which collates all real-time data on public transit and road conditions to help you better plan your journey.

At much the same time as the first BigApps contest, Mayor Johnson launched the London Datastore (www.data.london.gov.uk), filled with information on everything from abandoned cars and education league tables, to the expense-account details of London government members. In time it also was allowed to display real-time data for the tube system, the police and local NHS. Emer Coleman, who launched the Datastore, told me that the demand for information was beyond every expectation, and that Londoners have used it in numerous, sometimes unexpected, ways.

The Datastore is not just a mechanism for transparency. While it is important that the city government proves itself to be open and accountable, establishing a sense of trust between the city and City Hall, the variety of information being offered to general scrutiny has a far more valuable potential in engaging the active citizen. Once data is made available, City Hall loses control of how that information is used, and by whom: hackers, activists, website designers, coders or app entrepreneurs. It can be utilised to start a political campaign or launch a new business. This donation of the control of information by the traditional government powers to whoever has a broadband connection and a special interest is at the heart of a new revolution in politics, Gov 2.0. And once again this new era is being driven by cities.

But as with all transitions, the dawning of the age of Gov 2.0 comes with certain anxieties and unexpected consequences. To date it has been a slow process of acclimatisation in the same way a cautious swimmer dips their toe into the cool water of the pool before deciding to dive in. To begin with there was much investment in the pushing of government services online in the attempt to streamline and make the management of such tasks accessible and convenient. Therefore, from early on, one could apply for a driver's licence, pay council tax, get involved with polls and surveys, or book a doctor's appointment. This is a facility that connects government with the citizen through technology but the user is still the customer: there is the possibility of feedback but the user cannot change the way things are done. This is hugely useful but is not the revolution that the web offers.

Many within government quickly understood the web as a sophisticated broadcasting tool – the means to get their message across. Politicians set up websites; government departments told people what they did in blogs, Twitter feeds and podcasts. Once again, however, this innovation encouraged a one-way traffic of information. This was made emphatically clear during the riots of August 2011 when the public-order division of the Metropolitan Police, CO11, set up a Twitter feed allowing them to give real-time information updates (@CO11metpolice); within days they had over 15,000 followers. The social network, therefore, was used as a highly effective communication tool, letting people know where the danger was. It is disappointing to see, however, that the Met team only ever followed eight other feeds, all exclusively public services. In 2012 they changed their address to @metpoliceevents and had 32,800 followers, but still only themselves followed forty-six other feeds, predominantly other branches of the force. In effect, they are talking but not interested in listening; they are happy to ignore over 32,750 potential sources of information, active citizens who could help them do their job.

It is this spontaneous potential of social media to galvanise the 'wisdom of the crowds' that stands at the heart of Gov 2.0 and will transform the way cities are run in the future. An indication of this can be seen in the launch of the 311 phone line in New York by Mayor Bloomberg. Before he was mayor, Bloomberg made his fortune developing a financial-data business, and he understands the value of information; as a result 311 has become the cornerstone of his mayoralty. It was started in March 2003 to provide New Yorkers with a single helpline combining all the other services within the city administration (excluding the emergency services), from noise pollution, food stamps and school applications to park maintenance. By May 2010 over 100 million calls had been logged.

By setting up an information line to create a dialogue between city hall and the street, one should be prepared for a huge number of complaints. Few people call 311 to thank the mayor for his work or to congratulate his departments on a good job done. In time Bloomberg also added new services to the line: in 2009 he campaigned for re-election on the ticket of adding real-time information on the transit system; that same year he also launched a stop smoking programme. The line also coordinates with the nyc.gov website and individual queries can be pursued online; there is now a 311 app as well, and questions can be asked via

SMS or Skype. The idea has now been adopted by other cities throughout the US.

Yet it is not just the politicians who are driving the initiative forward. Technology also allows the traffic of information to travel from the street to city hall. While schemes like 311 are hugely popular, they are still in the hands of the civic administration.

In contrast, a number of open-source campaigners such as OpenPlans and Code For America have raised funding for projects such as Open311, a programme to develop a universal information line, a platform that is accessible and democratic for all. So far the project has been launched across America and adopted by twenty-four cities, including San Francisco, Boston and Baltimore. As open source, this means that anyone can access the data files in any of the participating cities; thus, for example, on 10 July 2012 there were eighty-three logs, from a 'How's my driving?' complaint (and one compliment) to reports of graffiti, parking violations, a missed recycling collection and calls for street repair. Similarly, in the UK, FixMyStreet, launched in 2006, offers a place to make a complaint, which is then sent on to the local council. On any given day, a visit to the site can involve the report of broken play equipment in Alexandra Park, north London, to an anonymous report of fly-tipping in Oxford.

The transition towards Gov 2.0 will not be smooth, particularly for government bodies who have always been wary of sharing too much, or being held too accountable. The difficulties associated with the differences between the old way of doing things and the new should not be underestimated. The story of how the London Datastore was established and how it has operated offers some insights into these difficulties and what the future might look like once such a project is up and running.

From the outset Emer Coleman, the director of digital projects at the Greater London Authority (GLA), believed that open government was not just about making information available but also engaging with the digital community who would be using the data, thus blurring the boundaries between a 'top-down' initiative and a 'bottom-up' campaign. Instead of hiring a big consultancy firm, a Twitter account was set up and a call for help was put out on 20 October 2009: 'a chance to get involved in design and build of London's Datastore – this Sat at City Hall'. Over sixty developers turned up that weekend and the process of breaking down the barriers began, between official reticence about sharing information with the hacker's natural suspicion of government. As Coleman later observed, bridging this divide was a challenge. On one side, the developers saw themselves as interested citizens, not politicians; as one confessed: 'I think really my goal in all of this is to make life a little less shit. If you can say, OK, this year I have made things a little less shit for people, then you have had a good year.'[22]

On the other side the average council worker had little idea of digital politics and an innate fear of letting anything get into the hands of the public. In a 2010 survey 69 per cent of those tasked with developing policy in central London borough councils neither used social media nor were familiar with the term Gov 2.0. This was despite a strong governmental drive as outlined in the Cabinet Office and HM Treasury Report *Power in People's Hands* and London mayors, first Ken Livingstone and then Boris Johnson, promoting transparency within London itself. In addition, the large public services were not keen on releasing their data. For some, the fear of losing control of the information and the prospect of painful scrutiny were too much to bear. In the case of much of the transport data, there was also a concern that it was too valuable to give away for free, as it could be used to generate considerable revenues.

Coleman worked alongside developers as well as the media to encourage the state agencies to release their data: 'they did this by writing, blogging, exerting pressure on their local/central government contacts or more formally in the media'.[23] The results are clear: already the free use of the information has inspired creativity and innovation, launching new businesses and apps to help the Londoner. From the outset there was a huge surge of apps transforming the information from the Datastore into useful tools, designed to help with real-time traffic reports, public-transport updates, and locating the 'Boris bikes' that are parked around the city. Cromaroma (www.chromaroma.com) uses the Oystercard payment system to devise a game that spans the city. Figurerunning (www.figurerunning.com) is an app that allows you to be creative while jogging with your smartphone. The phone works as a GPS monitor and your movements are then pencilled onto the map so that as you run around you can create shapes, pictures and figures on a huge scale. Some people have been able to jog the figure of a rabbit onto the street pattern.

Eventually, the opening-up of government changes government itself. On a personal level this can be transformative, as noted by Coleman in an interview with a career civil servant: 'Now I am exposed to a whole bunch of people who are at the cutting edge of the web so it would be really odd if it hadn't changed me . . . now I communicate through blogs, I never did that before, you know, I am an old-school treasury civil servant, we didn't tend to do that sort of thing. The biggest shift for me was we saw change by actually going out and presenting the human face of government, turning up at things and going, "Hello, I'm Richard, I'm from the Cabinet Office and I'm not horrible."'[24] In her survey of government workers and developers, Coleman discovered that 51 per cent felt that the release of data would lead to a different form of government and 64 per cent believed that it also encouraged participation in government; only 7 per cent disagreed.

Yet technology is not a panacea, a cure-all that just by its application heals every wound. This was particularly true during the London riots: technology undoubtedly had a powerful impact on the organisation of the rioters: private-group SMS on BlackBerry were used extensively, and once the violence began Twitter and Facebook were used to spread news and images of the looted trophies. At the same time, on 9 August, a Twitter feed (@riotcleanup) was launched with the message:

We're live. Locations to come very very shortly. #riotcleanup

Within minutes the feed detailed gatherings of local residents who were coming together with brooms and bins to clean up after the previous night's violence. The feed soon became the information post for clean-up groups throughout London, in Manchester, Wolverhampton, Liverpool and further afield. It became the platform for the collective response to the riots, coordinating efforts, sharing emergency information, launching collections for shopkeepers who had lost everything. Stories soon appeared in newspapers about this spontaneous 'citizen action' and in time even the politicians were keen to be seen to be involved: all three leaders of the main political parties were photographed with groups of good-hearted citizens brandishing brooms. Here was an example of how bottom-up politics works and a signal of how things might be in the future.

In the aftermath of the August riots, politicians and journalists fought over who could be the most damning of the generation of 'feral' youth who had rampaged through the London streets. It was only once emotions had calmed that anyone had anything useful to say about the social context that sparked three days of violence and destruction: education, housing, the prospects of employment, the systematic betrayal of the young by the authorities who do not understand and instead interpret desperation for criminality.

Yet it is sometimes worthwhile reminding ourselves that riots are rare occasions, proof that we do not live in Hobbes's vision of the state of nature, and that the city offers a complex self-regulation which emerges from the street, governing our everyday interactions far more than any control from above. New technologies allow us to think about this relationship again, as we are far more in contact with each other than ever before. In time it will change the nature of government itself but first the talking government must also learn the skills of being a listening government. This is a city based on trust.

Meanwhile Mark Duggan's mother is still waiting for an explanation of what actually happened to her son that night.

3

BUILDING BETWEEN BUILDINGS

Whenever I arrive at a new city for the first time, I scour the map and read through the guidebook in order to find the centre point from where the rest of the metropolis circles. As a historian, I look to see how a city tells its story through its buildings and architecture. It is as if the spirit of the place is captured, like whispers, within the stones of the great buildings.

In 1817 the French author Stendhal visited Florence and suffered from a bout of inexplicable dizziness, fainting and even hallucinations. As he wrote in his diary of the tour: 'I was seized with a fierce palpitation of the heart . . . I walked in constant fear of falling to the ground.'[1] The sensitive author was overpowered by the artistic wonder of the city, the crucible of the Italian Renaissance, where within a walk of a few hundred yards one can come across architectural masterpieces from Brunelleschi's Duomo and Ghiberti's Sacristy of Santa Trinita to the façade of Santa Maria Novella by Leon Battista Alberti as well as some of the most beguiling work by Michelangelo; meanwhile in the Uffizi Gallery, where Stendhal had his first fit, one can see works from Cimabue, Giotto, Pisano, Fra Angelico, Botticelli and Leonardo. In 1979 the Italian psychiatrist Graziella Magherini named the condition Stendhal syndrome, having observed over a hundred similar cases of urban vertigo.

Like all tourists, I begin my sorties around the centre by charting the great public spaces and most notable buildings – a city advertises itself and its power through grand squares, its cathedral and palaces. It is these places that become your compass as you learn to navigate the unfamiliar cityscape. Thus when I arrived at the train station in Florence for the first time, I headed towards the exquisite Santa Maria Novella, and then went in search of the Duomo and from there was able to make my way to the hotel. As I wandered in awe for the next few days, I crossed the Piazza della Signoria as if it were the starting point of all journeys. In time, streets and features – a church, a statue, a café – became as familiar as places that I pass every day at home. Yet the buildings, the streets, do not lose their power as I walk around the city.

Being in a place like Florence, it is impossible not to be affected by the surroundings, by the grandeur and history of the architecture. Each street corner seems to have a story encased within the marble and brick. Yet, as I wander around Florence, or any other city, I begin my day with a list of places that I want to see, an architectural to-do list, as if ticking off the glories of the city like exhibits in a museum. However, my peregrinations never work out so efficiently and often I am distracted by the unexpected delight that does not appear in the guidebook. More often than not, I am drawn away from my agenda by the life of the city itself.

And yet Renaissance Florence was in some ways the first modern city and what remains, stretching across over 500 years, appears to be the forcing ground of the ideas and designs informing the cities we live in today. There are things that are so familiar: the way the streets are planned, the height of the houses, the mixture between the marketplaces, the public squares and the more private spaces. As seen in the towers and dramatic religious buildings, the design of the city is political; it is more than a place of habitation or exchange.

The city is also a happiness engine. From Plato's notion of *eudaimonia* (flourishing) in *The Republic*, the pursuit of happiness has been one of the most important identities of the metropolis. The urban world magnifies our best aspects and it has been the task of successive generations to find the city form that releases these qualities rather than stifles, suffocates and destroys the human spirit. But how does this pursuit of happiness express itself in the relationship between ourselves and the buildings we construct? What is the relationship between the way we live and the places we inhabit?

The patron saint of the internet, seventh-century Spanish archbishop St Isidore of Seville, was the last scholar of the ancient world, the final flicker of the candle of learning before the Dark Ages descended. The youngest son of a distinguished family which included three other saints, he was at the forefront of the attempt to convert the conquering Visigoths to Christianity. He was also the author of the *Etymologiae*, a volume that aimed to preserve the sum of human knowledge before it was lost to barbarism. In this compendious encyclopedia his entry on the city is of particular note:

> A city (*civitas*) is a multitude of people united by a bond of community, named for its 'citizens' (*civis*), that is, from the residents of the city. Now 'Urbs' is the name of the actual buildings, while *civitas* is not the stones, but the inhabitants.[2]

Even 1,300 years ago, Isidore recognised a division between the stones of the city and the people who lived among them. Yet the Spanish saint also suggested that there was a connection between the two, that *civitas* could be embedded into the very stones of the city, Urbs, and the properly planned place could stir the emotions and influence our behaviour. From the grid layout of Augustine Rome regulated by the Caesars, Medici Florence, Baron Haussman's elegant boulevards that tore through the dilapidated streets of nineteenth-century Paris, to the re-imagining of Shanghai as the capital of the twenty-first century, architecture and political control have gone hand in hand.

But just as the judicious planning of urban space can enforce compliance and order, can architecture also liberate and nurture? Can a well-planned neighbourhood encourage a sense of community? The narrative of modern urban planning is the story of turning philosophy to stone. The twentieth-century planner was nothing if not ambitious: confident that he (for he is almost exclusively male) had found the technological panacea for the ills of society, convinced that building the city afresh would offer mankind a new start, accelerating people into the sublime realms of modernity: free from want, pain or unnecessary emotion.

The new city, he proposed, was rational, based upon the latest observations of the human condition, made solid into measured streetways and housing, and a considered balance between nature and civilization. The complexity of the ordinary street scene was to be ordered, while the exuberance of the dance of the street was criminalised and controlled out of existence. History shows us that there have been a lot more failures than successes.

Almost by accident, planners formed their own priesthood, wrapped up in ritual and arcane liturgy; every type of neighbourhood was anatomised and catalogued from 'inner-ring suburbs' to 'central business districts', 'exurbs', 'sun-belt cities', creating zones that were regulated into stasis, horrified by the seeming anarchy of an evolving, vibrant environment. The planners stopped talking to the people whose lives they were attempting to improve; they knew better; they spoke in an idiom that no longer connected; and as a result their expertise was no longer challenged.

This desire to know and control the city has its origins in fear and disgust. In 1853 the English art historian John Ruskin published the third volume of his work *The Stones of Venice*, a historical exploration of the Italian city at its moment of glory. He paralleled this Gothic masterpiece with his home city of Victorian London. Industrialisation, he argued, had turned the city into a factory and men into spiritless machines; only the revival of the robust, Gothic beauty of fourteenth-century Veneto could breathe life back into the soul of modern man. Ruskin's cry was heard in Britain, the United States and across Europe; it transformed railway stations into cathedrals, sewage pumping stations into Byzantine fantasies, and factory workers' houses into rural cottages.

Ruskin sourced his ideas from history, but this was not the only well of inspiration for urban thinkers. In the coming decades evolutionary theory, fantastical fiction, the desire to shock, the latest findings from newly forged sciences – psychology, sociology, psychoanalysis – would all be legitimate seedbeds for germinating ideas of the new city. However, as can be seen in the lives of three of the founding fathers of modern urban planning – Patrick Geddes, Ebeneezer Howard and Le Corbusier – the street was too often forgotten.

Just below the castle at the end of the Royal Mile in Edinburgh stands the Outlook Tower. Originally home to Short's Observatory, Museum of Science and Art, the tower was purchased in 1892 by the then professor of botany at University College, Dundee, Patrick Geddes. Often considered the father of modern town planning, Geddes began life as a zoologist and as a young man was influenced by Darwin's radical ideas of evolution, later lecturing on the life sciences at Edinburgh University. While he was there, he watched with dismay as the medieval parts of the old town were being demolished to make way for new buildings.

Knowing the importance of the environment and heredity as factors of Darwin's theory of natural selection, Geddes began to campaign for the preservation of historic buildings, believing that the city was the form that best housed man in his most evolved state. To destroy the natural urban ecosystem, he argued, was to risk mutation and degeneration. Instead, Geddes offered a policy of 'conservative surgery' to the ailing city. Work should be done where buildings could be preserved and improved, and only the places past saving should be demolished.

In his attempt to save old Edinburgh he salvaged the Outlook Tower near to the castle and turned it into a museum that promoted his ideas of the philosophical science of cities. The building was split into six floors, each divided into topics, from bottom to top: the world, Europe, language, Scotland, Edinburgh, and finally the tower containing the camera obscura through which visitors could view the city and the countryside beyond. Thus he presented the story of the city, the 'amphitheatre of social evolution', within the wider context of history, region and geography. This idea was at the heart of his system of regional planning, which examined the relationship between place, history and region and the best conduct of the ideal citizen.

In his 1915 book, *Cities in Evolution: An Introduction to the Town Planning Movement and the Study of Civics*, Geddes set out his idea of the city as an instrument of evolution. He proposed that the development of the city was just one part of a wider network and that city planning therefore was not just the relationship between streets and public spaces, but also the city and the surrounding

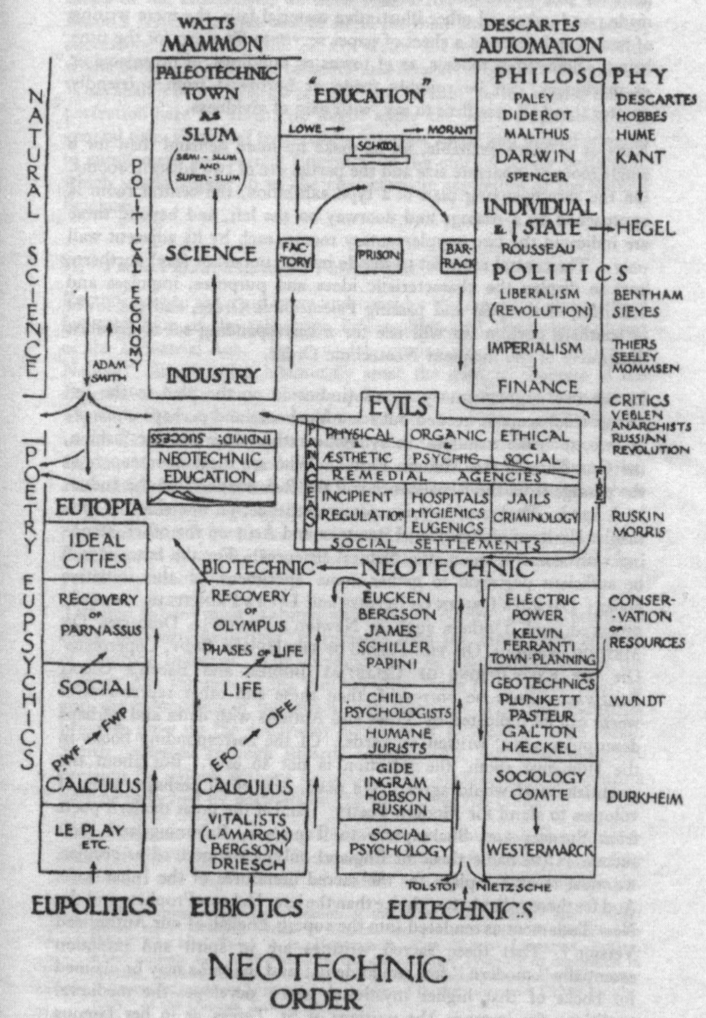

Geddes's plans for the Outlook Tower, the orders of society divided and ordered

countryside, the drama of human history being as important as geography. This may have made sense when preserving old Edinburgh but Geddes also predicted the continued growth of cities. He was the first to develop the concept of 'conurbations', ever-expanding urban communities, estimating that the east coast of America could turn into one vast city stretching for 500 miles. This growth needed to be organised.

Geddes's ideas were put to the test far from the ancient capital of Scotland in the Holy Lands in the aftermath of the First World War. In 1919 Geddes was asked by the newly appointed Zionist government to develop plans for a university, as well as new schemes for Jerusalem and the settlement of Tel Aviv in order to cope with the influx of arrivals. He began the process by walking around the site 'at all times of the day and night . . . As he went to this hillock or that, examined a *sukh*, peered into a house, reverently touched a tree, Geddes had no set plan in his mind but he followed some inner vision.'[3] Into the mix he also stirred childhood memories of reading the Bible. The result was a 36-page report, *Jerusalem Actual and Possible*. It is said by some that if the government had listened more to Geddes, and his understanding of 'the harmonisation of social customs and religious ideas with the work of modern reconstruction',[4] the subsequent history of Palestine would have been very different.

His notions were inspired by the science of life, moulded by empirical observation and deductive intuition. Nevertheless, Geddes was a poor communicator of his own ideas, and was no architect who could give shape and form to his philosophy. Instead he found the perfect disciple in Lewis Mumford, an American writer who later became the most influential architecture critic of his generation. Mumford would turn Geddes's looping, mental peregrinations into coherent and urgent theory, ensuring that regional planning was one of the dominant ideas of how a city should be.

As a leading member of the Regional Planning Association of America (RPAA), Mumford transformed and popularised Geddes's theories: allowing cities to grow unchecked was intolerable; people, industry and land were an integrated network that needed to be planned. Following the Great Depression, the RPAA was perfectly placed to give shape to the urban projects of Roosevelt's New Deal, combining practical directives of urban planning and a positive social agenda that drove forward the rebuilding of America out of adversity. Many of the New Deal towns, constructed by schemes such as the Tennessee Valley Authority, saw whole communities emerging according to regional planning.

In turn, Mumford's synthesis of Geddes's regional planning found fertile ground back in Britain in the work of Sir Patrick Abercrombie, the man who campaigned in the 1930s for a greenbelt around London to halt the spread of the city. Abercrombie was also in charge of rebuilding London after the Blitz, developing his 1941 masterplan. This grand scheme for the rebirth of the city included the de-slumming of the old neighbourhoods, reducing density and breaking up communities into new towns on the outskirts of the city, and reconfiguring the city for the new age of the motor car.

The influence of Geddes was therefore felt around the globe long after his death. However, Mumford and Abercrombie's philosophy of planning proposed a process without defining a model, and they needed to look beyond Geddes to find a shape for the new city. What they both found, in the work of a young English planner, was a design that did not look like any city previously seen; in fact, the new city was not a city at all, but a garden. They came to believe that the only way to preserve the city was to escape it altogether.

At the turn of the twentieth century Ebeneezer Howard was a stenographer at the Houses of Parliament in Westminster. Having spent his youth travelling through America, he was inspired by Edward Bellamy's utopian novel, *Looking Back*, which imagined a young Bostonian, Julian West, waking up after 113 years' sleep in AD 2000 and finding a perfect society in which everything was equally distributed.

Howard believed that this ideal could be founded in a new Garden City, planned from the ground up outside the industrial metropolis, but connected to the centre by the latest rail technology. The new city would have all the urban advantages but also benefit from the qualities of the countryside, as he wrote in *Tomorrow: A Peaceful Path to Real Reform* (1898): 'Human society and the

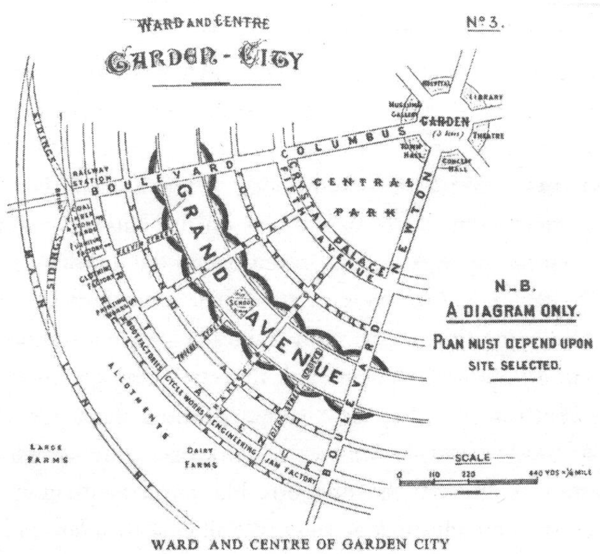

A detail from Howard's Garden City

beauty of nature are meant to be enjoyed together ... Town and country must be married, and out of this joyous union will spring a new hope, a new life, a new civilisation.'[5]

The future of the city was to be found by turning one's back on the city and starting again, breaking new ground in the countryside. Reborn on such bare ground there was no need to take the past into consideration and the city could be planned from the first brick to the final form. In Howard's vision the city was planned on a concentric grid with a library, town hall, museum, concert hall and hospital all gathered into the centre and set in parkland; this civic heart was ringed by the main shopping zone, designed as a glass arcade. Moving away from this were rings of housing, based around a 420-foot grand avenue, which also enclosed schools; and after that, centrifugal zones of factories, dairies and services. There was to be no smoke and every machine was to be driven by electricity. Needless to say, however, there was little discussion of life on the streets within the new Garden City; as Lewis Mumford would later write in his 1946 introduction to *Garden Cities of Tomorrow*, Howard was more interested in physical shapes than social processes.

Howard's dream was turned into reality at Letchworth, Hertfordshire, 34 miles to the north of London, and has been recreated around the world ever since. Work began in 1903 at Letchworth, with the purchase of 16 square kilometres of land outside the town of Hitchen. The first thing to be built was a platform for the railway, and later a station was completed. Under the supervision of the great suburban architects Barry Parker and Raymond Unwin, who had become famous as the leading campaigners for the Arts and Crafts movement, the community grew, if not exactly following Howard's exact concentric designs. It was said that only one tree was felled in the process of building.

The same philosophy was also tested in laboratories closer to

London at Hampstead Garden Suburb, a scheme sponsored by the philanthropist Angela Burdett-Coutts, who wanted to develop a harmonious community with housing for all classes. In time, there were Gardenstädte in Germany, Cité-Jardins in France, Cuidad-Jardínes in Spain as well as other communities in Holland, Finland, India and Palestine. Forest Hill Gardens, in Queens, connected to Manhattan by the newly electrified Long Island Railroad, was the first Garden City in America.

In their own separate visions Mumford and Abercrombie gave a modern shape to Geddes's philosophy of regional planning and Howard's hopes for the Garden City. Mumford's greatest achievement, in the end, was a book, *The City in History*, one of the most influential urban histories of the post-war world. Abercrombie saw his 1941 plan informing the rebuilding of London following the devastations of the Blitz. So it was that Mumford and Abercrombie influenced the lives of millions on both sides of the Atlantic.

Geddes and Howard both believed city building could deliver a new society. The Swiss architect Le Corbusier, on the other hand, first established an architectural theory and then went in search of the society to impose it upon. As a result his solution was very different in effect. While Ruskin, Geddes and Howard rallied against the horrors of the dense city, Le Corbusier desired to make it denser; as they sought to find refuge outside the city walls, Le Corbusier wanted to tear down the centres and build them up again; just as they wanted to put the city into the countryside, Le Corbusier decided that the parkland should come into the city. In addition, he did away with the street altogether. Le Corbusier thus hangs over twentieth-century architecture like a dark thundercloud.

Born Charles-Édouard Jeanneret in 1887, he changed his name

to Le Corbusier in 1920 after an early career travelling, teaching and working on small-scale commissions. In 1923 all his ideas, observations and experiences thus far were summed up in *Vers Une Architecture*, a manifesto for modernist design: architecture was a machine, he declared, that was severely out of sync with society: 'the primordial instinct of every human being is to assure himself of a shelter. The various classes of workers in society today no longer have dwellings adapted to their needs; neither the artisan nor the intellectual. It is a question of building which is at the root of social unrest of today: architecture or revolution.'[6] Thus a revolution in design was the only thing that could halt the coming catastrophe.

Already, Le Corbusier was imagining a new type of city: a regulated metropolis of skyscrapers, in which the plan was at the centre of the work because 'without a plan you have lack of order and wilfulness'.[7] The idea thus became more important than the place, theory superseded life itself. The rightness of the plan ensured the evolution of a peaceful, happy society, whose voices were not encouraged. In addition, this revolution demanded men 'without remorse' who could see the project to its end without swaying to public opinion: 'the design of cities are too important to be left to the citizens'.[8]

In 1925 Le Corbusier hoped to test his ideas with projections for the Plan Voisin that was the centrepiece exhibition in the Pavillion de l'Esprit Nouveau at the World Fair, Paris. His dreams demanded the levelling of most of the historic neighbourhoods of the French capital, north of the Seine – from the Marais to the Place Vendôme – and replacing them with long avenues, organised into a rigid grid system, filled with parkland and gardens. At the centre of each island was a vast tower block – the new machines for living. Thankfully the Plan Voisin was nothing more than an attempt to shock and was never intended to see the light of day; that did not mean, however, that Le Corbusier was not absolutely serious and his ideas further evolved into the concept of the Ville Radieuse, published in 1933.

Le Corbusier's 'City of Tomorrow' was the supposed solution to the apparent problem of the street. The architect saw poetry in speed and so how could the massed chaos of the city be reordered to allow for maximum velocity? While Geddes saw the relationship between the past, landscape and present as integral to any city plan, Le Corbusier wanted to smash history, 'burn our bridges and break with the past'.[9] Where Howard desired the marriage of city and nature, Le Corbusier saw the city as the enemy of uncontrolled nature, a machine to defend man against the vagaries of the unpredictable and inhuman, including human nature itself.

Unfortunately Le Corbusier's ideas did not fall on deaf ears but were embraced as a most exciting vision of the future. Le Corbusier himself was fêted as a prophet and was invited to build and design across the world. In addition his words were translated into every language and treated as gospel in most architectural schools and town-planning departments. He was the founding member of CIAM (Congrès International d'Architecture Moderne) which was started in 1928 and continued until 1959, bringing together the leading architects of the era and attempting to unify the whole discipline, offering one solution to every city's problems. In particular, this solution was encased within a single text, the Athens Charter, that Le Corbusier compiled in 1943. The charter set in stone the laws of 'the Functional City'.

The ideas could not have found more fertile ground; while Le Corbusier himself moved from the political right to the left during the interwar period, his philosophy was adopted by designers of all stripes. Thus it worked just as well in Soviet Russia, Fascist Italy, Vichy France, India in the aftermath of Independence, as well as Clement Atlee's 1945 Labour Government that oversaw the beginning of the rebuilding of Britain following the Blitz. One of the unexpected outcomes of the war was the diaspora of numerous European designers to America, where CIAM's ideas found an eager market, speculative developers saw the commercial advantages of the planned city, while civic authorities could accumulate huge powers by creating central planning departments. In effect, Le Corbusier offered a one-stop solution to the urban problem; the solution, however, involved complete destruction. It was a bitter pill, and we are still trying to get rid of the taste.

The irony can be seen in one of Le Corbusier's earlier projects: Les Quartiers Modernes Frugès, on the outskirts of Bordeaux. In 1926, three years after the publication of *Vers Une Architecture*, Le Corbusier was invited by the eccentric industrialist Henri Frugès to design 150 new houses for his workers. Le Corbusier saw this as an opportunity to turn his theory of the modern 'house-machine' into reality and came up with a series of ideas. In the end only fifty of the houses were completed but each one conformed to the four basic designs he had projected. Each house had direct light, a roof garden, good ventilation and windows as well as a small frontage; inside, all was standardised and regulated. The designs expressed Le Corbusier's passion for the mass-produced house; as he noted in his book, the workers should be forced into appreciating such uniform standards for it was 'healthy (and morally so too) and beautiful in the same way that the working tools or instruments which accompany our existence are beautiful'.[10]

Except nobody told the workers who were meant to move into these new machines that their houses were tools and not places of domestic bliss. The first group of proud homeowners refused to come, disliking the look and the style. The houses were thereafter given to poorer workers. Almost immediately these new tenants started to adapt and personalise Le Corbusier's designs: traditional wooden shutters were added to the plain façades as well as stone cladding; window boxes bursting with flowers blurred the clean, modernist lines; walls were knocked down and rearranged to make more space for internal rooms; sloping, tiled roofs replaced the flat concrete coverings that had started to leak; windows were replaced to let less light in, and keep the houses cooler.

This is a story that is often washed out from the history of architecture, but it should not be ignored. In time, the Le Corbusier Foundation blamed not the architecture but the sales methods that allowed a lower class of house buyer into the neighbourhood; meanwhile historians have used the example often as a way to vilify bourgeois ignorance. Le Corbusier himself said with some irony: 'You know, it is life that is always right and the architect who's wrong.'[11] Unfortunately, so much of the history of urban planning has displayed this kind of disinterest in how people actually live; yet, as can be seen, life has a way of coming up from the streets and making itself felt. This was made clear in one of the most famous confrontations in the history of city planning.

If things had turned out differently, Robert Moses might, perhaps, have been celebrated as one of the greatest urban thinkers of the twentieth century. Until 1961, he was without question the leading urban planner in America, transforming New York to his will with a ferocious desire for power and an uncompromising architectural vision. Yet, in that year, he clashed with Jane Jacobs, a journalist and campaigner who was forced into action as her neighbourhood became under threat, over the very nature of the city itself.

Since his youth Moses had ambition to burn; educated at Yale, Oxford and with a PhD in politics from Columbia, he threw himself into civic government. Committed, modern, an idealist, his passion for the improvement of the future can even be found in his juvenile poetry:

> To-Morrow!
> But the morrow sure
> To-Morrow!
> The lashes slumber lure;
> Ah! Shall we greet the dawning day,
> Perchance in vain we longing say,
> To-Morrow![12]

It is a sentiment that he shared with almost every architect and urban planner of the period: a determination to corral the future, a dogmatic need to bring order to the unknown, a steely conviction of certainty in the face of all opposition. Moses's first task was reorganising the systems of hiring and purchasing across New York's City Hall departments. In the wake of this bureaucratic revolution, he was offered any job he wanted and plumped for the Department of Parks, hoping to implement a statewide scheme of green spaces. Between the 1920s and 1960s he more than doubled New York's parkland, adding 658 playgrounds and 17 miles of beach. Yet his methods were overbearing from the start; as he told one Long Island farmer whose land infringed on his plans: 'If we want your land, we can take it.'[13]

Moses's schemes then became ever more grand, fuelled by F. D. Roosevelt's New Deal dollars. He held twelve government offices at the same time, coordinating projects across the city. In the 1930s he turned his focus on how to get traffic in and out of the city; by 1936 he had already completed the Triborough Bridge system that linked Manhattan, Queens and the Bronx. The next year, the Marine Parkway-Gil Hodges Memorial Bridge opened, spanning Jamaica Bay between Brooklyn and Queens. A new network of expressways and parkways were devised and driven through the old neighbourhoods; roads were expanded and widened wherever congestion appeared. When he was not allowed to build a bridge between Brooklyn and Battery Park at the southern tip of the island, he was given permission to dig the Brooklyn Battery Tunnel.

At the end of the decade he was able to dream of a completely new city when he was put in charge of the 1939 World Fair, held at Flushing Meadow, and dedicated to the 'world of tomorrow'. Moses co-opted General Motors to sponsor the Futurama display. It was a city, inevitably, that was created around the car: the city centre was replaced by vast highways lined by skyscrapers, embedded in parkland; suburbs were linked together by clean expressways. As the designer Norman Bel Geddes announced, 'Speed is the cry of our era'; the ease and security of a life sealed within the carapace of the automobile, hurtling through the city without obstacles, the perfection of velocity replacing unpredictable human contact.

In the aftermath of the Second World War, Moses continued his ambition to bring this city of the automobile to Manhattan, imposing his new order upon the chaos of the cityscape. In the 1940s and 1950s, Moses was the King of New York and began by focusing on housing in his autopolis, replacing old and out-of-date blocks with over 28,000 apartments set in high-rise towers. He laid plans for the Lincoln Center on the Upper West Side, as a cultural hotbed; he converted the road system of the metropolis, with Columbus Circle becoming the New York Colosseum. He also campaigned to bring the UN headquarters to the city, designed by Le Corbusier in 1950, resulting in one of the most iconic symbols of the modern city. By the mid-1950s, Moses could do no wrong; and the whole world not only agreed with his diagnosis of the city's ills, but also his radical surgery. It seemed, for a brief moment, as if he had the answer to the long-standing question: how to build a happy city.

Jane Jacobs, despite her chunky bohemian jewellery and broad smile, was nobody's fool. Born in 1916 in Scranton, Pennsylvania, she arrived in New York during the Depression and found clerical work while at night she honed her journalistic skills. Her work was picked up by *Vogue* and the *Sunday Herald Tribune*, where she gained a reputation for writing about the life of the city. She also signed up to study at Columbia University extension school, where she took a variety of courses, yet left before gaining a degree. During the war she worked at the Office of War Information, and it was during this time that she met her husband Robert H. Jacobs. In 1947 they moved into a flat above a convenience store at 555 Hudson Street, a run-down neighbourhood in Greenwich Village.

Jacobs was a pioneering homemaker, moving to a part of the city that many had left, the old nineteenth-century houses

NEW YORK WORLD-TELEGRAM AND THE SUN NEWSPAPER PHOTOGRAPH COLLECTION, LIBRARY OF CONGRESS

Jane Jacobs triumphant

subdivided and down at heel. Some of that clutter and chaos made its way into the Jacobs's flat that friends remember as deeply untidy but with a huge amount of personality. It was here that Jacobs began to observe the Ballet of Hudson Street and came to understand the complex patterns of the neighbourhood that she later described in *The Death and Life of Great American Cities*.

By the late 1950s she was also working at *Architectural Forum* magazine, where she met William H. Whyte who shared her concerns about the dangers of city planning. While architects were in thrall to the grand projects, they both asked, where were the people? In a groundbreaking collection of essays, *The Exploding Metropolis*, both Whyte and Jacobs expanded on their ideas. In 'Downtown is for People' Jacobs reflected on the future city: 'They will be spacious, park-like, and uncrowded. They will feature long green vistas. They will be stable and symmetrical and orderly. They will be clean, impressive and monumental. They will have all the attributes of a well-kept dignified cemetery.'[14]

From then on, the clash between Jacobs and Moses seemed inevitable. There was an early skirmish in the 1950s when Moses proposed driving a highway through Washington Square Park in order to ease congestion. Jacobs joined in with the campaign of energetic letter-writing, using her contacts to get high-profile support, including Whyte, the urban historian Lewis Mumford, who then wrote an influential column for the *New Yorker*, and even Eleanor Roosevelt. She brought her own children to the weekend protests on the square, providing perfect photo opportunities. On 25 June 1958 the New York *Daily Mirror* published a picture of Jacobs holding one end of a tied ribbon, symbol of a 'reverse ribbon cutting', signifying that Moses's scheme had been delayed into oblivion in the face of determined opposition. Moses could only complain: 'There is nobody against this, nobody, nobody, nobody but a bunch, a bunch of mothers.'[15]

Three years later Moses and Jacobs were at loggerheads once

more when Moses proposed building the Lower Manhattan Expressway (LoMex) to ease congestion in the city. The only problem was that Jacobs's home lay nearby and was thus under threat. Moses's expressway connected the Hudson River Tunnel and the two East River bridges and would hand Lower Manhattan to the motor car. In consequence the ten-lane raised roadway would dispossess 2,200 families, 365 shops and 480 businesses as well as a number of historic buildings, breaking into some of the most renowned neighbourhoods: SoHo, the Bowery, Little Italy, China Town, the Lower East Side, as well as Greenwich Village.

It was a fair bargain, Moses thought, as he wrote that 'the route of the proposed expressway passes through a deteriorating area with low property values due in considerable part to heavy traffic that now clogs the surface streets'.[16] He had done this before: the Cross-Bronx Expressway relocated over 1,500 families yet was considered a revolutionary success. It was only later that commentators started to date the decline of the Bronx to this act of destruction.

Jacobs would have none of it; as she would later write, it was pure folly to think that Futurama was a real place: 'Somehow, when the fair became part of the city, it did not work like the fair.'[17] In addition, she refused to contemplate the break-up of her own neighbourhood. Jacobs threw herself into the campaign, becoming the chairperson of the Joint Committee to Stop the Lower Manhattan Expressway and intent upon putting an end to LoMex.

Yet perhaps her greatest weapon, which destroyed not just Moses's project but his very reputation, was *The Death and Life of Great American Cities*, published in 1962. As the first line of the introduction makes clear:

> This book is an attack on current city planning and rebuilding. It is also, and mostly, an attempt to introduce new principles of city

> planning and rebuilding, different and even opposite to those now taught in everything from schools of architecture and planning to Sunday supplements and women's magazines . . . In short, I will be writing about how cities work in real life, because this is the only way to learn what principles of planning and what practices in rebuilding can promote social and economic vitality in cities, and what practices and principles will deaden these attributes.[18]

At the heart of this 'real life' was the street, the complex interweaving of people within the public spaces of the city. It was the street itself that was the principal object of study, and the metropolis's organising force. The city needed to be reconstructed from the bottom up, not projected from the imagination of a grand wizard planner. This hopefulness may have seemed as vague as any previous vision of the city, another brand of utopianism about the self-organised neighbourhood, but it was powerful enough to force Moses to defend the LoMex project against a growing opposition. When Jacobs took the microphone at a public meeting in September 1968, the officials tried to turn off the sound. When Jacobs invited protesters onto the stage, the chairman called for the police to arrest her. Instead she led a procession out of the meeting, only to be met by a plain-clothes officer who escorted her to a patrol car.

Jacobs's victory was sealed, while Moses hoped to keep the debate alive by writing ever more deranged memos and sending self-justifying packages to the *Daily News*. The project did not die, however; rather, in 1971, it dropped off the list of proposals eligible for federal inter-state funding and fell into a bureaucratic black hole. Moses lost his crown and his regal bearing; once the epitome of the master planner, America's very own Baron Haussmann, he was soon held up to be the example of how not to build a city.

The stories of Geddes, Howard, Le Corbusier and Moses do not mean that all planning is bunk, and that all 'top-down' management for urban renewal is flawed. Neither should we see Jane Jacobs as a white knight or a small-time Nimby defending her patch against the forces of progress. Cities should be built for people, and architecture must concern itself with the many different ways of building communities, not breaking them apart. Urban planning often ignores the human element when in fact it needs to be at the centre of any project. We must be as careful to plan the spaces between buildings as the buildings themselves.

In *The Death and Life of Great American Cities*, Jacobs asked people to look again at the city, and enquired how we might improve what we have in hand rather than rip up the street and start again from scratch. She began her sermon with a plea to appreciate the life of the streets as the true signifier of the vitality of the metropolis. Secondly, the streets, parks and public spaces of the city, the places where people meet, were more important than traffic flow, efficiency savings and the creation of zones. Finally, all planning should be developed through an understanding of how people used spaces, what made them happy, and how they adapted these places for themselves.

Jacobs developed many of these lessons while working with and writing for William H. Whyte, the executive editor of *Fortune* magazine, who commissioned her first articles. In 1956 Whyte had written *The Organisation Man*, which had evolved out of a study of the rise of Corporate Man. In a devastating analysis Whyte suggested that the post-war generation had been encouraged into conformity, happy to exchange their own individuality to participate in the corporate dream, which not only dictated how they worked but also offered them the banal ideal of a secure life, the comforts of suburbia, the steady accumulation of unnecessary things. In conclusion, Whyte controversially claimed that the culture of Organisation

Man, the surrender of self to the mythic corporation, was the very opposite of the rugged individualism that once built America.

Whyte's fascination with how Organisation Man lived led him to investigate every aspect of corporate life, including the allures of suburbia. In a 1953 essay, 'How the New Suburbia Socialises', he used his own neighbourhood of Forest Park outside Chicago to show how the design of play areas, driveways and stoops affected interactions; how keeping the front lawn clean leads to strong ties to neighbours across the road rather than over the back-yard fence; why owning a house that was built in the early stages of the development can make you more popular. In time, however, he began to focus his attention away from the suburbs on to the city centre, which culminated in the 1958 series of articles edited by Whyte, *The Exploding Metropolis*, including Jane Jacobs's first call to arms.

It would be almost a decade – the time in which Jacobs bested Moses – before Whyte put his ideas into practice. In the vacuum left by Moses's decline, the New York Planning Commission hired Whyte to develop a new approach to thinking about the city. Whyte began by looking at previous best practice but was surprised to find no research on the efficacy of any of the most recent projects; he was stunned that there was 'no person on the staff whose job it was to go out and check whether the places were being well used or not, and if not, why'.[19] How could a city improve if it could not learn from its mistakes, or even find out if it had made any?

Whyte hired a group of sociology students from nearby Hunter College to start conducting some serious studies into how people actually used places; and so began 'the street-life project', probably the first time that a method was brought to bear on the ballet of the streets. As was to be expected, the results were revelatory. From this study of 'the river of life of the city, the place where we come together, the pathway to the center',[20] Whyte built up his new idea of how the city really worked.

How do people walk down the street? How often do they bump into friends? Where do people stop to chat? Does bustle or a quiet space make a happy place? How much space should you leave as you pass someone? Who can you touch and what kinds of gesture are acceptable in public? Does a vendor get more business, or a busker more change, on a narrow street or a wide thoroughfare? Far more than the philosophical or aesthetic musings of visionaries, these were the real-life questions that can transform a city. Whyte produced his results in two books, *The Social Life of Small Urban Spaces* in 1980 and *City: Rediscovering the Centre* in 1988.

In both books he saw the decline of the city as a reflection of the changing economic relationship between people; as our lives became increasingly mediated, we were less likely to interact, to bump into each other, and as a result the city was losing its most fertile function: the place where strangers meet. First studying the street, then making a series of observations on the social life of our public plazas, Whyte explored the ways in which these public spaces were used, how they developed their own ecology, what worked and what caused problems. Thus he set out some opening observations on how people used the street:

> Pedestrians usually walk on the right. (Deranged people and oddballs are more likely to go left, against the flow.)
>
> A large proportion of pedestrians are people in pairs or threesomes.
>
> The most difficult to follow are pairs who walk uncertainly, veering from one side to another. They take two lanes to do the work of one.
>
> Men walk faster than women.
>
> Younger people walk somewhat faster than older people.

People in groups walk slower than people alone.

People carrying bags or suitcases walk about as fast as anyone else.

People who walk on a moderate upgrade walk about as fast as those on the level.

Pedestrians usually take the shortest cut.

Pedestrians form up in platoons at the lights and they will move in platoons for a block or more.

Pedestrians often function most efficiently at the peak of rush hour flows.[21]

Whyte was surprised to note, watching the flow of human traffic outside Saks on Fifth Avenue, that most people stop to talk either on the street corner in the centre of the flow, or right outside the shop entrance. He also observed lunchtime in Seagram Plaza and how the spaces of the plaza were populated – men more likely to sit closer to the pathways and on benches while women prefer more secluded places; lovers rarely hide themselves; if there were movable chairs they tended to be dragged in all directions, each new occupant

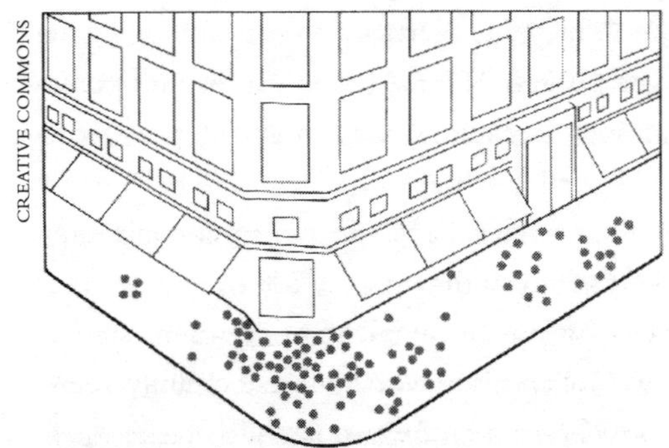

Location of street conversations lasting two minutes or more at Saks Fifth Avenue and Fiftieth Street. Cumulative for five days in June. Note main concentration at corner, secondary one outside entrance.

A diagram showing William Whyte's study of crowds outside Saks Fifth Avenue

choosing to find their own site; particular groups were likely to rendezvous in the same places. In his most memorable phrase Whyte concluded: 'What attracts people most is other people. Many urban spaces are being designed as though the opposite were true.'[22]

Whyte proved that people used the city in different ways than the experts had thought and often did the exact opposite of what the planners intended. Like the residents of Le Corbusier's Quartiers Modernes in Bordeaux, people on the street don't always behave as you want them to, however hard you try. Instead, Whyte highlighted the need to find a more open-ended, and engaged, planning policy that can make a real difference to how we use and feel about the city.

Since Jacobs's epic battle with Moses and Whyte's studies of everyday life on the city streets there have been a number of attempts to transform planning from an arrogant performance in which the architect knew what was best for the people, adhering to strict dogma as the necessary medicine for society's irrational nature. Instead, many planners now recognise the value of a street-up approach, of designing for the way that people actually live rather than the way one might hope they behave.

One way of opening the potential for street-up communities is by doing away with planning restrictions altogether: let the people decide what their neighbourhoods look like. If you believe in the wisdom of crowds, the result is likely to be more complex and interesting than a community built from the imagination of one architect. In the district of Almere, on the outskirts of Amsterdam, such an experiment is underway. Holland is one of the most densely populated nations in Europe, so every inch of land needs to be managed and planned to cope with the demands of a growing population; yet in this unique neck of the woods it is still thought that allowing people to self-build their own homes may be the best way forward.

Almere itself was a planned city, started in the 1970s, designed to cope with the rapid expansion of the Dutch capital, Amsterdam. As communities were built out of a polder, land reclaimed from the watery marshes on all sides, the growth of the districts surprised even the developers and it was not until 1995 that the local government decided that Almere should be more than a series of dormitories with a scattering of centres, and become a centre of its own. Nothing if not ambitious, the authorities commissioned Rem Koolhaas to plan a brand-new city centre, to give the periphery its own cultural, business, retail and government focus. The results are impressive, including buildings by leading staritects such as Will Alsop, SANNA and Koolhaas's very own OMA; but even more intriguing was that while this great project of creating a city out of nothing in as short a time as possible was underway, in another corner a completely different experiment was being conducted.

In 2005 local planner Jacqueline Tellinga initiated the Homeruskwartier, the self-build project, in the south-western Poort district. Covering over 100 hectares, the newly reclaimed land was divided into fifteen sub-districts to provide infrastructure, and then divided further into 720 plots. Each district was given a theme – low rise, live/work, sustainable development, shared and mixed accommodation – and the community was given a central zone to develop retail and office space. The initial costs of land were fixed at €375 per square metre, and some plots were bigger than others. The new owners were then given a passport as proof of ownership and left to their own devices; Tellinga hopes that 'self-build leads to more socially cohesive cities whose inhabitants have a much stronger attachment to their surroundings'.[23] Many cities are watching to see how Homeruskwartier grows and develops as a potential solution to the current housing crisis.

While it might be common sense to offer people more say in the way they build their own homes, do the same rules apply when thinking about public spaces? For so long our streets and public squares were barren places, to be traversed without hesitation, reminders of our anonymous smallness. We have lost touch with the city, as proven in a report conducted by Transport for London in 2006, which revealed that most people only understood London's geography by the underground railway map, which presents a spacially distorted picture of the city; as a result one in twenty people exiting Leicester Square station on the Piccadilly Line had hopped on to the train at one of the two nearest stations, both of which are only 800 metres away. It is for this reason that when we think about cities we must concentrate not just on the design of buildings but the encouragement of life between the buildings.

This is exactly what the Danish architect Jan Gehl thinks. Gehl has long campaigned to redesign the city by putting the pedestrian first. Starting in his home city, Copenhagen, he was the driving force behind the Stroget Car-Free Zone, the longest pedestrian area in Europe, devised in the 1960s. Like Whyte, Gehl believes that the city can rediscover its original functions in the hypermobile world: the city as a place for discourse, for bumping into strangers and old friends, for the exchange of information and goods, for formal occasions like feasts and festivals as well as private pleasures. While new technology has allowed us to do many of these things remotely, they do not replace the human urge to be where other people are. As he writes: 'Life in buildings and between buildings seems in nearly all situations to rank as more essential and more relevant than the spaces and buildings themselves.'[24]

It started off as an experiment. At Christmas time it was customary to cut off the central street, Stroget, that ran through the middle of Copenhagen, for a couple of days. Yet in 1962 they extended the closure to engage public reaction. For some the plan could only lead to disaster, with complaints that 'we are Danes, not Italians!'

CORBIS

Stroget – the joys of a car-free city centre

and 'no cars means no customers and no customers means no business'.[25] Yet the opposite proved the truth. Slowly the street was renovated with new pavements and fountains; and the Danes became accustomed to street life: on sunny days cafés began to put tables out, performances were staged, shops changed their window displays to attract the ambling browser. The scheme was widened throughout Copenhagen until by 2000 there were already 100,000 square metres of the city centre pedestrianised. A bicycle scheme was devised with 2,000 bikes available for hire.

But what was the purpose of all this planning? If it was just a retail opportunity, it was a lot of effort for an open-air mall! Rather, the new street plan did not dictate how people should behave but offered them a theatre for their urban lives upon which the identity of the living streets emerged. The street was allowed to develop its own complexity, to be regulated but open, evolving.

This was not always so obvious. In the early years when musicians started to busk on Stroget they were moved along by the police, who presumed that their performance was a disturbance. Yet it soon became apparent that the streets were more than conduits of consumption but rather the 'country's largest public forum'.[26] In a study in 1969 Gehl noted not only how people moved along the streets but where they stopped, what they looked at, what attracted their attention. While banks, offices and showrooms attracted the least interest, there was a marked slowing down in front of gallery windows, the cinema board, shop displays. The most arresting spectacle, however, were other people, from the man dressed in a Viking outfit advertising a sweater shop to jugglers and musicians: the various human activities that went on in the street space itself.

Yet where does this tipping point occur – when does the life of the street become the life of the city? Empty streets can be intimidating, and they do not become natural places of complex interaction without some effort. According to the Project for Public Spaces in New York, a group that was created by Fred Kent, who was involved with Whyte's City Streets project in the 1960s and has worked on developing numerous public spaces, each space should have at least ten things to see to make it a vibrant place. As the PPS website explains, the power of ten can be scaled up in any way you like:

> If your goal is to build a great city, it's not enough to have a single use dominate a particular place – you need an array of activities for people. It's not enough to have just one great place in a neighborhood – you need a number of them to create a truly lively community. It's not enough to have one great neighborhood in a city – you need to provide people all over town with close-to-home opportunities to take pleasure in public life. And it's not enough to have one liveable city or town in a region – you need a collection of interesting communities.'[27]

It is only the people on the street, however, who can tell whether a place achieves its purpose; a community will soon show whether it has embraced or adopted a new project. In the book *How To Turn a Place Around*, Kent tips the traditional relationship between architect and client on its head and shows that the community is the expert when it comes to the usage of a place. This has been taken to its logical conclusion with the increasingly popular practice of 'crowd-sourced place-making', which uses social media and the wisdom of the group to develop new places. It is indeed a radical alternative to the twentieth-century view of how to build a city.

Stroget in Copenhagen started out as an early example of a 'pop-up' community experiment – a temporary project. Often, the best ways to change the city are for only a short amount of time and on a small scale: improve the city block by block, allow people to own their own streets, make people the catalyst for change. The Better Block campaign was set up in the US in 2012 when a group of local activists and planners decided to do something for themselves and started to improve a single block in their neighbourhood. The location was an unloved stretch of asphalt which the group were able to transform into bike lanes, café-style tables and chairs, trees and pop-up businesses to encourage visitors. After the initial success, the group decided to up the challenge and have since conducted a number of 72-hour pop-up interventions where they turn a block around over a weekend. Thus in June 2012, their twenty-sixth project included an unloved warehouse district of Fort Lauderdale called FATVillage Art District. On one day, Professor Eric Dumbaugh and a group of students from Florida Atlantic set about to improve the neighbourhood, changing the 1950s industrial park into a temporary arts destination with murals, food trucks, a dog park and a farmers' market.

Initiatives like Better Block are all part of a larger movement embraced by 'tactical urbanism'. Here the emphasis is on incremental change from the bottom up, with a focus on five main goals:

A deliberate phased approach to instigating change
The offering of local solutions to local planning challenges
Short-term commitment and realistic expectations
Low risks, with a possibly high reward
The development of social capital between citizens and the building of organisational capacity between public-private institutions, non-profit and their constituents.[28]

Such tactical urbanism can be found in many places: Depave is a group from Portland, Oregon that tears up unwanted asphalt and returns the land to gardens. The Open Street Initiative has pedestrianised thoroughfares for the weekend to open up American cities to walkers and cyclists; the scheme now runs in over forty cities across the US. The mayor of New York has turned Times Square into a car-free plaza. The change in legislation on food trucks has allowed a new vibrant culinary culture in many US cities. Guerrilla gardening has turned forgotten corners of the city into blooming borders.

Making a city for the people makes a difference. After a century of architectural visionaries and their dreams of transforming human nature to the destructive nightmares of autopia that ripped up the old neighbourhoods in the name of efficiency and cleanliness, we have learnt that if we do not take account of the people who use them, it has every chance of failing. To rebuild the city, one must start from the street up and involve all those who live there. It is often where the best ideas come from.

4

A CREATIVE PLACE

Silicon Roundabout. I exit the subway and part of me expects to see something resembling Superman's Fortress of Solitude, a palace of crystalline shards pointing into the London sky. This place is meant to be the centre of the action, a hub for the future capital. In November 2010 Prime Minister David Cameron came here and announced the launch of Tech City, an initiative that hoped to turn this stretch of east London – which starts in Shoreditch and in time has come to include the Olympic Park 3 miles to the east at Stratford – into the technology capital of Europe. In his speech he set out what the government could do to nurture a vibrant new economy based upon creativity and knowledge to challenge the rest of the world:

> Right now, Silicon Valley is the leading place in the world for high-tech growth and innovation. But there's no reason why it has to be so predominant. Question is: where will its challengers be? Bangalore? Hefei? Moscow? My argument today is that if we have the confidence to really go for it and the understanding of what it takes, London could be one of them.[1]

As I walk up to street level, I am curious to see what has changed since I lived near this neighbourhood fifteen years ago. Back then, it was a down-at-heel backwater, only yards from the financial business district yet a community that was struggling to stay afloat. Once an enclave of light industry with factories, workshops and warehouses, it had been abandoned and allowed to rot; the once-elegant town houses had been turned into sweat shops. It was not a safe place to be at night.

Yet even in this state, something was stirring and the seeds of transformation were being sown. As I wander, I am struck by how very little has altered on the surface; however, there is a different, more purposeful feel to the place. I note that the ironic street art that had once stood above the roundabout – Banksy's early stencil of Travolta and Jackson in full *Pulp Fiction* get-up, arms outstretched gripping bananas instead of guns – has been painted over. Instead, nearby, a new mural seems to sum up the neighbourhood: CHANGE.

As I circumnavigate the roundabout, I stand in front of the window of What Architects that has a witty display of models built out of

'Change' is coming. Near Silicon Roundabout

Lego. Down Leonard Street, there are banners for the eCity apartment block boasting state-of-the-art furnishings, a sauna and 24-hour concierge service. Also, there are coffee shops everywhere, every chain café imaginable, jostling for real estate in this small corner of the city. It appears that caffeine is the fuel of the new era; where once the coal dug out of the ground powered the first Industrial Revolution, today the creative economy runs on the double espresso. I feel as if history is repeating itself: just as the first coffee houses in the seventeenth century marked the dawn of the globalised world, so this new generation of cafés is fuelling the Information Age.

There are many connections between the coffee houses of the 1600s and places like Silicon Roundabout today. As centres of information and trade, the first coffee houses established a forum for the new kind of urban, creative economy. It was here that people came together from different places and met as equals; information was exchanged from the docks – what ships had come in, what cargo was on the quay – and the first stock exchange was created, the first insurance list formulated, where one would come to digest the daily printed news. Clubs were formed, politics debated, 'penny universities' established to educate those who did not have time for school; the coffee house was a place for auctions, trials and even scientific experiments.

Consider the relationship between creativity and the city: so often it has been assumed that one needs to be alone, and in a quiet place, to find the inspiration for something new, yet throughout history the best ideas have often emerged from the complexity of the city. Are cities more creative places? Where do good ideas come from?

The leading American novelist Jonathan Franzen famously claimed that he sometimes wrote his novel *The Corrections* at a desk facing a blank wall, the internet cable to his computer disabled and even occasionally wearing a blindfold to aid his concentration. This may sound like a method of extreme isolation, while others feel at their most creative sitting in Starbucks, but both take their inspiration from the bustle of the city. In another example, the economist Adam Jaffe examined the impact of technological neighbours being close to each other and the knowledge 'spillover' that occurs with proximity. It makes sense to be close to your competitors; there are creative advantages to being in the same place, which evolve into clusters of innovation.

If cities are the natural environment for innovation, is this something that we can nurture? And what is the best way of doing this? Silicon Roundabout was attracting creative companies long before David Cameron and his quango cavalry arrived. Does government have a role in promoting initiatives like Tech City? In other instances, culture itself has been used to transform the city, turning a place from a backwater to a cultural destination. Can the promotion of the creative city help revive fortunes or should we be wary of investing in white elephants?

In the last couple of decades numerous cities have begun to rebrand themselves as 'Creative Cities'. As of 2011, at least sixty cities around the world have initiated creativity policies; Britain alone has twenty. In these instances, the city has seen culture as a means to improve the profile and economy of the place. Liverpool One has attempted to revive the fortunes of its abandoned Albert Docks area with a collection of attractions, museums and enticing modern apartment blocks, with mixed critical response, hoping to bring people back into the city centre to live and visit. In Berlin, the development of the Pariser Platz, which once ran along the line of the Berlin Wall between East and West Germany, had the complicated task of both attracting crowds of visitors but also becoming a place of national significance, the symbol of the united nation. Many of these new schemes are in pursuit of the 'Bilbao effect'.

At the end of the 1980s the Basque city of Bilbao was a long way down the list of European cultural centres. It was a shabby industrial and fishing community on the north coast of Spain, where one in four working adults was unemployed and it had a meagre tourist revenue from the 100,000 or so visitors a year. As architecture curator Terence Riley noted: 'No one had heard of Bilbao or knew where it was. Nobody knew how to spell it.'[2]

It was indeed an unlikely place to site a signature work of high-tech modern architecture and a world-beating collection of contemporary art. Yet, through determination and planning, the local government was able to persuade the Guggenheim Foundation to share its collection and to launch an architectural competition attracting bids from the world's staritects. A site was then chosen that was once Spain's leading steelyard, the centre for the ship-building industry that moved to Asia decades ago.

In the end, the LA-based architect Frank Gehry was selected, and the result was less of a building, more of a glistening tumult of curves, metal and glass. The Guggenheim, Bilbao is the architectural equivalent of Marilyn Monroe singing 'Happy Birthday'. Costing over $100 million to build, it was never a project for a faint-hearted municipality. In addition to the architectural auto-icon of the museum itself, the city was committed to provide transport – a new airport and subway – as well as improve sanitation and air quality to make the destination more attractive.

Visiting the city today and seeing the building for the first time as it spirals above the surrounding blocks is a thrilling experience. Bilbao has grown accustomed to the hordes of visitors and is starting to look comfortable with its new status, perhaps even taking it for granted. The River Nervión that curls around the museum is now less polluted and is ribboned with parks, while the main streets of the city have been widened and pedestrianised, filled with boutiques and cafés. The graffiti has gone. Bilbao itself has benefited from the museum. It is calculated that the project was so successful that it had paid for itself within seven years. In 2010 visitor numbers continued to rise despite the economic downturn, reaching 954,000, at least 60 per cent of these coming from abroad and therefore adding a calculated €213 million to the region, €26 million tax revenue to the local government and offering employment to over 3,000 local workers.[3] Bringing the Guggenheim to Bilbao was therefore one way of breathing new life into the city.

The 'Bilbao effect' has been much copied but not often bettered. It heralded an era of superstar architects who were commissioned to build eye-catching cultural destinations that would put a once second- or third-tier city onto the map. The rise of visitor figures, new income for the city as well as a revived civic pride are the kind of factors that have persuaded other cities to attempt the same trick, albeit with mixed results. While such grand projects have raised the status of big-name architects – Gehry, Foster, Hadid, Meier, Koolhaas, Libeskind – they have not always seen the city itself blossom. For every Sydney Opera House, whose burnished-sail roofs have become so iconic that they are shorthand for Australia itself, there is the National Centre for Popular Music in Sheffield.

Funded by the National Lottery to the tune of £15 million, the new centre was to be a celebration of British pop music. Sheffield is one of the unsung centres of pop, having produced bands as diverse as perm rockers Def Leppard, Goths the Cabaret Voltaire, 1980s synth bands Human League, ABC and Heaven 17, to Britpop deities Pulp, crooner Richard Hawley and the Arctic Monkeys. It therefore seemed the perfect place to celebrate local creativity and the organisers commissioned a piece of instant-icon building designed by Brandon Coates Associates that looked like four interconnected metal drums.

Yet the project did not fail so badly in the design but in the business plan – the original estimate of visitor numbers was far too high and when the collection opened in March 1999 the owners were expecting 400,000 through the door a year. When, after seven months, only 104,000 had come, the media started to sense a white elephant, and the day-to-day operation was handed over to PricewaterhouseCoopers to find a way to reduce costs. In June 2000 the project was closed with losses of over £1 million. By 2003 the building had been converted into the Students' Union building for the local Sheffield Hallam University.

Disasters like this have not put off emerging cities from still attempting to establish themselves as cultural capitals. It is easy, however, to confuse creativity and what Deyan Sudjic calls the 'edifice complex', the uses of architecture to show the world how powerful or rich a place is.

In January 2007 the Abu Dhabi government announced the launch of Saadiyat Island, a new development to make the UAE a cultural powerhouse in an instant. At the launch, the royal family stood next door to some of the world's leading architects. Gehry had been hired in the hope that he would repeat the magic of Bilbao with Guggenheim Abu Dhabi. Zaha Hadid was also in the photo line-up with plans for an arts centre; French architect Jean Nouvel, famed for his Islamic Centre in Paris, was given the task of developing the Gulf outpost for the Louvre, while Tadeo Ando had designs on a maritime museum to complete the set. The whole complex will not be finished until 2017.

While many involved felt that this was an opportunity to use art and culture to cross borders, it is difficult not to believe that its primary purpose is not so much creativity as tourist dollars;

Saadiyat includes plots for a Hyatt Hotel, a Monte Carlo Club, the Mandarin Oriental and St Regis beach villas; as Barry Lord, one of the developers noted: 'Cultural tourists are wealthier, older, more educated and spend more. From an economic view, this makes sense.'[4] It might make sense, and has clearly worked in Bilbao, but this is not the only way to define a creative city, nor does it truly tell us why they will become so important in the future.

Recall Geoffrey West's study into the metabolism of the city. Gathering together all possible data on the urban world, West and his team at the Santa Fe Institute discovered that cities display a superlinear power law when it came to size and output. Thus the city that grows by, say, ten times does not just improve its performance by ten but by sixteen times its original. This was, they proposed, true of the city's economic power, energy efficiency, even crime rate and levels of disease; surprisingly, it is also true for the city's creativity: 'wages, income, domestic product, bank deposits, as well as rates of invention, measured by new patents and employment in creative sectors all scale superlinearly with city size'.[5]

Thus, the complex interweave of connections and people, the agglomeration of knowledge and ideas, is an amazing incubator of innovation. Being in the city, part of the crowd, does not make us individually smart but can help us collectively to be remarkably creative.

Cities are the ideal laboratories of innovation: there are more people here, so the likelihood is that more ideas will bubble to the surface. It is not just the size of the population, however, but the density of the connections that matter. The network of weak ties that help one to find a job more easily, and makes it so hard to be lonely in the city, is also the powerful crucible of innovation. Good ideas often do not come from solitary moments of contemplation but from sharing; of rubbing two notions together to produce something new; they are hunches that have lain dormant for long periods which are rolled over and examined in a new light; moments of serendipity that cause a surprise symbiosis; the result of a friend of a friend offering essential help at the right time.

The city also offers diversity and competition, the best forcing grounds for turning seeds into blossoming success. This is what Adam Smith calls the 'invisible hand' of capitalism: the market's demand for the new, the supplier's desire to reduce costs and scale up profits has always fuelled creativity. Competition forces innovation, finding the new edge or improvement that makes the vital difference. Best of all, good ideas breed other good ideas; creativity develops its own virtuous circle. It has always been this way, and is one of the reasons why people have continued to leave home and take that perilous journey, willing to risk everything, to make their fortune and reputation within the metropolis. Take, for example, the capital of seventeenth-century Holland, Amsterdam, which in its day was the greatest city in the world.

Amsterdam's Golden Age arose out of chance, timing and geography, but it reveals how the complex city flourishes. The capital of Holland, principal state within the Dutch Republic, was ideally located, naturally positioned at the centre point of the burgeoning Atlantic world: connecting the Hanseatic states to the north with the Mediterranean south; making it the hub of the maritime trade, the marketplace for American gold, spices brought by Portuguese ships from the east, Venetian treasures, English wool, French wine, silks from Lyon, timber from the forests of the north, wheat from Poland, herring and hemp for strong rope from the Baltic States, metals brought overland from Germany, and even rare, fragile tulips from Constantinople.

For example, on one morning in June 1634, ships returning from the east displayed their bounty on the wharf before carting it all to the Bourse:

326,733½ Amsterdam pounds of Malacca pepper; 297,446 lbs of cloves; 292,623 lbs of saltpetre; 141,278 lbs of indigo; 483,083 lbs of sappan wood; 219,027 pieces of blue Ming ware; 52 further chests of Korean and Japanese porcelain; 75 large vases and pots containing preserved confections and much of it spiced ginger; 660 lbs Japanese copper; 241 pieces of fine Japanese lacquer work; 3,989 rough diamonds of large carat; 93 boxes of pearls and rubies; 603 bales of dressed Persian silks and grosgrains; 1,155 lbs raw Chinese silks; 199,800 lbs of raw Kandy sugar.[6]

The local merchants themselves invented a new way of doing business, setting up joint stock ventures such as the East India Company, sharing the risk of long, expensive voyages as well as the prospective rewards. This offered a scale of business that was previously only within the grasp of a king. Founded in 1602, within twenty years the

CORBIS

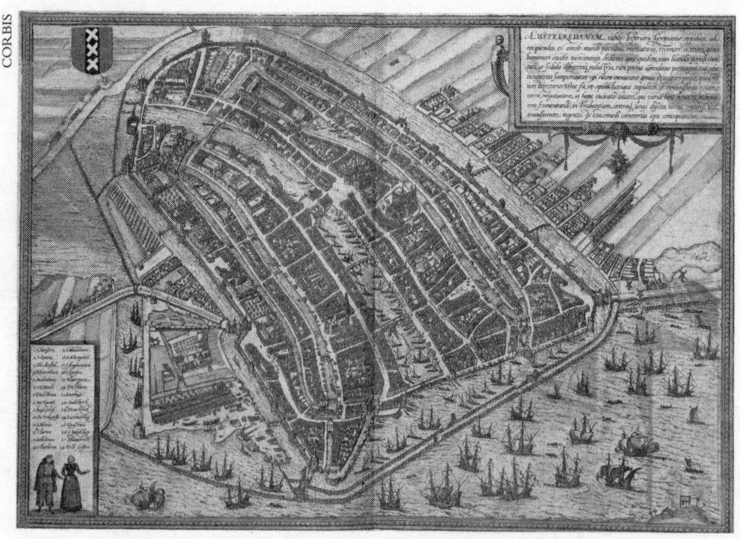

A map of Amsterdam in the seventeenth century

East India Company controlled the majority of the Asian spice trade with colonies throughout Indonesia, and later adding ports in Malaysia, Sri Lanka, the Indian subcontinent, Thailand, Japan and mainland China. By 1650, it was the richest company in the world with 190 ships, a private army and an annual dividend of 40 per cent.

In time, the port saw the value of not just being a place of trade but also a place that finished and improved the raw materials that were dropped at the quay: wool was turned into fabric, metals were beaten and moulded into finely wrought goods. Banking followed, chased by the most valuable commodity: information. Amsterdam became an intellectual bourse as much as an exchange for commodities. And as merchants looked for commercial advantage and intellectuals went in pursuit of the new truth of the changing world, innovation and creativity interweaved, collided, flourished.

Walking around Amsterdam today, one can still read the explosion of creativity of that moment in the ambitious canal-building schemes. The city itself was dug out of the marshy banks of the River Amstel with a system of concentric canals that encircled the centre. These were cut in the early seventeenth century in response to the rapid urban growth and proof that even the very ground the city was built on was the result of ingenuity and innovation.

This was also reflected in the architecture of the age. As the seventeenth-century traveller Melchior Fokken wondered: 'All the buildings stand tall ... some of them two, others three and four storeys high; sometimes their great cellars filled with merchandise. Within, the houses are full of priceless ornaments so that they seem more like royal palaces than the houses of merchants.'[7] There was money to build ambitious projects: merchant houses were made from brick or stone and rose high above the canal waters. The façades were modestly decorated, reflecting the Calvinist restraint that bundled religion, trade and polite behaviour into insurmountable unity. There were also significant public buildings commissioned at this time: the town hall, the Bourse, the grand plaza of the New Market centred around the important Weighing House. All these new buildings set the city's magnificence in stone and were designed in a new Dutch Baroque, an idiosyncratic interpretation of Roman splendour adapted for northern European taste; a reflection of how a city can take ideas from a far-off place, adapt, mutate and make them native.

But business does not occur in a vacuum; most of the best ideas come from somewhere unexpected, the chanced connection. Thus the determination for profit within Dam Square in seventeenth century Holland also brought forth a creative revolution. As people came from across Europe to enjoy the benefits of the Bourse, the city itself was transformed. A silent tolerance of religious difference became the norm, so that as long as people worshipped in private they were mostly left alone: as a result the Jews who had recently been persecuted in Portugal and Spain found a haven. French and Flemish Protestants who were hounded out of their homes also made the journey north in the hope of peace. English Puritans ran there after the Restoration and it became a hiding place for radical thinkers looking for political sanctuary. Meanwhile, on Oudezijds Voorburgwal, a Dutch Catholic merchant built a chapel in his roof, later named Our Lord in the Attic. This mixture of nationalities, faiths and practices were all equal on the trading floor but allowed for a level of social complexity, connections and networks that made the city a powerful engine for good ideas.

Alongside the invention of the first stock exchange, Amsterdam was also the nest for new methods of accountancy and banking; financial tools for leveraging stock, banknotes and promissory notes, systems of credit that we still use today. But this innovation was more than just the moment of the deal: it infused the whole city. Amsterdam ship builders led the way in new maritime technology ensuring their vessels, the Fluyt, could carry the largest cargo safely by reducing the number of cannon aboard while employing block and tackle hydraulic systems to ease operations and reduce labour costs. The return of novel goods from the New World incentivised sciences such as sugar-refining and metallurgy. Meanwhile the expansion of the cities demanded innovations in crop rotation and dairy farming to feed all the citizens.

Being masters of the oceans encouraged a mushrooming of legal ingenuity, in which, for example, Amsterdammer Hugo Grotius set out the tenets of international law as he attempted to establish Holland's primacy over foreign lands. Maritime science also engaged scientists to think about astronomy, horology and nautical innovation, resulting in the development and improvement of telescopes and microscopes, star charts and celestial predictions, lens grinding and time pieces as engineers hoped to find a mechanical solution to the longitude problem. These new machines allowed people to look further, deeper, higher and more clearly at things that were once invisible, launching new fascinations in chemistry, biology, astronomy, engineering, microbiology, entomology and geology.

And alongside technology, there was also a revolution in culture, which thrived on the sea of new influences, ideas that washed up in the port, as well as a tide of surplus cash that needed to be spent. Painting became the rage for wealthy Amsterdammers and even farmers invested in the art market. In particular, there was a fashion for domestic, still life, portrait and civic paintings, especially in the hands of masters such as Rembrandt van Rijn and Frans Hals; while Johannes Vermeer, working in nearby Delft, seemed to be able to turn ordinary life into a moment of beauty.

This market in art was reflected by the flood of print and paper that accompanied a turning point in publishing and books. Here ideas were traded and exchanged in an atmosphere of freedom that allowed John Locke to write his works on toleration, the basis of government, and the substance of human knowledge; here also René Descartes, hounded from France, put down on paper his *Discourse on Method* and Benedict Spinoza shocked the world with his *Theologico-Political Treatise*, but despite widespread opprobrium the book was not banned. Here, upon the cobbled streets beside the canals, were the stirrings of the first information revolution.

All the same energy and innovation that could be felt amongst the canals and squares of seventeenth-century Amsterdam can be found today at Silicon Roundabout. The metropolis has a unique propensity for new ideas, improvement and adaptions, the cross-fertilisation of good notions. For centuries the city has been the perfect place to develop the killer app. Yet there is one noticeable difference.

Walking around Amsterdam 350 years ago, it would have been impossible not to notice that the majority of the business conducted within the city was the exchange of things. The smell of the spices permeated the warehouses; porters carted wheelbarrows of goods from merchants' warehouses to stores; wagons were overloaded with bales of fabric; meanwhile in Shoreditch, almost every transaction is invisible. The factories have been renovated and the industrial machines replaced by rows of shining Apple Mac screens. The production line has been superseded by the critical path; the moment of invention no longer takes place in the workshop but in the cloud; the engineer has abandoned joists and sprockets and has picked up XML, Adobe Flash and Mathematica.

In the Industrial Age we made and traded things; today in the Information Age we create and sell ideas. As John Howkins, who coined the phrase 'creative economy', states: 'Creativity is not new and neither is economics, but what is new is the nature and the extent of the relationship between creativity and economics.'[8] In 2001 Howkins predicted that the creativity business was worth $2.2 trillion worldwide and was set to grow 5 per cent a year; he was almost right. This sector was the one area of the global economy that was least affected by the credit crunch; in 2008 it generated $592 billion, more than double its turnover in 2002, which suggests an annual growth of 14 per cent. The knowledge economy forces us to think again about how we work, and what we do; it could also allow us to think about the city anew.

According to Richard Florida, the extent of the creative classes is having a profound impact on the success of cities. Using the broadest definition of the knowledge economy as possible – 'science and technology, arts and design, entertainment and media, law, finance, management, healthcare and education'[9] – Florida shows that since the decline of industry in the west, this new class of worker has risen at a gallop: 5 per cent of all employment in 1900, 10 per cent in 1950, 15 per cent in 1980 and more than 30 per cent by 2005. And almost all these jobs will be found in the city. However, they are not evenly spread out between all cities.

Imagine a twenty-first-century Amsterdam and you may do well to think of Bangalore. Until recently, the Bay Area – Silicon Valley – has been considered the mecca of all coders, hackers and technology entrepreneurs. People came from around the world to access the super-charged atmosphere and assorted expertise of the Santa Clara Valley: in 2010 it was calculated that 60 per cent of the scientists and technologists working there were born outside the US.

Amongst the most successful group in Silicon Valley are from the Indian subcontinent, constituting approximately 28 per cent of the entire workforce. Between 1980 and 1999 15.5 per cent of all start-ups in Silicon Valley were run by entrepreneurs who had moved to the Bay Area from India; combined, these new companies generated $17 billion in annual revenue and 58,000 jobs. Today, however, many in the valley are nervous that the flow of dedicated, educated and ingenious coders from India is slowing down. It appears that one might not have to go all the way to San Francisco to make one's fortune any more. India itself has developed its own Silicon Valley.

In the 1990s Bangalore gained a reputation for IT services and today the city is a destination for thousands of educated young scientists every year. The talent pool is considerable, educated in a highly competitive and rigorous system; a 2009 Ernst and Young survey discovered that there are more scientists in India than anywhere else in the world: 2 million students overall, including 600,000 engineers, graduating from over 400 universities every year. When an average school teacher earns 100,000 rupees, a graduate from an Indian institute of technology can expect forty times that sum. Yet this was still far lower than what a coder in the Bay Area would expect and as a result American companies began to set up their own offices there in three business parks on the outside of the city, shiny satellites on the outskirts of the old colonial town, which is becoming increasingly congested as more and more engineers arrive to make their fortune. Since 1971 the city's population has grown from 1.6 to 8.4 million.

A reputation for excellence, efficiency and low cost was confirmed in the 1990s when the world was faced by the Y2K virus. At the time there was a global concern that the operating systems of most computers had been programmed in such a way that on the stroke of midnight, 1 January 2000, planes would fall out of the sky and banks would collapse. Companies such as Infosys were tasked with testing and repairing over 2,000 billion lines of code. The operation proved that Bangalore could deliver on time, on cost and was home to some of the smartest engineers in the world. With the dawn of the internet age, many businesses realised that they did not need to create their own IT departments, and when it came to ordinary, mundane tasks nor did they have to rely on the relatively high costs of paying for the lifestyles of Californian coders. By 2005 Bangalore became the outsource capital of the Information Age, worth at least $5 billion a year in revenues and growing at an astonishing 30 per cent a year.

In 2007 the city was home to over 1,300 ICT firms; every major global company, bank and developer had offices there and were dependent on the skills and dedication of the local workforce of 250,000 engineers. In addition to the American, British and European headquarters, many local firms had started to dominate the field. The industry was now spread out across a series of suburban parks built to cope with the rush of growth. The International Tech Park was the first to be developed in 1998 with its own power station and set around six buildings named Discoverer, Explorer, Navigator, Creator and Pioneer, and a shopping mall giving the impression that a chunk of America has been directly transplanted to the subcontinent. Electronic City, to the south of Bangalore, is now home to over 120 companies such as Hewlett Packard, Infosys and Siemens as well as a number of educational institutions churning out managers, coders and budding entrepreneurs.

In the words of many commentators, Bangalore is now competing with Silicon Valley itself as the tech capital of the world. But there are problems with such aspirations. The local HAL airport only started to service international flights in 1997, and at that point it had capacity for 3.5 million passengers a year; a decade later it was straining with 7.5 million visitors. It was replaced by the Bangalore International Airport but in 2005 the new airport had to change its development to deal with a potential 12 million customers. As a result the project was delayed by three years. Today it is India's fourth largest airport. But when I visited, as my taxi drove me away from the new shiny terminal I was warned that it might take three hours to get to my hotel. They were still building the road between the city and the airport. The fabric of the city was failing to keep up with the demands of the burgeoning creative economy it has spawned.

The economist Enrico Moretti has been charting the new geography of jobs in America and his research reveals that the new knowledge workers have a multiplier effect wherever they work. Creative jobs often attract other creative workers; in addition they increase employment and salaries for those who are providing local services: 'for each new high-tech job in a city, five additional jobs are ultimately created outside of the high-tech sector in that city'.[10]

The creative economy has a powerful impact on its host city, but not all cities are equal. Some are more creative than others, while some attract a certain kind of entrepreneur. For despite Geoffrey West's equation telling us that size is the main determinant of the complex city, individual places have very distinct personalities and reputations.

For example, some places are more liveable than others. There are at least three seperate liveability indexes that rank the economy, health, lifestyle and culture of the world's cities; in 2012 *The Economist* decided that Hong Kong was the ideal hometown; elsewhere Mercer's 'quality of living survey' decided that Vienna topped the rankings; meanwhile *Monocle* magazine plumped for Zurich as the number-one spot. Liveability has a huge impact on where people want to move to in pursuit of the perfect job; and making a city more open, cultural, clean and safe can change its economic fortunes.

Perhaps more importantly, cities are becoming increasingly

specialised. It is for this reason that we talk about Hollywood and movies, Milan as the centre of Italian fashion, and Wall Street as the world centre for banking. Within a globalised market it makes no sense to attempt to reinvent new industries within each individual city. Take, for example, the iPhone, a product that is developed truly globally: devised in Cupertino, California, the silicon chip inside it is designed by ARM (a company that has its main offices in Cambridge, as well as Bangalore); the chip itself is developed in Korea; and the phone handset is assembled by hand in the FoxConn factory in Chengdu, China.

Each stage of the iPhone's production highlights the advantages and costs of globalisation: that the world is being divided up in terms of local specialism connected through a network that links cities ever closer. Why, for example, should one try and develop a microprocessor industry from scratch when it is easier to invest and trade in the latest technology from Incheon or Seoul in South Korea, where the scale of production is unbeatable, and there is a level of expertise and infrastructure that is hard to compete with? Similarly, why go anywhere other than Bangalore for your end-to-end software problems?

This inequality amongst cities gives people more choice about where they want to live. As urban economist Richard Florida observes, 'The place we choose to live can determine the income we earn, the people we meet, the friends we make, the partners we choose, and the options available to our children and families.'[11] An 2008 survey of 8,500 people in fourteen major cities showed that 75 per cent of residents had 'chosen' their city. As the world's population becomes ever more fluid, the personalities of the world's cities, and the question of how they can attract the best workers, is going to become more urgent. What, for example, will happen to the Bay Area if young Indian entrepreneurs feel that they can stay at home and start up new enterprises in Bangalore without going to Silicon Valley?

As individual cities become increasingly specialised, people are going to travel across the world more to get to the centres of excellence. The future city therefore must be an open and adaptable place. It needs to continue to attract the best workers from afar, to accommodate the latest ideas wherever they come from. The creative city needs creative people, and this is becoming an increasingly mobile marketplace that has to cope with many changing dimensions. With all this passion for newness and mobility, it is often easy to forget what is already there.

This brand new, hypermobile vision of the future comes with a warning: things are not as fluid, open and fresh as the economists would have us believe. Richard Florida was the first to coin 'the creative class' as a new, dynamic social and economic group who were having a profound impact on urban regeneration. The new human economy, he proposes, will be split between those who are mobile and those who are stuck. Knowledge workers will move around the world in search of places of excellence: 'The mobile possess the means, resources and inclination to seek out and move to locations where they can leverage their talents.'[12] It was this creative class that David Cameron had in mind when he launched Tech City in 2010. It is these burgeoning 'hi-tech nomads' that are causing congestion in gridlocked Bangalore. The 'creative class' is the human equivalent of the 'Bilbao effect', developing a place where small start-ups and multinational companies can share the same car park, attracting talent from around the world.

Such schemes can be tremendously successful. Within a year of Cameron's announcement, Tech City had attracted huge attention from global companies. The high-profile push has raised the international standing of the project. For big-tech companies looking

Silicon Roundabout

for a place to site their European office, the publicity drive has worked, as confirmed by Georg Ell, European general manager of US company Yammer: 'The Tech City initiative was the catalyst for our move to east London. It provides a nucleus which drives momentum, opportunities to share and learn from others. It also attracts a talent pool.'[13] Google has also signed a lease on a seven-storey office overlooking the roundabout, proposing to set up a 'launch pad' for innovation and start-ups. Amazon has promised to set up a large European 'digital hub' to house its design teams as well as the recently purchased tech businesses Lovefilm and Push-button. There are plans afoot as well for what to do with the Olympic Village and the media centre that was designed to cope with 20,000 international journalists, which will become part of Tech City after the 2012 Games.

Does this high-level investment in the gospel of the creative class help grass-roots creativity? Richard Florida's ideas are not without their critics. For some, his new intellectual nomads are not a special breed apart, but generally more educated and therefore always more likely to be able to go in pursuit of the best jobs. For others, mobility itself is no proof of success or creativity, and 'the stuck' could easily be reinterpreted as happy.[14] Still more warn against the worship of the 'creative class' as the only means of developing a competitive economy, dismissing all that has happened before as irrelevant, promoting a doctrine preaching that 'the history of a city is at best of little use, and at worst an obstacle to entering the advanced knowledge economy. The prescription is to bring the economy from up high into one's city.'[15] It is sometimes too easy to be seduced by the new, rather than really looking and seeing what is happening on the ground.

Creativity does not evolve out of a vacuum; it does not emerge from a photo opportunity or a government initiative. No project has ever worked when it has been imposed against the grain of the place. The notion that building a business park and a good road to the airport is sufficient to inspire economic revolution is a foolish one that has trapped many cities which have rebranded themselves as 'creative'. When considering Silicon Roundabout as a creative place, or Bangalore as a centre of innovation, therefore, the long-term history of the neighbourhood has a more powerful influence on the future than the government brochures might imply.

I have come to the Roundabout to visit TechHub, situated on the ground floor of a 1960s office block. The space was started by businesswoman Elizabeth Varley as a focus for tech entrepreneurs and start-ups. It looks undistinguished compared to some of the newer buildings that have begun to sprout up in the neighbourhood. There is, however, a sense of energy, of can-do, makeshift potential about the place. The offices now cover the complete ground floor; demand for space has been so strong since opening in spring 2011 that it has been almost impossible to convert the floor plan. The ceiling panels have been taken out, exposing heating and electrics, leaving strip lighting and dangling cables hanging down like ivy.

In the front there is a large open-plan space with movable tables; it is, according to the marketing blurb, a place for tech entrepreneurs to touch down, work, plug their laptops in and use the fast wifi.[16] It is also here that the Hub organises meetings, drinks, get-togethers, seminars and information swaps. Investors and angels can come and see what is happening and offer advice, perhaps even investment, connecting new entrepreneurs with the wider Silicon Roundabout community. There are small office spaces for private meetings and, for the more regular workers, a permanent desk. The project is geared to promote connections and good ideas. And looking around on my visit, despite the quietness and atmosphere of concentration within the main spaces, this place is as active as the Amsterdam Bourse on a busy day.

Inside TechHub

Silicon Roundabout was born out of enterprises and good ideas like TechHub; however, this new community has not been built on a blank slate but upon decades of history. When I first came here in the early 1990s, only a few people I knew had mobile phones. Starting my first job in publishing, the office did not yet have the internet and as the editorial junior I was tasked with going to the Cybercafé in Whitfield Street whenever we needed some online research; with a dial-up connection, it could take all afternoon. At that time Shoreditch was emerging from decades of neglect, abandoned by government, business and hope: an inner-city white working-class ghetto. It had been heavily bombed during the Second World War and was developed as a test bed for numerous social-housing schemes, tearing through the traditional community and uprooting the neighbourhood.

Yet some of the old fabric remained: disused factories that were now empty and decaying; warehouses that stood vacant; Victorian terraces that now housed sweat shops. And all this only a matter of 500 yards away from the edge of the world's most powerful financial capital. From the once dilapidated Old Street roundabout, one could look south and see the glistening glass and steel of the City, shimmering in the afterglow of the Big Bang. It was the perfect time and location for regeneration.

They were exciting times when there was only one place that everyone congregated – the Bricklayers Arms on Curtain Road – and a burgeoning artistic culture was born, soon to be associated with the YBA movement. It was near here that artists such as Gavin Turk, Tracey Emin, Gilbert and George lived. Here Joshua Compston set up the first East End gallery, Factual Nonsense, and organised happenings such as the Hoxton Square Hanging Picnic, where the artwork was exhibited along the railings surrounding the central garden area. Cheap rent afforded large studio space and a DIY ethos so that many exhibitions were self-curated, such as

The Shop at 103 Bethnal Green Road, opened by Emin and Sarah Lucas. In time, Shoreditch began to attract other creative industries: design, fashion, magazines such as *Dazed and Confused*, architecture and early innovators in web technology.

A similar story – the deep roots of the city's innovation – can be found in Bangalore, which on the surface appears to have emerged as an IT superpower out of nowhere in the 1990s. However, the truth shows that the southern Indian city had a long history of investment in science and technology. During the Raj, Bangalore, the capital of Karnataka, was renowned as a retirement paradise for ageing colonials who did not wish to return home. The city was an attempt to create 'a bit of England in India' with its Turf Club and the elite Bangalore Club.

In the aftermath of Independence in 1947, Bangalore remained blessed; the departing British leaving their legacy of the English language and law, which would be useful in the future. In addition the government of Jawaharlal Nehru (1947–64) ordained the community India's 'City of the Future', the intellectual capital of the subcontinent, and plans were set to build three universities, fourteen engineering colleges and forty-seven polytechnic schools. These in time attracted a number of research institutes in all manner of things such as science, health, aeronautics, food and even, in 1972, two years after Neil Armstrong set foot on the moon, the Indian Space Research Organisation. As a result many of the nation's most important public-sector agencies – Hindustan Aeronautics, Bharat Electronics, Indian Telephone Industries – were established there. Then the private sector moved in: Wipro, which first started as a producer of vegetable oil but went into IT in 1980; Infosys, set up in 1981 with an initial investment of $300 and now employing 133,000 people in over thirty-three countries; and the transistor manufacturers, Namtech.

Even before headlines began to celebrate Bangalore's new IT dawn, the city had a deeply ingrained relationship with technology and innovation. I was reminded of this as I talked with Dr S. Janardham, who had come to the city in the 1960s and soon became a leading pioneer in computing at the National Aerospace Laboratories. When he first arrived, Bangalore had a population of only 600,000, and he watched as it became the place for the best engineering minds of the whole subcontinent. He is proud of his legacy and felt that India would soon rule the IT world.

It is only from such long-term creativity that the present-day innovation emerged. In 2008, two years before Tech City, it was estimated that there were no more than twenty start-ups in the Old Street area; by the end of 2011, this number has risen to over 300. Location, agglomeration and the right atmosphere has helped form this natural cluster of firms. It is here that Last.fm, Moo, Dopplr and SoundCloud started; in 2011 local heroes Tweetdeck were bought by Twitter for £25 million. The most recent success story can be found at Mind Candy, creators of the online sensation Moshi Monsters, which has encouraged over 50 million children worldwide to adopt their own pixelated pet. On merchandising alone, the company expects to make £60 million in 2011.[17]

According to a 2012 report by the Centre for London, it is clear that the top-down initiative needs to be taken with a pinch of salt. It appears to be something of a rebranding exercise with the aim of attracting foreign investment rather than stimulating grass-roots activity. Silicon Roundabout is not a science park that has been raised up on the outside of the city; it is located in the heart of one of the most creative neighbourhoods that has organically grown in the past two decades. The government project appears to be more of an attempt to find a purpose for the Olympic Park following the Games.

In contrast, around the roundabout itself, there has been little actual investment: the tube station (one of the least attractive in the city) has not been upgraded; there has not even been an improvement to the broadband capacity to the region. There are fears that the cheerleading will simply raise rents and squeeze poor commercial space in an already fragile emerging economy. The report concluded:

> One of the most striking characteristics of the East London cluster is its organic growth. It has been evolving for years under the policy radar, and only now – as it reaches critical mass, and becomes the figurehead of London's digital economy – is it receiving much public attention ... Tech City should be about taking what inner East London already has and helping it get even better.[18]

When I asked Varley what was the most pressing issue in the area, however, she did not demand change to infrastructure, or marketing campaigns, but instead bemoaned the lack of bottom-up investment in start-ups. She called for the government to invest with small grants in the people rather than the place, 'so that a young entrepreneur can eat for six months' at the crucial prototype stages of starting a business rather than being forced to work on new projects around the day job. In addition, Varley suggested that we should stop comparing Silicon Roundabout with Silicon Valley. The comparisons make little sense, she noted: Santa Clara is a one-industry town while London is creative in so many different ways. It is unlikely that the UK will develop a new Facebook or Twitter, but with initiatives like the DCE (the Digital City Exchange) connecting Silicon Roundabout with academics from Imperial College, London, there is hope of finding innovations in health-care, sustainability or data management.

Similarly, I hoped to find the same story in Bangalore, and had travelled to see whether the city was more than a highly skilled service provider for the hi-tech companies of the world, or whether it had the potential to start up its own economic revolution. According to Dr Janardham, the city's computer business had begun as a commercial venture; it was only in the 1980s that engineers began to be interested in computing science and the field became more focused on solutions, architecture and code. While this developed a generation of brilliant coders, it lost its entrepreneurial spirit. Compared to many other centres of excellence, the number of registered patents coming out of Bangalore are small, and in most cases belong to the multinational corporations. In addition, the number of start-ups are surprisingly few compared to, for example, Shoreditch. Perhaps, I suggested to him, innovation went against the grain of the place; perhaps Bangalore was the home of the 'cyber coolie'.

Can this spirit of entrepreneurialism be rediscovered or would Indians continue to fly to Santa Clara to get their good ideas off the ground? At the Centre for the Internet and Society, I met Kiran Jonnalagadda, who runs HasGeek, one of the leading blogs watching the burgeoning start-up community. Previously he had been a founder of Barcamp, a self-organising 'unconference' where the audience decided what to discuss, an unexpectedly fertile environment which had spawned Headstart and Start-Up Saturdays, two initiatives that have now expanded nationally.

Jonnalagadda was optimistic. He highlighted that the community – just as in Silicon Roundabout – had yet to reach critical mass in terms of technology, capital or the size of the market. India was still waiting for its Moshi Monsters to launch local innovation internationally. At present, most of the successes were national: FlipKart and Indiaplaza were popular e-commerce sites; Interviewstreet was a smart recruiting site that set up coding contests to find the best hackers for the job; HarvestMan is a Bangalore-developed open-source search bot.

But there are a number of obstacles, both bureaucratic and cultural, in turning a good idea into an international business. It has been said that there is not enough research and development in Indian domestic companies, which affects the level of patents; why innovate when there is so much money to be made from providing services? There is also a big debate on intellectual property legislation that rewards and protects innovation. In addition, starting up a business in India can be a labyrinthine problem. In Singapore, it takes twenty-four days to set up a business; on his blog Kiran Jonnalagadda recounts with incredulity the tortuous 110 days it took for HasGeek to become a limited liability partnership. Then there is the fact that investment is sometimes difficult to come by, especially when most enterprises were traditionally set up within the family.

Nevertheless, Jonnalagadda believes that, despite the obstacles, Bangalore is a vibrant place, and he told me to visit Jaaga on Double Road, in the centre of the city, to see how exciting start-up culture in the city can be.

Jaaga, the TechHub in the Garden City, promises much. Set back from the street, it was established in 2009 by Freeman Murray and Archana Prasad as a cultural centre, architectural space and idea incubator, with the essential caffeine-chugging café attached. It is a place where good ideas come together. The building is made from pallet racks which create a flexible space that can be used for work, performances and collaboration. On the afternoon I visited, there were a group of young coders quietly tapping away at their laptops. Later, there was going to be a performance from a group of visiting graffiti artists. Two days after that the studio on the first floor would be hosting the live webcast of the latest TEDx conference.

It is places like this that act as crossroads between the history of a place and the development of the new, providing a 'bridge between university and the start-up world'. As Freeman Murray told me, in Bangalore 'there is a large population that has been raised on the idea that IT is a path to success, and these people are reading all the same websites as people in Silicon Valley and watching the success that is happening there'. But just as in Silicon Roundabout, that talent needs to be developed. Good ideas come about as a result of the interconnections between people, places and notions. If Bangalore is going to become the creative city that it undoubtedly promises to be, places like Jaaga are as important in nurturing the possible as the legislative and entrepreneurial support that give life to business.

As I return to Silicon Roundabout once more, I am forced to rethink my assumptions about the creative city. I need to reconsider how the long-term history of the neighbourhood is as significant as the latest round of headline investments and news stories. The creative city is not a simple promise of the future prescribed with press conferences and impressive marketing. The overselling of the 'creative class' as a cadre of supermobile stormtroopers, who can flip a place into the twenty-first century with the holy doctrine of the knowledge economy replacing anything that looks old, does not wash.

At Silicon Roundabout, I sense that the neighbourhood is thriving without the branding of Tech City. This is not because of large corporate behemoths who come in and raise the rents on office space; rather it is driven by the people who are busy launching their start-ups, looking for investment angels or searching for the next big thing, sharing a desk and cross-fertilising half-notions, making connections at meet-ups; it is in the energy of this proximity, fusion and network that the future of the creative city is born.

5

REBOOTING THE COMMUNITY

Everyone had been given directions in advance, as well as the number passcode for the security gate. It was a short walk from the Métro down rue Acacia and then a few yards to the large, green iron doors that blocked off the entrance to the mews behind. Already one could hear the murmur of activity on the other side as I punched the number into the touchpad and waited for the click of the releasing lock. With a push the gate opened, and as I stepped through I felt as if I was passing from the city into a new, unfamiliar place.

Every Sunday evening for the last thirty years, 38 rue de la Tombe Issoire, Paris, has been a city within a city; for here Jim Haynes has held an endless supper party, the door open to anyone who wants to enter, the table ready for all who wish to eat, the conversation a babble of different languages, accents, generations and sensibilities – by reputation this is a place where once everything, and anything, was permitted. But it was Thanksgiving 2011 and, after hanging up my coat and with a plastic glass of red wine thrust into my hand, I made my way into the main room where forty or so people were already bumping into each other, introducing themselves, finding connections and listening to each other's stories.

I introduced myself to Jim, who was sitting on a stool near the kitchen area where an oversized turkey was standing ready for carving. Jim is a remarkable lightning rod for the last forty years. Born in Louisiana in 1933, he enlisted in the US Air Force after university, and was sent as a Cold Warrior to a small listening base close to Edinburgh, Scotland. He soon became more interested in the life of the city than preparing for World War Three, and was given permission by his superiors to live in the centre and study at the university. Later he travelled around Europe and returned with plans to set up a bookshop that quickly became a hub for radicals, writers and publishers. He then became involved with the emerging Edinburgh Fringe Festival, setting up the Traverse Theatre, organising it as a club to circumvent the censoring Lord Chamberlain's office.

Moving down to London in 1967, he founded the Arts Laboratory, the avant-garde epicentre of the swinging capital, publishing the *International Times* and hosting the UFO events at the Roundhouse with its house bands Pink Floyd and the Soft Machine. A trailblazer for the Free Love movement, he produced the magazine *SUCK* from Amsterdam and curated the first Wet Dream Film Festival there. At the same time he moved to Paris and began to teach at the university, during which period he moved to rue de la Tombe Issoire. At first, he and a friend Lenny Jensen rigged up a local cable TV station, linking together all the neighbours along the mews, sharing films and videos. He renamed his atelier the Embassy of the World and started to issue world citizenship passports to replace national documents, until he was taken to court by the French authorities. He also began to hold dinner parties and picnics for the community. Over time, these Sunday evening salons gained a reputation and became an institution; today, they are a barely kept secret that people have spread across the world.

Jim Haynes at home, 2009

On the evening I was there, I was immediately approached by an American woman in her fifties. Many people had turned up alone and this sense of fellowship set out the rules of the room – you were free to talk to anyone you wanted, to introduce yourself and ask questions: How did you hear about Jim? What are you doing in Paris? Groups of people huddled together and then moved on, interconnecting and creating a network that quickly weaved through the whole room, and then outside into the night air where other groups bunched together, smoking. This was a city in the making – strangers meeting strangers, developing the rules of engagement as the evening progressed; finding the language and practice of community as we went along.

The American woman had moved to Paris six months ago, and heard about Jim's parties through a friend. I then spoke to a young French banker who had previously worked in London but had returned home and was looking for work. He was with his girlfriend, and was talking to Colin, another American from California, a music scholar who was setting up a chamber orchestra in Paris. He introduced me to a Swedish couple, who were in the city, like me, for the weekend. There was also Pat, who wrote the subtitles for French films and was trying to get a novel published; Suzi, a South African architecture student who had spent the day in Montparnasse Cemetery; two sisters, Stef and Pam, who had been coming to Jim's for over fifteen years and conducted tours for rich Americans around the ateliers of the leading haute couture designers and fabric shops.

Throughout it all, Jim himself sat on his stool and surveyed the scene he had created. When I asked him why he still did this, despite one heart attack and another health scare, he admitted that he was still interested in people, still wanted to share with strangers and make friends, that this making of a community, for however brief amount of time, was a reason for living.

At rue de la Tombe Issoire, a community comes together, shares food, drink and conversation and departs in the course of an evening. The ecology is simple to define and the rules of engagement are quickly acquired despite any initial shyness. Above the seeming chaos of the kitchen quarters, this evening is a momentary community, self-organised and complex, but a community in every sense of the word.

The idea of people coming together, sharing the same space and getting on with each other sounds simple, but 7,000 years of urban history often disproves this. It was once far easier to know who you were and where you came from; the definition and requirements of citizenship were set out clearly. Yet, as the city grew beyond the boundaries of the first walls, the question of belonging became more problematic. How can you prove you are who you say you are? What are the codes of practice, the behaviour of 'cityness', and how do they evolve? How can you define community when people are on the move so much?

As the population of the world becomes increasingly urban, redefining community is an ever urgent question. People, families and groups are coming to the city now in greater numbers than ever before; they are arriving at places that are so large and diverse that they cannot simply be defined by one identity. Community may be many things: a shared space, a way of behaving, as well as people; yet the process of belonging is more than any one of these things alone. It is an ecology that combines place, people and the way they interact.

But it seems that living together creates serious problems, that jamming so many people into such a tight space makes the city a ticking time bomb ready to explode. Somewhere between the experience of an evening in a Paris salon and the full scale of 9,000 years of urban history, the problem of community had become an intractable crisis. How can we challenge this scenario?

We are hardwired to be together. Despite the fact that we have been told most of our lives that we are all individuals and that survival of the fittest was the only rule of the game, we have been genetically designed to seek each other out and form communities. We are social animals and, as a result, the city is the most natural place for us to be. Our personalities are formed by our relationships with others; our language is shared; it is the connection with others that makes us happy, smarter and more creative. It is only our ability to cooperate that has allowed us to survive thus far. Collaboration is the engine of complexity, connecting us with each other, strengthening the social bonds. As evolutionary biologist Martin Novak writes: 'Cooperation is the master architect of evolution.'[1]

The way and the extent that we work and live together is often surprising. Take, for example, a crowd. In 2011 a team at the Zurich Federal Institute of Technology wanted to see whether they could scientifically work out the collective behaviour of a large group of people walking down the street. They asked whether people followed certain rules or whether a busy sidewalk was a picture of chaos as people bumped into each other like random billard balls cascading across a table. Using tracking devices, Medhi Moussaid's discoveries were unexpected: in each scenario the crowd quickly adopted the characteristics of a complex system and began to self-organise. Almost from the outset two lanes started to form to allow for bodies to flow in opposite directions; where a bottleneck was encountered an unwritten rule of how to step to one side was adopted.

One particular result, however, revealed that although this movement was purely based on probability – guessing in which direction the other was going to go – where you come from had an influence on which side you chose. In most countries in the west, we will instinctively move to the right; in Asia, to the left. Most of the time this causes manageable problems but at moments like the Olympics, or at the Hajj, when visitors from around the world congregate in one space, it can cause chaos.[2]

The added dilemma to this scrum is that many people within the crowd are not acting alone: 70 per cent of any crowd is part of a smaller group. When three or more people are walking together they often adopt a formation depending on their speed. If they are walking fast they usually adopt a penetrating Λ shape, with one leader cutting ahead of the two wings. If the pace is a little more relaxed, the group often forms a U or V with the central figure hanging back.

In addition, just as Oscar Wilde declared that everyone in London looked like they were late for a train, it is the case that people from different nationalities walk at different speeds. In a groundbreaking experiment, Robert Levine of California State University in Fresno timed the average walking speeds in thirty-one different cities and found that nine out of the top ten – Dublin, Amsterdam, Bern/Zurich, London, Frankfurt, New York, Tokyo, Paris, Nairobi, Rome – were wealthy cities and economic factors such as earning power, cost of living and time accuracy were key factors.[3] When time is money, we tend to pick up the pace.

We have a biological need to be together but the exact measurement of what that togetherness means is up for grabs. There are rules that govern how we come together, but they are different dependent on where you are. The problems of community are often what is lost in translation.

One thing that connects the crowd with a more permanent community is the problem of proximity. For Jean-Paul Sartre, hell was other people, but the chain-smoking existentialist was wrong. Returning to Jane Jacobs's neighbourhood on Hudson Street, the transformation of a random gathering of people into a community is formed through a combination of the routines and relationships that accumulate over time, mixed together with the more immediate connections made in the moment. A community is not a family with its strong ties and obligations but an evolving, turbulent network of weak links, familiar faces and rehearsed rituals.

Density, the necessities of shared space, has a big part to play in this process. In Jacobs's Greenwich Village

> a good city street neighbourhood achieves a marvel of balance between its people's determination to have essential privacy and their simultaneous wishes for differing degrees of contact, enjoyment or help from the people around. This balance is largely made up of small sensitively managed details, practised and accepted so casually that they are normally taken for granted.[4]

Density defines a city, and therefore the community. It is the key problem when there is overcrowding, the network through which diseases can decimate a neighbourhood; when things get too crammed, density turns old parts of the city into slums, where poverty huddles and becomes stuck. It is the overfull bus that forces you to wait for the next one. It is the social-housing waiting list that leaves some children in poverty only a few hundred yards from the richest enclaves of London. It is the equation behind the queue for the water tap in the Mumbai slums, and the ten-hour traffic jam in Lagos. With the prospect of increased urbanisation in the next thirty years, particularly in parts of the world where there are already problems of managing the infrastructure, density could easily be the biggest challenge of our age.

However, we should also look at the advantages of living close together, and make sure that as we attack the problems of overcrowding we do not do away with the benefits of living cheek by jowl. We now know that large, dense cities are more creative, that the network of weak ties, diversity of parts and the added competitiveness encourage innovation. But urban density also has an impact on fertility rates, reducing the number of children within a family. It can reduce the amount of energy that one uses, and improves the efficiency and productivity of everyday life. Perhaps most surprisingly, and despite many misconceptions, being close together also makes people behave better. Although there is a long-held assumption that the faceless crowd is an aggressive mob, density actually encourages civility.

In a 2011 report by the Young Foundation, three communities were tested for levels of politeness: Newham, one of the poorest and most diverse boroughs in east London; Cambourne, a county town in Cambridgeshire with a growing young population; and Wiltshire, one of the least densely populated counties in the south-west of England, 90 per cent of which is classified as rural. Over a series of tests and observations, the study looked at levels of basic civility and politeness, from saying 'good morning', to issues of honesty, respect and trust.

The results were unexpected; where it is often assumed that incivility is linked to disadvantage, diversity and poverty, the opposite was found to be true: 'We found very high levels of civility in some disadvantaged, diverse places, as well as instances of serious incivility, in the form of intolerance and rudeness, in more prosperous and homogeneous contexts.'[5] As an example of how people who lived close together were forced to be kind and observant of each other, the researchers highlighted Queen's Market in Newham:

> We observed how shoppers of a range of ethnicities queued patiently and stepped out of the way of prams and elderly shoppers. Shopkeepers were adamant that maintaining civility was critical to their commercial success. Those who treated customers from different cultures or ethnicities rudely soon went out of business. Stallholders had adapted with the times – in east London it is not uncommon for Cockney salesmen to speak fluent Urdu, for example.'[6]

The city forces people to adapt their behaviour, to be more open and civil; the diversity of the community does not have to nurture divisions but accommodation and politeness. However, there is no golden mean of density that produces a well-balanced community. For example, even as we look disparagingly at London or Paris for being too cramped it is worthwhile remembering that the most densely packed society in Europe is not one of the giant industrial northern cities but Malta, a place that many people from the larger cities escape to for peace and quiet. The pursuit of urban density, therefore, is only one of the means to develop the ecology of community. It can deliver benefits, moderate and modify how a community develops, it can encourage diversity and innovation, enrich the communal life through weak links and associations but it is not the gift of happiness itself.

Detroit is a stark example of how changing levels of density can impact on a community. In 1932, amidst the aftershocks of the Wall Street Crash, the Mexican artist Diego Rivera was invited by the Detroit Institute of Art to draw a series of vast murals to celebrate the city that was at that time suffering heavily from the Great Depression. Before the crash, Detroit had been the home of the American automobile industry; situated by the Great Lakes and linked by the new railway, the city established itself as an industrial centre in the late nineteenth century; in the 1900s Henry Ford took advantage of the thriving carriage trade and set up his first workshop there in 1899. Soon he was joined by General Motors, Chrysler and American Motors. By 1912 the Highland Park plant, the largest industrial complex in the world, was producing over 170,000 Model Ts a year.

In response Detroit's population exploded, rising from 466,000 in 1910 to 1,720,000 in 1930. Yet that year demand for new automobiles plummeted, and there were massive lay-offs from the factories; half the workforce were dropped, pushing over two-thirds of the city under the poverty line. Into such a febrile atmosphere, it was perhaps dangerous to commission the renowned Marxist artist to devise such a massive work of art – charting the history and development of the city's industry from its agricultural roots to the modern assembly line. Rivera worked on the mural for the next eleven months. In a series of twenty-seven panels he devised a temple to industry, with the car as the highest form of man's achievement. It presents Detroit's history as manifest destiny, facing the problems of the Great Depression and conquering all obstacles; but the city would soon be seen to be fragile indeed.

By 1950 Detroit had a peak population of 1.8 million, attracting a new army of workers from the south and becoming the second-largest metropolitan area in the US. The arrival of these – mainly black – migrant workers had its own catalytic impact as the richer white residents got into their cars and moved to the suburbs – white flight, as it was called – making the city rich but dangerously divided. The industrial success of the American empire was built in the factories of the city, but the spoils were unevenly shared. The wealthy white families dominated the centre of Detroit as well as the exurbs, the neighbourhoods outside the city boundaries, linked by expressways that bounded over the suburbs, where many black familes found themselves increasingly stuck. Following brutal riots in 1967, which killed forty-three and destroyed 1,400 buildings, there were attempts to break down the racial barriers with a new plan for Midtown that aimed to integrate the disparate

CORBIS

The fall of Detroit

communities. However, as the city started to decline, the first signs of deprivation were seen in the black suburbs. Jobs were lost, mortgages became unserviceable and foreclosure soon followed; in time demand for housing flatlined.

Today, Detroit is in trouble: the orders for American automobiles have slowed while international competition has undermined US supremacy; the city has turned into an industrial ghost town. This has had a devastating impact on the population, which was reduced by 25 per cent between 2000 and 2010. The average income there is half of the national median. In 2009 the unemployment rate stood at 25 per cent and the murder rate ten times worse than New York. The average house is worth little more than $10,000 and over 50 per cent of all children live in poverty.

As a city built on cars, Detroit was also a city dominated by freeways leading to suburbs that now are almost empty. In a 2009 survey it was found that many neighbourhoods were almost abandoned, 91,000 lots in total were standing open, 55,000 of these had been foreclosed. Therefore the city was in the impossible situation of being forced to spend $360 million a year to provide services to houses which were empty and were not generating tax revenue. What was the mayor, businessman and former All-Star professional basketball player Dave Bing, to do? Desperate circumstances called for dramatic measures.

To start, people looked at ways to revive downtown, hoping that if the centre of the city could revive then the rest would follow. One early response was to develop the Detroit People Mover (DPM), a monorail that runs in a circuit around the downtown region aiming to deliver swift transit around the city. There was also a concerted effort to develop the Detroit International Waterfront, a collection of plazas, riverside walks, hotels, music halls, theatres and cultural centres. The Renaissance Center is a cluster of interconnected skyscrapers including the headquarters of General Motors, and numerous banks.

But surely the problem was not just about reviving the centre? Reducing the city to its central business district does not offer homes, schools and security. In addition, Detroit is cursed by a wealthy outer belt of exurbs, connected to the centre by fast-flowing freeways. The problem is the wasteland, the inner suburbs, caught between the centre and these exurbs. Once these neighbourhoods were the forcing ground of the city, home to its workforce and community, but now stand as empty land. In response many planners proposed that Detroit use the bulldozer and shrink the city back into a liveable density. Using the 2009 neighbourhood survey, it was decided that Mayor Bing needed to select the winners and losers, the communities that would be leavened to the ground, and those that would receive government funding, with the warning 'If we don't do it, you know this whole city is going to go down.'[7]

Since then, although there has been much discussion about 'right-sizing' Detroit, the bulldozers yet have to move in. Unlike Barcelona, where Joan Busquets was encouraging increased density in a traditionally dense community, the people of Detroit do not have a history of living close together. As some critics point out, even a depopulated Detroit is more dense than many of the sunbelt cities like Phoenix or Houston, therefore the issue might not be density alone. Others, like economist Ed Glaeser, say the problem is not just about bringing people together but also providing them with something to do, as well as the education and social tools that might encourage them to want to be there.

Still others have complained about how one could effectively conduct this 'right-sizing' which would force people to leave their houses, and close services and neighbourhoods. As a result even

Mayor Bing admits that the Detroit Works Project has taken longer to start than hoped. After taking the opinion of over 10,000 stakeholders into account through endless neighbourhood meetings, there has also been a concerted rebranding exercise to get locals on board, convincing people that this was a shared vision for the city rather than one imposed from city hall. In the meantime, the public-transit system has been privatised, and therefore taken off the government's books. The new owner, 25-year-old Andy Didorosi, promises to run the scheme at cost, but has reduced the service to one bus riding a loop through the main neighbourhoods.

There are some positive signs of regrowth even as discussion of right-sizing continues. Although not the solution in itself, downtown Detroit is becoming attractive once more to businesses. In summer 2011 Quicken Loans moved into the Chase Tower from the suburbs, bringing 4,000 employees into downtown. Owner Dan Gilbert has gambled heavily on the rebirth of the city centre, buying real estate, investing in retail, as well as encouraging other businesses into the area. One of the markets that could see real growth is technology start-ups and Gilbert has also set up Detroit Venture Partners to take advantage of the new culture. This is reinforced by Tech Town, established by Wayne State University Research and Technology Park, General Motors and Henry Ford Health System as an incubator for innovation. In 2010 Detroit was the largest market for hi-technology engineers – even more than Silicon Valley – as the car industry tried to find a route out of its depression.

Detroit is a painful reminder of the relationship between the fabric of the city and the development of a community. This is not simple or straightforward, however: one can find strong communities in slums and terrible loneliness in the richest enclaves. Yet the interaction between ourselves and the places around us is so complex that it has fascinated architects, psychiatrists and politicians. On a panel at the LSE in 2010 the architect Will Alsop described a visit to Lyons, France, where a new art gallery and historical district – in pursuit of the Bilbao effect – had transformed the city centre. Sitting in the town square, he continued, he noted there were many young kissing couples, canoodling away oblivious to the other passers-by. Was this the effect of architecture? he asked; can we create a place that encourages people to kiss?

Psychological experiments often reveal unexpected connections between ourselves and the environment. In one example of psychological priming, a group of people were asked to walk along two equal walkways: along one walkway were displayed pictures of old and infirm people; on the other were images of younger, more vital models. In every study, people moved faster along the second walkway. Priming is the study of how external stimuli can influence behaviour or responses, but how far can this go? A place can have an emotional impact on people – a church has a sense of the sacred, a palace resonates pomp and power – is the same also true of the public spaces of a city?

With tongue firmly in cheek, the homepage for the Cardiff University Sociology Department describes Georg Simmel as 'rather like Gary Barlow out of Take That, the one that had all the good ideas and did all the work but none of the fans fancied or could remember what he looked like'.[8] Born the son of a wealthy chocolatier in 1850s Berlin, Simmel was rich enough not to work and so took the role of a private lecturer at the university, where he became popular amongst students and befriended other thinkers such as Max Weber, Rainer Maria Rilke and Edmund Husserl. The forgotten father of sociology, he is now remembered for his philosophy of money; however at the time it was his 1903 essay, 'The Metropolis and Mental Life', which highlighted the ills of urbanity, identifying the struggle between the individual's need to be free and the demands of the 'socio-technical mechanism' of the city.

Simmel's work soon made its way across the Atlantic and in the 1920s was adopted as a bible by the Chicago School of Sociology. The group, which included Nels Anderson, Robert E. Park and Ernest Burgess, gained fame for their 'ecological' approach to studying urban life: that the city was a place of differences, and the environment was a key factor in determining human behaviour. In particular, they were fascinated by the relationship between cities and their anti-social or marginal communities, and how this could endanger or stimulate a community. As Park, who had studied with Simmel in Berlin and later translated his work, wrote: 'The city magnifies, spreads out and advertises human nature in all its various manifestations. It is this that makes the city interesting, even fascinating. It is this, however, that makes it of all places the one in which to discover the secrets of the human heart, and to study human nature and society.'[9]

The Chicago School saw the city was a problem, a place that forced people into new behaviours. Park himself was interested in the process of immigrant assimilation into cities, and the resultant racism that met new arrivals. Similarly, Nels Anderson wrote about the hobo, highlighting the problem of homelessness; Ruth Shonle Cavan in 1929 wrote a book about young women coming to Chicago to work and the opportunities and problems that they faced. Meanwhile the black researcher Edward Franklin Frazier contextualised the issues of life within an African-American family in *The Negro Family in Chicago*. The Chicago School not only gained attention because of the subject matter of their work but also as a result of their method: promoting close and systematic observation rather than philosophical speculation on the formation of human nature or what people want. This scientific study of where cities went wrong went hand in hand with a reformist agenda: exploring not just how the city did not work, but also how it could be fixed.

The current incarnation of environmental psychology began in the 1970s, when the emphasis moved from grand planning schemes to a more refined study of the relationship between the individual and the wider environment. In particular, this new discipline was interested in the role of place identity, how a certain environment feeds into a sense of self; the impact of density upon a sense of well-being; the problems of noise, weather and pollution; how women and men perceive the urban environment; how design improves a sense of place. This movement therefore combines the results of studies in environmental psychology and psychological priming with the latest ideas in architecture. As Harold Proshanksy of the New York Graduate Center noted, the discipline is hard-wired with the hope of improving the city and as a result has developed a number of strategies that underpin our ideas of urban renewal.

In general these efforts focus on well-meaning areas such as healthcare, crime reduction and combatting poverty. What does a healthy city look like? Can we build places that make us safer? What are the changes to infrastructure that make a real difference to people's ability to succeed? It is often the small or unexpected moments that make up our experience. Thus the height of a window, letting in the sun at only certain parts of the day, can have an impact on happiness. Our proximity to green spaces can have an impact on our moods as well as a child's social development. Street lighting can make one feel safer when walking at night. How can we change a streetscape to make a city more walkable? Take, for example, the problems of shadows in the modern metropolis.

Recall the sense of joy that comes from sitting in a city square with the sun on your face. It is sometimes easy to forget how important sunlight is in our everyday lives. In the nineteenth century social engineers such as Florence Nightingale promoted the idea of fresh air and sunlight as health-giving conditions. For the Victorians, sunlight, clean water and pure air constituted the principal components of the ideal city. This was particularly a cause of debate in New York for, as architect Michael Sorkin observes in the wonderful hymn to his home city, *Twenty Minutes in Manhattan*: 'Much of the modern history of New York's physical form is the result of debates over light and air.'[10] By the 1870s there were complaints that the high tenements that had been built to house the rising population were obscuring the sky and filling the air with a putrid stink. As a result a height limit was put on all residential buildings in the 1901 Tenement Housing Act.

But this did not stop architects who were developing the business district and in 1915 work started on the Equitable Building in Lower Manhattan to replace previous offices that had recently burned down in a fire. Out of the ashes the architect Ernest R. Graham designed a neo-classical block that stood sixty-two storeys tall above the city. As it was being built it soon became clear that the vast edifice would cast a shadow across 7 acres, plunging the neighbourhood and the surrounding buildings into permanent darkness. In response the New York government set out the 1916 Standard State Zoning Enabling Act which imposed limits on the maximum height of buildings, where they might be built, as well as devising a code for 'setback', designing a building so that as it grows skywards, it also tiers inwards to reduce its shadow, as can be seen in the iconic designs for the Chrysler or the Empire State Buildings.

In the post-war period, architects once again began to question these regulations. The modernist aesthetic, inspired by Le Corbusier, demanded bold, regular blocks of pure glass and metal; rather than being 'set back', these new skyscrapers were being built within

Shadows and the city: Manhattan, 2012

plazas so that the shadow would not interfere with other buildings. This new approach to the city was encapsulated by the Seagram Building created by Mies van der Rohe and Philip Johnson. Now there was less emphasis on the experience of the city beyond the plaza that hugged the ankles of new skyscrapers, because it was assumed that everyone was in their cars; what sunlight one might encounter could be reflected from the shining glass of the modernist monuments onto the streets below where it would palely glisten along the chrome finish of a polished Cadillac.

Yet, even as Robert Moses was planning his Futurama city, there was opposition. In addition to Jane Jacobs's successful protests against LoMex, others were starting to discuss the idea of 'solar access', the essential right to sunlight as a key quality of life. In particular, Californian architectural thinker Ralph Knowles was developing the notion of planning cities around 'solar envelopes' which determined the height and orientation of buildings according to the cyclical solar movements.

It seems unlikely that this would ever be put into practice in Manhattan but in 2010 Mayor Bloomberg picked up on many of the key notions of the right to solar access, and how the persistent presence of shadows would impact on public life in the city, as set out in the excitingly titled CEQR Technical Manual: 'Sunlight can entice outdoor activities, support vegetation, and enhance architectural features, such as stained-glass windows and carved detail on historic structures. Conversely, shadows can affect the growth cycle and sustainability of natural features and the architectural significance of built features.'[11]

Environmental psychologists have spent a long time studying the impact of sunlight and shadow, conclusively showing that more natural light affects the well-being of workers or families within the space. In particular, scientists discuss the importance of sunlight for the body's cicadian rhythm, or nature's alarm clock. This is the natural process that regulates the daily biological rhythms, regulated by the hormone melatonin, secreted from a gland in the centre of the brain, which can have an impact on conditions such as Seasonal Affective Disorder. This has encouraged many architects to rethink the importance of sunlight within their design.

It is this kind of experiment that informs environmental psychology, the link between place and behaviour. The power of this connection is also the thinking behind the well-known 'broken windows theory' that first appeared in a 1982 article by James Q. Wilson and George L. Kelling in the *Atlantic Monthly*. In the essay, the authors reported on the relationship between disorder within a community and crime: a chaotic environment in which vandalism is a reflection of a 'don't care' attitude. There, the authors proposed that it is better to repair broken windows in a run-down block than to wait for vandals to trash the whole building: 'One broken window is a signal that no one cares, so breaking more windows costs nothing . . . "untended" behaviour also leads to the breakdown of community controls.'[12]

When Kelling went to work for New York City Hall the policy became part of a wider 'zero-tolerance' policing strategy. In his own account, William Bratton, the police chief who adopted Kelling's ideas, reports: 'Ten per cent of New Yorkers experienced violent crime. But 100 per cent experienced the city's disorder: fare-beaters and drunks on the subway, mental patients off their meds wandering the streets, prostitution operating in the open. Long lines, high taxes, poor service. Broken neighbourhoods, broken people, broken windows.'

Bratton felt that while the police spent most of their time responding to crimes, they did nothing to prevent it. He started not with windows but the petty crime of fare-dodging. At the time it was calculated that over 17,000 fares at $1.15 were being avoided every day. Using plain-clothed police and a system of 'mine sweeps', he got dramatic results: 'Fare-beaters tend to have character flaws. One in seven are wanted on warrants or probation violations. One in twenty-one carried an illegal weapon . . . Now it was about making felon collars. And when fare-beating went away, crime fell, and so too did the sense of disorder. And when it did, ridership returned . . . Take care of the small stuff, and you head off the big stuff.'[13] The sight of a daisy-chain of offenders being pulled through the station became a highly effective deterrent and recovered nearly $70 million in lost revenue a year.

Some critics believe that the repairing of windows happened to coincide with a falling crime rate in New York, so that small interventions were amplified by wider social changes. Others felt that Bratton was heavyhanded. Nonetheless the results were emphatic: crime rates dropped by 0.3 per cent in 1990; 4.4 per cent in 1991 and 7.8 per cent in 1992. By 1996 serious crime had fallen by 32 per cent, the murder rate dropped by 47 per cent and car theft by 40 per cent.[14] It is a powerful example of how changing the environment can influence behaviour; and it does not just work with broken windows. Experiments in Holland concerning graffiti suggest that allowing one tag to remain on a wall often leads in time to the complete surface being covered. The Dutch research team discovered that in some cases, a disorderly environment increased the likelihood of criminal behaviour by nearly 50 per cent.[15]

Being able to manipulate or manage people through design does not come without concerns. Just as one city can plan for better community, others can use the same scientific principles to reinforce political control. In addition, any project that provides planning solutions in the form of strong medicine, without consultation of the people it is going to affect, is also likely to confront unexpected consequences.

Solutions from planners, developers, architects, politicians and urban bloggers are legion; but what if the community wants to reboot itself rather than have transformation imposed upon it from well-meaning decision-makers? Robert Putnam's classic study of community, *Bowling Alone*, offers a disheartening view of modern society. With an abundance of observation material and statistics, he makes the watertight argument that our sense of community and our participation in communal activity has collapsed. Using the image of the lonely bowler throwing his ball down the alley, where once he would be part of a team, our sense of who we are and where we fit in has atomised and become dangerously small. As he calculates, more Americans are bowling than ever before but league bowling has plummeted. This is, however, a symbol of a wider malaise: 'We spend less time in conversation over meals, we exchange visits less often, we engage less often in leisure activities that encourage casual social interaction, we spend more time watching and less time doing. We know our neighbours less well, and we see our friends less often.'[16]

Putnam goes on to show how the loss in communal participation has unexpected impacts elsewhere within the city, affecting levels of honesty and trust, attitudes to others within the group, establishing the weak ties that make a city complex and creative, and potentially the foundation of democracy itself. He raises this spectre in order to confront it, to warn against the decline and to show that it is not necessarily inevitable. In particular, he promotes the notion of 'social capital', the benefits that come from association and being part of the group, the idea 'that social networks have value', that they deliver both private and public good.[17] He argues that being a good neighbour makes us better people; conviviality is the tradeable commodity that creates a better place around us.

But this is often very difficult in the hectic modern world. We have become accustomed to our solitary ways: travelling in cars cuts us off from others and we find waiting for a bus or strap-hanging on the tube an unpleasant experience. Work is so all-consuming that we have little time for our families let alone helping out in the community; or even doing things we like, such as going to the theatre or listening to music. Most of us now live in suburbs where there are fewer people and sprawl allows us to live behind fences. We no longer go to church in the same way we did before. We are still interested in sports, but now we are more likely to be a spectator than get involved. It is far easier to run on the treadmill when one has time rather than organise life around weekly practice when others rely on you to turn up. Membership of political parties has plummeted just as voting figures have dropped. Putnam calculates that television itself is responsible for at least a 25 per cent drop in social interaction. Modern life is driving us apart, it seems.

Perhaps it is not surprising, therefore, that although cities are shared spaces, yet we have become increasingly obsessed with privacy. At the end of a hard's days work there is a certain joy in closing the front door and locking the city out. Even as we use the city in the course of an ordinary day we have become suspicious and unsure of the shared spaces: the public square is often a place that needs to be traversed, head down, at a speedy trot rather than somewhere one might want to linger and kiss. We are often uncertain of who owns these places, what they are for.

It is this lack of sense of ownership that might explain why we feel so uncertain in such open spaces. I remember as a child being told not to go into certain play areas because they were dangerous. One often sees patches of green which should be giving a sense of delight to the neighbourhood but in fact are no more than ignored drifts of garbage. Much social housing is designed around public spaces, but there are often signs prohibiting pets or ball games, and there are regulations that no more than three youths may congregate in a certain place at any time. It is no wonder that these places become the conflicted territorial boundaries between gangs, or between youths and the authorities. It is in these vacuums, designed to enhance the environment, but which discourage sharing or ownership, that the most assaults and robberies occur. In the official reports on the 2011 London riots, much analysis was given to the lack of 'ownership' felt by the disaffected generation who rampaged.

In addition to this there are a number of places within the city that are being privatised without our knowledge. In January 2012 the City Corporation of London won a legal battle to evict the Occupy London protesters who had pitched their tents on the north side of St Paul's churchyard. Before the court case there had been much debate over who actually owned the land. For many it initially seemed obvious that it belonged to the cathedral Chapter and that it was up to the Dean to decide whether to push for eviction. As a result the canon, Reverend Giles Fraser, asked the police to leave the churchyard as he was happy for the protesters to express their legitimate rights. When the Chapter decided that they wanted the protesters out, Fraser resigned, followed later by the Dean, Right Reverend Graeme Knowles. But, in fact, the question of ownership was more complex.

When I first visited the site in November 2011, the sense of energy and diversity of the new settlement was overpowering. I had previously written a book about St Paul's Cathedral and had visited the churchyard on numerous occasions, but wandering around the camp was an electrifying experience. I was taken aback by how well organised and orderly the community was: there was food, together with recycling bins for all different types of waste; nearby there was a group of musicians thumping bongos and the lowing churn of the didgeridoo. By the statue of Queen Anne a soap-box evangelist was allowed to prophesy the end of the world without interruption while students in Guy Fawkes masks chatted away. There were posters protesting the imprisonment of Kurdish leader Abdullah Öcalan, while on the pillars of the colonnade were adverts for film-showings, debates, calls to arms, as well as scrawled, hare-brained conspiracy theories. There was a lot of wit in many of the signs, and one even made the connection between St Paul's Churchyard and Tahrir Square.

CORBIS

Occupy London, St Paul's churchyard, 2011

There was also what had been named the Tent University, home to a series of talks planned by academics, activists and even some high-profile supporters like the fashion designer Vivienne Westwood. On my first visit I slipped into the back of the marquee and listened as one speaker explained how to use social media to generate protest groups.

When I tried to walk around from the protest site, however, to nearby Paternoster Square, a place I had visited on numerous occasions, I was stopped by security guards and told to turn around. The square, part of a recent regeneration project completed in 2003, was home to a number of large offices including multinational banks Merrill Lynch and Goldman Sachs, as well as the London Stock Exchange, the target of the Occupy protesters. But I was still bemused as to why I was being stopped. My initial reaction was anger; why was I being banned from a part of my city; surely I had the right to go wherever I wanted? Apparently not; the square was not a public space at all but owned by the Mitsubishi Estate Co. It turned out that there was no public right of way and the company could grant me access or not, without explanation, whenever they wanted.

The privatisation of public spaces is more prevalent than I could ever have imagined. Not only are large tranches of the city being sold by the corporation to developers, there are also gated communities who prefer to live their lives behind electric fences. As the architectural campaigner Anna Minton explains:

> Who controls the roads and the streets is, as Victorian protesters were well aware, enormously important to how cities function. Today there has been no public debate about the selling of streets at all. Instead, as ownership of British cities goes back to private landlords, the process of removing public rights of way is buried in the arcane language and technical detail of the most obscure parts

> of planning law . . . there is an adage in highway law which says 'once a highway, always a highway' . . . In many British towns and cities, this common-law right is being quietly eroded.[18]

It is difficult to reboot the community if our public spaces are being closed off. Where shall we meet if everywhere we go is mediated by CCTV or private security guards with hi-vis vests and walkie-talkies? At a recent talk at London's Southbank Centre, the urban sociologist Richard Sennett, who had supported the Occupy movement since the outset, told the audience that the threat to public spaces is one of the most dangerous attacks on our civil liberties and had to be defended by any means. The audience applauded as he called for 'more occupation of spaces', encouraging the listeners to 'go where you don't belong'. It is only now, once we have lost these public spaces, that we mourn their passing.

We have become afraid of shared spaces and are inclined to ignore their importance; as a result they are disappearing without a whisper of protest. This is something that we might come to regret when it is too late. To reboot the community we need to find the spaces that we have, 'the commons', and make them places worth sharing.

A 2011 survey conducted by the Cooperatives UK group showed that, despite the fact that 80 per cent of people questioned said that sharing makes us happy, 'except sharing a toothbrush', sharing has declined over the last generation.[19] The will to share exists: one in three said that they would share their garden to grow vegetables; six out of ten claimed that they would car pool if it were possible (filling the 38 million empty car seats every year) and 75 per cent agreed that sharing was good for the environment. Inevitably, however, there is a huge gulf between the will and the actuality.[20] What is holding us back?

In 2009 Elinor Ostrom became the first woman economist ever to be awarded the Nobel Prize for her work, sharing the accolade with Oliver E. Williamson. Having made extensive field studies of how Swiss farmers share mountain pasture, as well as how local villages set up water-irrigation systems in the Philippines, Ostrom's particular arena of expertise is the 'common pool resources', in which she has modelled the best ways to organise a local community around a finite set of resources.

It is rare that economists ever go out to observe how people actually behave and this is what made Ostrom's research so counterintuitive. Previously it was assumed that while people tend their private property with care, they often abuse common resources with the assumption that if they did not take as much as they could, someone else would. What Ostrom observed, was wholly different: in whichever group she studied, however, the commons were looked after with the same care, if not more, as private property. What her studies show is that each community develops long-term strategies and norms of behaviour that preserve the sustainability of the resource better than any institution that can be imposed from above. A sense of ownership does not have to be exclusive in order to be real: the collective or cooperative sharing of communal property can on many occasions be the best way.

Critics might say that while this might work in a village where everybody knows each other's business, does it work for the city? In 2011 the website Shareable.net, dedicated to promoting the cause of the commons, announced twenty policies for a shareable city by identifying the local places and activities that could have an inspiring impact.[21] Working alongside the Sustainable Economies Law Center, the project strove to find the legal framework to underpin the enterprise. For example, in order to promote urban agriculture, it was suggested that the government create property tax incentives for the conversion of vacant plots to farm land; other proposals were the inclusion of 'community gardening' and 'personal gardening' into the standard zoning code; allowing commercial food farming in all city zones; subsidising water, and finally: 'De-pave paradise and put a tax on parking lots'.[22] All these initiatives could be started from the ground up by groups coming together and campaigning on a single issue in the local area. The only impediments are the will, the time and the places to plan and launch.

In addition to the commons we need places to meet up, kick back and develop the brilliant schemes that will increase our shared enjoyment of the metropolis. The city is filled with such 'third spaces', places supercharged to reboot the community, if only we looked harder. As sociologist Ray Oldenburg explains: the café table on the Parisian street, the English pub, the Brooklyn coffee shop where you can sit by the window for the whole day, the secondhand bookshop that offers conversation as well as the unexpected volume, the barbershop where the hours of the day are marked with banter, the candy store at the corner of Jane Jacobs's Hudson Street, the coffee houses of seventeenth-century Amsterdam where ideas circulated like money – these informal spaces are at the heart of the community; they are the incubators and the forcing ground of society.

When I was in Paris visiting Jim Haynes's salon, I took the opportunity to go to one of my favourite bookshops, Shakespeare and Co., situated on the Left Bank facing Notre-Dame. The shop was opened by George Whitman, who first came to Paris in 1948 under the GI Bill and soon launched himself in the literary scene. As a younger man he had travelled in South America and when he fell seriously ill, he was nursed back to health by the locals; a kindness that he never forgot.

As a result, Whitman was determined to make his shop something different, driven by the motto: be not inhospitable to strangers, lest they be angels in disguise. And as you walk amongst the bookshelves stacked with titles in different languages, secondhand, antiquarian and fresh from the publishers, there are small beds where some of the bookshop staff rest, who have come to Paris to live the bohemian dream and are happy to find a respite where they can. This is more than just a bookstore – it is an idea, a culture, an example of how the world could or should be.

As I picked at titles in an almost random fashion, I overheard snatches of conversation: a flirting couple in the photography section; one of the shelf-stackers was complaining about another of the staff because they spent too much time on their poetry. Outside a small crowd had gathered and a man who looked strangely familiar was playing guitar with two young, grungy tourists. It was only later that I worked out that the man was Lenny Kaye, guitarist with Patti Smith and author of a book on crooners, who was doing an impromptu reading and concert.

Places like Shakespeare and Co. are highly potent spaces that draw people together and turn individuals into groups. The combination of the commons and the third place has found a particularly potent home on the internet, technology bringing larger groups of people together than ever before. While spending all one's time on Facebook or Second Life is bad for you, technology has the capability of turning observers into actors, of aggregating interests, developing groups and coordinating community.

This mixture of networks, between the real and the digital, is particularly suited to the vast cities that will rise through the coming century. This connectedness does not mean that the electronic community replaces human contact, but the opposite: that technology can nurture a sense of citizenship, the sharing of information and knowledge, which is then taken to the streets.

The gap between the digital protest and actually making it

happen in the street is the most difficult to breach. The Arab Spring was not won by people tweeting from their Cairo bedrooms but by the use of technology encouraging people out onto Tahrir Square. This relationship between media and stimulus to action is the source of great debate. For some commentators, such as economist Paul Mason, author of *Why It's Kicking Off Everywhere*, technology has the potential to be one of the key tools for revolution; on the other hand, writers such as Malcolm Gladwell feel these hopes are unjustified: weaks ties are not strong enough to maintain a protest.

In other spheres, the efficacy of online organising has been clearly successful, as I discovered when I visited Bangalore.

It felt as if I was on a secret mission. I had contacted the Ugly Indian (theuglyindian.com) three times from the UK before I travelled to Bangalore, but it was only once I had arrived that the group contacted me. I had an email waiting for me as I reached the hotel. I was then given a phone number, which did not pick up when I rang. Instead I got an SMS asking me to text them. Finally they gave me an address and directions for their next 'fix-up' the following morning. And so at eight the next morning I found myself in the back of an autorickshaw in search of a very unusual type of happening.

The Ugly Indian are an anonymous group of successful Bangalore businessmen from the IT and financial services industry who were fed up with waiting for the local government to make their city clean and liveable. As I got out at my destination, a quiet residential street in one of the toniest neighbourhoods in the city, the first thing they asked was that I not quote any names or give away any identities.

Already there was a group of volunteers, employees of the office block opposite, who with gloves, picks and shovels were starting to move the pile of rubble and rubbish that was overflowing from the pavement onto the road. In the words of one of the office managers,

Working with the Ugly Indian in Bangalore

who was taking a cigarette break, for many of these educated desk jobbers, this was the first manual labour they had ever done. But as they scraped away in their weekend gear and business shoes, surgical face masks protecting them from the dust, they were already starting to make a difference. They had cleared and cemented a new, even pavement with a well-crafted kerb. They were now starting to talk about planting some bushes and perhaps flowers.

The Ugly Indian started in frustration. While I was standing there, I got talking to an older gentleman, Dr S. Janardham, dressed in a polo shirt and chinos. As well as being one of the leading IT pioneers in Bangalore, now retired, Janardham was former secretary of the HAL Second Stage Civil Amenities and Cultural Association. He told me about the neighbourhood, which was one of the first to be built as the city rapidly grew in the 1970s. The houses and streets were extremely well kept, yet there were always problems, such as the site where the rubbish was dumped and allowed to fester. As a leading light in the local association, his job was to collate a list of the trouble spots and force the local authorities to act. When I asked him whether there was ever any response, he raised his eyes to the sky and, with an apologetic smile, made it clear that my question was a bad joke. 'What was one to do?' he asked.

For the Ugly Indian, the solution 'starts with the 50 feet in front of your house or your office'. The local authorities were clearly not about to change, but this did not give the ordinary citizen any excuse not to take care of the city themselves, albeit with 'no lectures, no moralising, no activism, no self-righteous anger. No confrontation, no arguments, no debates, no pamphlets, no advocacy.'[23] The project was completely voluntary, and promised nothing more than a morning or two of hard graft. Nonetheless, as one of the group that morning told me as we stopped for a cup of tea poured from a canister on the back of the bike of the chai wallah, the simple act of moving earth, clearing rubble and turning cement 'sensitises' the group to their neighbourhood; it showed that the ordinary citizen could organise change and take control of the places around them. Just by doing something, 'that' problem had turned into 'our' problem, which was eventually transformed into our 'neighbourhood'.

When I finally asked how the Ugly Indian could expand and spread into other cities, the organiser looked at me and shook his head. 'Many people ask us how they can set up their own Ugly Indian group,' he reported. 'I tell them that they don't need to, they just need to get on with it.' It seems that rebooting the community can start with the smallest of things, and the tools to revive the neighbourhood can be found all around.

6

TRUST IN THE CITY

On the late afternoon of 26 February 2012, a seventeen-year-old boy called Trayvon Martin was walking back from the local convenience store to the house of his father's new fiancé, having bought a bag of Skittles and a can of Arizona Iced Tea. The youth, who was around 6 feet tall and in good health, was crossing The Retreat, a gated community in Twin Lakes, Florida, a congregation of 263 elegant town houses, ideally located ten minutes from downtown Sanford and the mall as well as good schools. The community was a symbol of the vagaries of development in the last years of the property boom of the noughties.

Each house – identical to the others – was built as an image of homely paradise, with a porch and a garage for one car. Inside, the future homemakers were promised the best materials and small luxuries for a hard-working middle-class family. The initial cost of an off-plan house in 2004 was $250,000. By that day in February 2012 more than forty houses were empty and over half were rented and advertised on realtors' websites for $119,000.

The purpose of gated communities was to offer added safety and a sense of belonging but since the recession foreclosures and the rise of rental properties were making it more difficult to pinpoint who lived where in The Retreat and who was an outsider. There was no way of knowing who had the gate passcode or whether it had been handed to the 'wrong type of visitor'. This sense of anxiety had risen along with the crime rate, which, through 2009–10, included eight burglaries, two bike thefts and three common assaults. In September 2011 the local police had set up a formal neighbourhood watch scheme in response to people's escalating fears.

At 7.11 pm the neighbourhood watch captain, George Zimmerman, phoned 911 to report a suspicious person: 'black male, late teens, dark gray hoodie, jeans or sweatpants walking around the area'.[1] The suspect was walking with his hand within his waistband. Zimmerman was well known to the police. He had arrived at the community in 2009 along with his wife, and from the start had been an enthusiastic member of the neighbourhood watch. The list of calls he had made to 911 covered twenty-two pages and included reports as diverse as 'Man driving with no headlights on'[2] to his neighbour's garage door being open.

At 7.13 pm, two minutes after his previous call, Zimmerman rang 911 again to report that the young person was 'now running towards back entrance of complex' and that he looked suspicious.[3] The dispatch told Zimmerman to stay put and not pursue the suspect. Despite this command, Zimmerman expressed his exasperation that 'these assholes, they always get away'; there is also some controversy whether he also swore 'fucking coons' under his breath as he followed the young man.

In the interim, at 7.12 pm, the young suspect, Martin, was called by his girlfriend. Later in an interview she claimed that he had reported someone was following him and he was scared. He began to run, about the same time as Zimmerman reported this to the police. The girlfriend heard Trayvon call out 'what do you want?' to someone, who had just asked 'what are you doing here?' She then heard a scuffle and the phone line went dead.

What happened next is contested. One eye witness, 'John', saw a young black man hitting another man in a red sweater who was crying out for help. Zimmerman would later claim that it was he who was being attacked. Listening to the 911 calls at the time, Trayvon's mother attested she could hear that it was her son who was in danger. A young boy also saw a man in a red jumper on the ground, but his mother later claimed the police pressured him to say this. There was a fight, and then there was the sound of a gunshot, leaving Trayvon lying dead on the grass while Zimmerman stood over him, possibly with cuts to the back of his head. The injuries are significant, as Zimmerman later told the police he had shot the unarmed youth at point-blank range with a pistol in the chest, in self-defence.

After initial inquiries Zimmerman was released by the police; his later prosecution and the wider debate of police procedure, race, gun

CORBIS

The gates of The Retreat, Twin Lakes

crime and the 'stand your ground' laws have all gained a huge amount of space on TV, radio and the news around the world. President Obama himself got involved when he stated, 'If I had a son, he would look like Trayvon.'[4] In the following court case Zimmerman pleaded not guilty for second-degree manslaughter, maintaining his claim of self-defence. Yet this is not just a narrative about gun laws, race and police protocol; it is a story about the city and trust.

It is impossible to divorce the relationship between the events that occurred on that day and the place where it happened. For not all places are the same and this has a powerful impact on how we behave, navigate and feel about the city. In 1973 the American architect and planner Oscar Newman, in a book called *Defensible Spaces: People and Design in the Violent City*, set out the concept of the gated community, where residents tend to feel a stronger sense of ownership or 'territoriality' when there are barriers. In contrast with the Broken Window idea, which sought to repair the violent city by action, Newman argued that the defensible space was a barricade to hide behind.

The idea has been hugely successful around the world, offering security, community and a sense of exclusivity. In many of the most violent and dangerous cities, urban fortresses have appeared where every movement in and out is monitored. 'Security by design' has become the bedrock of a securitisation industry that protects our homes using heavily armed private guards, and the latest innovations in surveillance, access control and hardware. Like The Retreat at Twin Lakes, the hi-tech apparatus and image of safety that the modern gated community promises as standard is one of the selling points of the new enclave.

The gated community is the opposite of Jane Jacobs's exuberant, flowing Hudson Street. The self-organised complexity has been managed into order; the eyes on the street are paranoically focused on invasion. In the US, the number of such communities has grown by 53 per cent between 2001 and 2009 and now are home to nearly 10 million people. They are often built as a response to rises, or the perception of a rise, in crime beyond the fence. But while the railings may give a sense of protection, they make the city a more dangerous and unequal place. They create mental spaces that encourage the anxiety of the George Zimmermans in us all as well as define that space as outside the normal city, patrolled by private security and regulated by private committee.

If Trayvon Martin had been walking on an ordinary street rather than within a privatised neighbourhood, where he was considered a hoodie-wearing 'outsider', there would have been no question of invasion or property infringement. There would have been different interpretations of laws concerning carrying guns and self-defence. He would still be alive.

The line between 'us vs them' is redrawn within the city. While our communities should be built on a solid foundation of trust, we seem to be living in an age of increasing suspicion, distrust and fear. John Locke said that 'trust' was at the heart of any society; and this notion of 'trust' has too often been ignored in the discussions of how to make a happy city. For Jane Jacobs, trust comes from the small interactions within the street's ballet: 'it grows out of people stopping by the bar for a drink, getting advice from the grocer and giving advice to the newsstand man, comparing opinions with other customers at the bakery and nodding hello to the two boys drinking pop on the stoop'.[5] But as the city grows, clearly these interactions can become more impersonal and brief. As our cities get ever larger, the question of trust becomes more urgent. We need to reconsider what trust is and where it fits within the modern metropolis.

You cannot see trust, you can only perceive the consequences of its absence, or the benefits of its influence. It is invisible, but it can be found in many different places: religious experience ('trust the Lord'), as well as the scientific laboratory ('trust your eyes'); it is to be hoped for by politicians at the stump ('trust in me') and with the handshake to seal the deal ('my word is my bond'). But it can also be found all around the city, in the small transactions and interactions that we daily navigate: between individuals and amongst groups and institutions, or in the relationship between the city and the citizen. It can come with obligations and strictures on time, behaviour, reciprocity or even threat. Trust assumes an order of things, and a universally agreed norm of behaviour. But how does it work?

For political scientists like Francis Fukuyama, trust forms the bedrock of a market economy: 'one of the most important lessons we can learn from an examination of economic life is that a nation's well-being, as well as its ability to compete, is conditioned by a single, pervasive cultural characteristc: the level of trust inherent in the society'.[6] This is illustrated by a thought experiment: a buyer and a seller decide to do a deal but agree that they will both bring a closed bag to the meeting and exchange bags without looking inside. What social pressures will encourage the buyer to put the full sum of cash into his bag? Will the merchant risk his reputation by defrauding his customer? Fukuyama suggests that a marketplace without a sufficient level of trust levies a disadvantageous reputation upon itself. In time a bourse that cannot regulate itself or honour transactions will lose its customers or have to pay a higher price to buy loyalty. The lack of trust will eventually cost a city dear.

In Fukuyama's city, everything has been reduced to the marketplace, everything has a price and can be exchanged; one invests in order to get something out: A trusts B so that X will happen. It is trust, Fukuyama argues, that underpinned the rise of the west and could be found in the development of the rule of law in opposition to absolutism, religious tolerance which allowed every merchant to be equal on the trading floor, as well as the rise of urbanism, which was a refuge of freedom away from the obligations of the ancient regime. It is trust that formed the crucible from which seventeenth-century Amsterdam was born.

Robert Putnam, author of *Bowling Alone*, proposes an alternative definition of trust. For Putnam trust and sociability are connected: trust grows out of us being together, and is nurtured in the associations, bowling teams and church congregations that bind a community. Trust disappears when we spend less time with each other: 'people who trust each other are all-round good citizens, and those more engaged in community life are both more trusting and more trustworthy'.[7] Trust thus accrues social capital, a form of currency that can be exchanged and put to profit in a number of different ways. In this view, one does not trust solely because of its instant advantages, but also for its long-term benefits.

Alternatively, for the German sociologist Niklas Luhmann trust is a means of controlling the future, a sophisticated symbolic way to mitigate risk. Others believe that trust results from rights, and can only exist in places where the rights of the individual are respected. Therefore, in totalitarian states or dictatorships trust becomes a defiant act, and on occasions can even be an act of revolution. Václav Havel in the face of Czechoslovakian suppression included trust as one arrow in the quiver of the 'power of the powerless'.

For Eric Uslaner, professor of government and politics at the University of Maryland, trust is not the result of business deals or social interaction; instead it is hardwired into our social selves, based on a basic belief in the goodwill of others. Trust came first. It is not based on a set of relationships at a certain moment – a calculation that trusting will produce benefits – but a general trusting: 'A trusts B to do X' is replaced by 'A trusts'. Trust is therefore connected to optimism, confidence, tolerance and well-being, not just strategic reckoning.

This type of trust, for Uslaner, leads to social engagement rather than the negotiated results of coming together. Better cooperation then leads to the promotion of equality, policies of democracy and a belief in generalised rights. Generalised trusters are 'happier in their personal lives and believe that they are masters of their own fate. They are tolerant of people who are different from themselves and believe that dealing with strangers opens up opportunities more than it entails risks.'[8]

But it seems increasingly difficult to expect to find trust within our everyday lives; this generalised trust has, for some reason, plummeted in the past decades. Most of the time the consequences are not as dire as the death of Trayvon Martin but the effects are as invidious. We have become accustomed to expect people to act selfishly, and as a result do so ourselves. This loss of trust has consequences which we can find all around us.

In 2011, following the collapse of the banks in the aftermath of the credit crunch, the revelations of MPs' expenses in the UK, as well as the phone-hacking scandal that forced News International to admit that it had illegally listened into thousands of private messages, Ipsos MORI conducted a poll on behalf of the UK Office of National Statistics to measure levels of trust within the major professions. As expected, it made for grim reading. In response to the question 'Would you tell me whether you generally trust them to tell the truth or not?' here is how each profession polled:

Doctors 88%
Teachers 81%
Professors 74%
Judges 72%
Scientists 71%
Clergy 68%

Police 63%
Television news 62%
Ordinary person in the street 55%
Civil servants 47%
Pollsters 39%
Trade union officials 34%
Business leaders 29%
Journalists 19%
Government ministers 17%
Politicians 14%.[9]

In a similar poll conducted by Gallup in the US in 2009 there had been a drop in trust in state politicians from 67 per cent to 51 per cent.[10] In 2011 the rating for the Supreme Court plummeted to 46 per cent[11] while trust in the executive branch hovered at 61 per cent, the legislative branch at 45 per cent, and politicians in general were awarded a meagre 47 per cent. Some 73 per cent of the American people, however, trusted themselves to get the job done right.[12] These are sobering statistics, indeed, that suggest that the relationship between the street and city hall, or the even more distant relationship between the street and Parliament, is in tatters and has been so for some time.

Another reflection of the erosion of trust in our cities can be seen on many street corners and high above the everyday hustle and bustle. Just as we no longer trust government, they no longer trust us. The state's use of technology to track, watch and enumerate our every movement has become a cause for concern for many who believe that civil liberties are under threat. The most obvious example of this is the ubiquitous presence of CCTV cameras. It is not known how many units are installed in the UK but it is estimated that there are at least 500,000 in London, on average, 68.7 cameras

The street artist Banksy's *One Nation Under CCTV*

for every 1,000 people in the capital. Thus an individual going about his business in the city is caught on camera at least '300 times a day'. Yet it is not just in London: it has been calculated that the remote Shetland Islands to the north of Scotland have more CCTVs than the whole of the San Francisco Police Department.[13]

In Europe, CCTV is less popular, perhaps because of the legacy of fascism and stronger privacy laws. In 2004 it was estimated that, in contrast to London, there were fifteen open-street surveillance systems throughout Germany, fourteen in former Soviet Budapest, one in Norway and none in Vienna or Copenhagen.[14]

In the US, things changed somewhat in the aftermath of 9/11, where there was a surge in the demand for surveillance in New York in particular. In 2006 a report by the New York Civil Liberties Union calculated that within the central districts of the city, the number of CCTVs had jumped between 1998 and 2006 from

446 to 1,306 in the Financial District and Tribeca; in Greenwich Village and SoHo the number has leapt from 142 to 2,227; in total an escalation from 769 to 4,468.[15] According to the geographer Stephen Graham, the city itself has become the battleground in the War Against Terror, and surveillance has become just one of the ways the state watches the enemy within: 'Contemporary warfare takes place in supermarkets, tower blocks, subway tunnels and industrial districts rather than open fields, jungles or deserts.'[16]

Many of these new techniques, learnt from the battlefields and Green Zones of Iraq and the on-going war between Israel and the Palestinian people, were brought to bear in the preparations for the London 2012 Olympics. In the spring months leading up to the Games, the city was put on high alert, with the UK's greatest mobilisation of troops and hardware since 1945: more soldiers than were stationed in Afghanistan at the same time, with an overall cost of £553 million. With manless drones circling in the air, an aircraft carrier docked in the Thames and undercover, armed FBI agents in the crowd, this sometimes gave the appearance more of a coup than a celebration. The city itself was wired with new CCTV scanners with face-recognition software, and a new central control where 33,000 screens are monitored twenty-four hours a day. Surface-to-air missiles stood on the roofs of council flats near the Olympic Village. During the Games themselves, the media gave up their usual cynical stance and embraced the occasion, even forgetting to report any of the many instances of legitimate protest that occurred. When the police arrested 130 members of the campaign group Critical Mass on the evening of the Olympic opening ceremony, few even noted the story.

The police services will go to any lengths to promise 'total security'. But even if one agrees that it is imperative that events like the Olympics should go ahead without the risk of attacks or protest, it is sobering to consider the probability that the tight security apparatus is unlikely to go away once the carnival has moved on; as one Whitehall official commented: 'The Olympics is a tremendous opportunity to showcase what the private sector can do in the security space.'[17] In effect, the city had been turned into an emporium for the industry, and while their wares were not as obviously advertised as other sponsors, it was clearly a very important shop window. In addition, it is difficult to believe that after the vast investment made by the city in the latest technology, it will all be turned off now that the Games are over.

For many, the argument that if you are not doing anything wrong then you have nothing to fear is sufficient balm to turn a blind eye to the increased technological intervention of the street by the authorities. Only thieves and terrorists need be nervous. The evidence, however, is not so conclusive. In 2005 a report from the University of Leicester showed that CCTV surveillance had little impact on rates of crime.[18] In the case of the neo-Nazi bomber David Copeland, who waged a thirteen-day campaign in 1999, there was so much surveillance around the first bomb outside a supermarket in Brixton that it took fifty detectives over twenty days to go through all the visual evidence; by the time they had finished, Copeland had already been arrested. In the end he was convicted on forensic evidence found in his bag.[19]

There is also a very high instance of abuse of surveillance equipment, with numerous examples of operatives using cameras to stalk women for voyeuristic purposes and to conduct illegal invasions of privacy. In particular, criminologist Clive Norris found that black youths in the UK were 'between one-and-a-half and two-and-a-half times more likely to be surveilled than one would expect from their presence in the population'.[20]

Surprisingly, the evidence shows that surveillance does little to assuage the fear of crime. The 2004 report from the University of

Leicester asks where was the inconclusive proof that CCTV makes people feel safer? How do we feel being silently watched by the authorities all the time? Does it change the way people behave? Does it influence our sense of trust?

In 1791, two years after the storming of the Bastille, the Utilitarian philosopher Jeremy Bentham developed the notion of the Panopticon, a prison in which the inmates were observed at all times by some unseeing eye. The design of the gaol meant that the prisoner never knew whether he was being watched or not; therefore he was forced to behave himself rather than be disciplined. In effect he became both the jailer and the incarcerated. Does CCTV have the same effect, forcing us to readjust our behaviour where we think we are being watched?

This does not just impact on the relationship between the individual and the state, but also on our relationships with each other, and with the technology companies that have become so central to our social lives. We have become very comfortable with giving our privacy away: on Facebook and Twitter, you can now locate where another poster is; in 2011 a survey by Jiwire reported that 53 per cent of mobile-phone users are willing to give away location information in exchange for content, coupons or product information.[21] Smartphones have GPS and while we can use Google Maps to find out where we are, this information can be shared with others. The ubiquity of new technology creates a new layer of surveillance, which raises a series of questions that are perhaps even more urgent than the relationship between the state and the streets. As digital theorist Rob Van Kraneburg warns:

> Your movements are watched, not by the use of crude cameras (which, it transpires, were rather poor at fighting crime anyway) but by tags embedded in your gadgets or in your clothes or even

under your skin. Transmitted wirelessly and instantly they, connect with satellite systems that record your digital footprint endlessly. Everything you buy, every person you meet, every move you make. They could be watching you.[22]

Think of the different places in the city where you are not allowed to go. Consider the 'Do Not Enter' sign; 'only authorised personnel allowed'. Recall the places where you need ID or are requested to sign in with security. Add to these the places that you need to pay to be in, and the ones that you have to pay to get to. There are gated communities which make sure that you cannot go inside unless you are known, and then there are the places without gates that still make it clear that you are not invited. Suddenly, the freedom of the city appears to be a maze of restricted places, streets, neighbourhoods. As a 2007 UN-Habitat report concludes:

> Significant impacts of gating are seen in the real and potential spatial and social fragmentation of cities, leading to the diminished use and availability of public space and increased socio-economic polarisation ... even increasing crime and the fear of crime as the middle classes abandon public streets to the vulnerable poor, to street children and families, and to offenders who prey on them.[23]

Distrust goes hand in hand with the rise of inequality, and becomes ingrained into the very fabric of the city itself. As Uslaner points out, inequality undermines the sense of common purpose and ownership, it attacks optimism and a sense of being in control of one's fate. This is the same conclusion that Richard Wilkinson and Kate Pickett came to in *The Spirit Level*: 'Think of trust as an important marker of the ways in which greater material equality can help create a cohesive, cooperative community, to the benefit of all.'[24]

In almost every statistic on the subject, however, society has been growing increasingly unequal since the 1970s, and we are only now starting to audit the consequences. This is particularly true of the city, where the super-rich and the impoverished are crammed together. Today 90 per cent of the world's wealth is held by the richest 1 per cent. And these divisions are not just between the first and the third worlds but within our very own societies. For example, in 1973 in the US, the richest 1 per cent earned 7.7 times the amount of the average wage; at the same time in the UK, that ratio stood at 5.7. By 2008 this had increased to 17.7 times.[25] London is the most unequal place in the UK: today the richest 10 per cent of the city have 273 times more than the bottom 10 per cent.

The economist Branko Milanović has attempted to calculate who was the richest person in history. Taking a measure of what an average income at any given moment and place might be, he was able to compare levels of wealth during the glorious Roman Republic, as well as the age of the nineteenth-century robber barons, early twentieth-century tycoons, to the present-day mega-billionaires.

Marcus Licinius Crassus, the money behind Julius Caesar's bid for emperor, was said to be worth 12 million sesteres. With the annual wage of an ordinary worker estimated at 380 sesteres, Crassus's fortune was equivalent to 32,000 people, 'a crowd that would fill about half of the Colosseum'. In 1901 Andrew Carnegie was worth about $225 million, equivalent of 48,000 people, so was richer than the richest Roman. John Rockefeller, in 1937, had a fortune close to $1.4 billion, equivalent to 116,000 people in the years following the Great Depression and just before the Second World War. Bill Gates, in 2005, was estimated to be worth $50 billion, but despite the vastness of the sum it put him at a lesser footing than Rockefeller, with the equivalent salary of 75,000 people. But the richest man in history is the Mexican billionaire Carlos Slim who, in 2009, was estimated to be worth $53 billion – about the same as 440,000 Mexican workers. Slim's wealth makes him almost as rich as the seventy-second largest country in the world, Belarus.[26]

In 2011, as the Occupy Wall Street protesters campaigned against the 1 per cent, it was sobering to note that even within this percentile there was a hierarchy. The top 0.01 per cent, comprising 14,000 families, had an average income of $31 million and accounted for 5 per cent of the total US income. The sector between the top 99.9 per cent and 99.99 per cent wealthiest in the US added another 135,000 families with an average income of $3.9 million, accumulating another 6 per cent of the nation's total income. The remainder of the top 1 per cent – those between 99 per cent and 99.9 per cent – held another 11 per cent of the total pie, and accounted for 1.35 million families. Therefore the top 1 per cent of the US population owned 22 per cent of the whole economy.[27]

The city can magnify inequality: it is here that wealth is made and it is also the place that the poor come to; and often they have to live desperately close to each other. In order to measure this many economists use something called the Gini Coefficient. On a scale between 0.0 (being the most equal) and 1.0 (total inequality), one expects a developed country to be somewhere between 0.3 and 0.4, the top figure considered to be the 'international alert line' when levels of inequality become a global concern. Very high inequality can be found between 0.5 and 0.6 and includes countries such as Chile, Zimbabwe, Ethiopia and Kenya. Few nations – Namibia, Zambia and South Africa – chart higher than 0.6 ratio.

However, cities offer a more extreme picture than countries. In Asia and Africa, the Gini Coefficient ratios for cities are higher and growing faster than the nation, showing that just because cities are becoming richer, this wealth is not evenly distributed. This same phenomenon can be found in the US: while the national Gini Coefficient is 0.38, more than 40 American cities have a ratio of above 0.5. The most unequal city in the US – Atlanta, Georgia, at 0.57 – is at a similar level of inequality as Nairobi, Kenya, which includes the largest slum in the world, and Mexico City.[28]

Yet income inequality within the city is more than just a register of varying levels of wealth. The consequences of inequality go to the heart of the city: they define the urban landscape and determine the distribution of opportunities, turning the right to the city that should be available to everyone into a rigged lottery. In an unequal city it is more difficult to get access to housing, healthcare, education and transport. Inequality is connected to higher crime and murder rates, a reduction in social mobility and the decreased likelihood of voting in an election. It also results in increased levels of mental-health problems, teenage pregnancies, obesity, poor exam results, and, most perilous of all, it lowers life expectancy.

When I lived in Santiago de Chile in the 1990s, I only went once to the Pudahuel commune that stands on the outskirts of the city, close to the airport. There seemed to be little reason to go there, one of the city's forgotten corners. Today hotels and convention centres have been built that are easily accessible from the terminus and highways that take you straight into the centre of town, giving the impression that this is a successful neighbourhood. However, there is another story that is hidden behind the shiny glass and well-tended forecourts of the business zone.

Pudahuel was first a shanty town that grew out of the rapid urbanisation of Santiago in the 1960s, when the government could not cope with the level of migrant workers flooding into the city. During the presidency of the left-wing Allende, places like Pudahuel became centres of radicalism and hope, and were therefore crushed when the military dictator Auguste Pinochet stole power in a coup in 1973. As well as torture, secret police and martial law, Pinochet used the city itself as a means to control the masses: those who supported him were rewarded with lucrative development contracts, as well as the opportunity to make a fortune in the privatised utility markets. For those who opposed the military regime, life became very difficult. Pudahuel was purposefully allowed to rot, denied services and overlooked for any development projects.

As a result, in 1983 the neighbourhood erupted in a series of protests against the lack of housing, including hunger strikes and illegal rallies as well as occupying embassies to gain international attention. Wanting to set an example to the other 'red' *poblaciónes* who dared to complain, the authority's response was brutal and ten locals were killed. Afterwards the regime continued to use the right to the city as a means to suppress the people: the housing market was opened up to speculators who saw profit in many of the regions of poor housing close to the centre, leading to brutal slum clearances and widespread movement of the poor away from the richer neighbourhoods.

When the regime ended in 1989, the new government continued the existing vision of the city by clearing the poor out of the centre of the metropolis and creating new under-developed communities at the periphery of the city where cheap land was available. There was no will and few funds to improve the poor neighbourhoods where they stood and by 2000 Pudahuel was the third poorest commune in Santiago, with over a third of the population living under the poverty line. One of the key problems that many commentators highlighted was not that there were no jobs, but that access to work was so difficult: people in the *población* could not travel into the city because there were no reliable services to deliver a ready workforce to the workplace.

In 2006 Marisa Ferrari Ballas conducted a survey into the problems faced by women who live in Pudahuel as they travel by public transport around the city.[29] She noted that while there had been improvements to the transit system in Santiago, these had mainly been aimed at servicing the richer parts of the city. Where the need was greatest – amongst the poor who had to travel the furthest and had the least income to pay – improvement had been slow. For some families transport costs to work could account for as much as 30 per cent of the weekly income.

Ferrari Ballas then measured the time spent on transit, revealing that 25 per cent of all women questioned spent over two hours a day riding to work, while nearly 75 per cent lived at least an hour away from the office or workplace. In addition it was revealed that many women felt unsafe on the bus, and were compelled to stand, holding their shopping and their children for long periods of time. From this study alone the case for safe, regular and well-maintained transit is compelling and could have a huge impact on the equality of the city; but it is too easy to overlook the plight of the silent and the invisible.

The problem of access to the city is shown in even more stark contrast when considering the Hukou system in China. In March 2003 Sun Zhigang, a 27-year-old graduate and a worker at the Daqi Garment Factory in Guangzhou, southern China, died suspiciously in the medical clinic attached to one of the city's detention centres. Sun had arrived in Guangzhou three weeks earlier and on the morning that he went missing had left his flat to visit an internet café. At the door he was stopped by the local authorities who asked to see his papers, including his temporary permit to work in the Hubei province and his ID card. He had not yet applied for residency, and his permit still indicated that he was a resident of his family home in Hubei. He had forgotten his ID but offered to call a friend to bring it to the shop.

After that, nothing was heard of him until a friend called his family to let them know that he had been found dead. The following day, Sun's father and brother arrived from Wuhan to identify the body, and were told that he had died of a brain haemorrhage and heart attack. At a later autopsy conducted by experts from Zhongshan University, anomalies started to pile up. They reported that Sun had died from injuries and traumatic stress; it turned out that he had been beaten across the back. The family took the controversy to the *Southern Metropolitan Daily* newspaper, but there was little reaction as the current SARS epidemic was monopolising the front pages. Instead, an internet campaign started, calling for justice for Sun. In the end, twelve employees of the detention centre were convicted for the crime.

However, the issue was not just the story of brutality against a student. As the news started to spread through the internet some academics also began to question the legal issue of the Hukou system, which was the reason for Sun being detained in the first place. The system had a long history in China but had most recently been revived in 1958 as a way to regulate the flow of immigration between the countryside and the city. In that year Chairman Mao had called for a 'great leap forward', with the hope of transforming China from an agrarian economy to an industrial giant in an instant.

In Mao's dream private farms were to be collectivised and the country would benefit from the increase in productivity: this would then feed a policy of rapid urban industrialisation. Except things went desperately wrong. In the cities, steelworks and industrial factories become the property of the state and there was a rapid rise in production in the first year. However, there was not enough grain to feed the workers, as the collective farms failed to fulfil demand; Mao decided that it was the rural farmer who would suffer the most and the ensuing famine and deprivation was widespread. The Hukou system was enforced to keep the rural workers in the countryside, although they could not survive there; only holders of the right papers were given food in the city. In the end, it is estimated that up to 45 million people died of hunger as a result of the policy.

In recent years the Hukou system has been used to restrict movement from the countryside to the city to share in the economic boom of the new economy. It has created a whole class of illegal workers, who have no rights or papers, ready to be exploited by the factories. Today nearly 200 million workers live outside their legally registered territory and therefore cannot expect any government services, healthcare or education. While they earn wages in the factories, they cannot gain resident status. Instead, they remain informal labour, threatened with expulsion. In addition to this illegal workforce there is an added 130 million 'home-staying children', as they are called, the next generation of workers whose lives are already blighted by this inequal policy.

There have been numerous calls to reform the system. Following the horrific death of Sun Zhigang, the process of C and R (custody and repatriation) was repealed, so the brutal treatment meted out to illegal workers was no longer possible. In 2005 there were news reports that the system was to be wholly abolished but there has been little more reform than devolving responsibility for regulation from the central authority to local government. This allows Beijing to blame the regional cities when things go wrong, but the cities are not keen to abolish a policy that would force them to provide services to an unknown new population. Instead, at any moment there are 40 million Chinese people flowing between the cities and the countryside, unaccounted for, unprotected. Today, workers don't fear being picked up by the authorities, they are just ignored.

When the recession hit the globalised markets in 2009, most of the headlines pointed to China's resilience and the bold new future for the Chinese economy, but this hid the terrible impact that was felt amongst the migrant workers who were not part of the economic boom. They would never become members of the Chinese middle class, sharing the spoils of the nation's fortunes, because they had been born in the wrong place.

In 2010 the American journalist Leslie T. Chang went to Ghangzhou and spoke to a group of factory girls who had come to the city, having paid a couple of recruiters who promised them jobs, and worked with borrowed ID cards and new names. They all started work on the assembly lines but hoped to move quickly up the factory hierarchy, never to return to the countryside. They slept in dormitories, sometimes twelve to a room. The rules were strict within the factory: no talking, ten-minute bathroom breaks, and numerous systems of fines and punishments. The risks are high but for many worthwhile: one earns enough to send some home to the village, one can also work hard, strike lucky and cross the class divide, get an education and become a member of the middle class. But for most, the threat of discovery, unemployment and desperation remain.

According to Kam Wing Chan, professor of geography at the University of Washington, the Hukou system has made impossible the development of the Chinese middle class. Shenzen, with a population of 14 million, has only 3 million registered urban dwellers. It is this very fluidity and informality of the labour market that has allowed the economy to grow so quickly: 'This system of official discrimination has enabled China to experience such economic growth – and what makes it unlikely that the second-class citizens will be able to become the sort of consumerist middle class outsiders are predicting.' In the long term this means that China will remain a nation of home-grown illegal immigrants, and cannot develop the domestic market to consume its own products. For 140 million (over twice the population of the UK), sharing the urban dream is impossible.[30]

Can we rebuild trust, or is it lost forever once it disappears? Is it a political question or can we design equality into the fabric of the city? Can we organise ourselves to rediscover our sense of community?

Sometimes the most pertinent observations come from unlikely places. More than any other section of the city, taxi drivers understand the way the urban world works. It is for good reason that the test every London black-cab driver must pass is called 'the Knowledge'. In a recent study amongst taxi drivers in segregated Belfast, blighted by decades of religious violence, the report stressed how important it was for the drivers to understand the human cartography of the city as much as the street map in order to stay safe.

One of the most unexpected taxi drivers in history was the French Marxist philosopher, famed resistance fighter and radical writer on the city, Henri Lefebvre. In his essays, *Existentialism*, he looked back on the influence that his job had on formulating his ideas. Having come to an impasse in his life, he had stopped working, given up on his latest manuscript, and broken from his philosophical comrades. He continues:

> I became (of my own free will, O champions of liberty) a manual worker, and then a taxi driver. And that really was a laugh. A huge volume could not contain the adventures and misadventures of this existential philosopher-taxi driver. The Paris underworld unfolded before him in all its sleazy variety and he began to discover the secrets . . . I want to remember only my contact with the infinitely more precious and more moving reality: the life of the people of Paris.[31]

David Harvey, one of the leading explicators of Lefebvre's work, concludes that this period behind the wheel 'deeply affected his thinking about the nature of space and urban life'.[32] Some years later, in 1967, Lefebvre published his essay 'La Droit de la Ville' which proposed that while the city was the place where inequality, injustice and exploitation were most apparent, it was also the site of its transformation. The city causes the crisis – the home of neo-liberalism, the banking community, hideous inequality – but also offers the best possible location for its salvation. Only the city could cure the city of its own ills, but this future could only come from the bottom up.

For Lefebvre, the 'right of the city' is 'like a cry, and a demand'.[33] In particular, the citizen has a right to participate in as well as to appropriate the city: that is to say, the people should be at the heart of any decision-making process about the creation and management of the city; as well as having the common right to use and occupy the spaces of the city without restriction. The emphasis on the physical spaces of the city being the theatre for everyday life, Lefebvre argues, changes our sense of belonging. Being part of the city is not determined by ownership or wealth but by participation, and in consequence our actions change and refine the city.

Yet Lefebvre's philosophical observations do not offer a map; rather they are an appeal to study and re-evaluate everyday life and examine how inequality shows its face in many different ways. Rather than policy, he offered the hopes of the city liberated from its shackles. A few months following the publication of his essay, that hoped-for revolution appeared to have exploded in Lefebvre's own city of Paris. In May 1968 protests broke out in the capital as students, trade unions and political activists took to the streets and demanded change from the conservative rule of Charles de Gaulle. Many felt that this was the moment when Lefebvre's vision of the city might come true.

But despite the failure of 1968 to deliver on the promise of revolution, the idea of 'the right to the city' has remained a potent hope.

The advantages of 'La Droite de la Ville' being a philosophical essay rather than a political road map has meant that the concept has been refreshed and refined by subsequent thinkers and campaigners. It was there at the Occupy camps in cities around the world, in the concept of taking public space and transforming it through their actions. As the American legal activist Peter Marcuse blogged, there was a strong connection between 1968 and Occupy: 'The spirit of 1968 has continued and is part of the DNA of the Occupy movement and the Right to the City movements . . . both reflect the underlying impetus for change, the congealed demands of the exploited, the oppressed, and the discontented.'[34]

Some cities have already adopted the idea of the right to the city as an expressive part of their constitution. For example, the 2001 statute of São Paulo states that each citizen is guaranteed 'the right to sustainable cities, understood as the right to urban land, to housing, to environmental sanitation, to urban infrastructure, to public transit and public services, to work and to leisure, for present and future generations' (although this does not seem to have changed the everyday life of the city, which is one of the most inequal in the world). Similarly, Argentina's third city, Rosario, has declared itself a 'Human Rights City'. In 2004 this idea was enshrined at the World Urban Forum in Barcelona in a World Charter of the Rights of the City that hoped to anatomise in articles and clauses the poetry of Lefebvre's philosophical position.

The fight for the right to the city is perhaps most obviously seen in the issue of housing, which was at the heart of the recent economic boom and subsequent bust in 2008. It was the subprime market and the massive extension of debt that allowed the market to 'privatise profits and socialise risk'. The basic need for housing was conjured into the dream of a family home obtained by a mortgage that was easy to negotiate and impossible to pay off. When the market was good, driven by spiralling demand as everyone was told that they could share the home-owning utopia, it was possible that your house was earning more than you were. Your house was no longer a home but a speculative commodity that you happened to live in. Inevitably, when thousands found that they could no longer make their monthly payments, this confusion collapsed with hideous consequences.

To take one example of a country affected by the housing market: between 2000 and 2006 house prices in Ireland doubled; and 75,000 new homes were being built every year to supply the demand. Much of this was encouraged by a keen mortgage market that was willing to take greater risks than ever before in order to fill the order books. In 1994 banks and building societies advanced 45,000 loans to a total sum of €1.6 billion; in 2006 lenders were willing to give out 111,000 loans worth €25 billion. In addition, those who applied for loans were changing. In 1997 only 4 per cent of loan applications came from 'unskilled/manual' workers; by 2004 this had risen to 12 per cent.

At the height of the boom some houses in Dublin were worth 100 times the owner's salary. But then, in 2007, the market began to slow and there were rumours of problems on the horizon; yet estate agents, economists and politicians continued to tell people to buy. The crash eventually came in 2009 and by the end of 2010 over 31 per cent of all properties were estimated to be in negative equity. Today there are large areas of Dublin that remain half-finished building sites, while other neighbourhoods and new developments stand empty.

The idea of a home in the suburbs (despite the unserviceable mortgage), of the security of living in a gated community, has long been at the heart of the contemporary dream, and, as events have shown – the empty neighbourhoods of Detroit, the death of Trayvon Martin, the increasing levels of inequality within the city – this dream has turned for many into a nightmare. There are now deserts of empty speculative homes in almost every city that was swept up in the boom years, while nearby thousands of people are desperate for proper housing.

In May 2010 the New York chapter of the Right to the City Alliance produced a report that gathered together the results of an eight-month survey conducted through seven neighbourhoods within the city – South Bronx, Harlem, West Village, Chelsea, Lower East Side, Bushwick and downtown Brooklyn – in order to calculate the number of vacant buildings or lots that could be used for housing low-income families. At that time it was estimated that 400,000 individuals were currently living in homeless shelters, including families and children; elsewhere 500,000 households were in rented accommodation but their housing costs accounted for more than 50 per cent of their monthly income.

The report found that a total of 450 residential buildings were completely empty, offering housing for an estimated 4,092 families. It also found that a further 3,267 units were under construction. Meanwhile, a large proportion of new luxury units being built in these neighbourhoods were being sold at a price outside the reach of the average resident. Many apartments had been for sale for months, empty and without a buyer able to afford the inflated price. In the meantime, the city government was chasing over $3 million in tax arrears from developers who were late or could not pay.

A similar injustice became apparent in April 2012 when Newham Council in the East End of London, the locale of the £9.3 billion Olympic Park, sent out letters to 500 families in local social housing informing them that they had to move out of London and relocate to the city of Stoke over 160 miles away. Months before, as part of the government's austerity measures, a cap on all housing benefit had been imposed which made it almost impossible for London's most needy to live in their home city. At the time, London mayor Boris Johnson caused controversy by calling the measure similar to Kosovan-style 'ethnic cleansing'. When the news was announced, 350,000 were sitting on the housing waiting list for the whole city. Homes for London, the project set up by the charity Shelter, calculates that 1.8 million people will be pushed out of the city as a result of rising rents and the cap.

Homes for London also calculated that 33,100 new homes need to be built every year, but the evidence on the ground is woeful. When he was first elected in 2008, Mayor Johnson called London a 'first-class city with a third-class housing system', adopting the policy of his predecessor Ken Livingstone and promising 10,000 new units every year to accommodate the continued rise of demand for assistance within a hyper-inflated market. Yet even at this rate, it is not sufficient. 'Affordable housing' itself is a term that can be interpreted in different ways, with the official definition pegging it at 80 per cent of market rate, and therefore still out of reach of the most needy. As rents rise ahead of the inflation rate, increasing by 11 per cent in 2011 alone, homelessness seems the only option for many.

The survey in New York and the news from London both reveal how far our major cities are from adopting the right to the city as one of the cornerstones of a modern metropolis. In the aftermath of the 2008 housing crash, the Temple Hoyne Buell Center for the Study of American Architecture at Columbia University, New York, published *The Buell Hypothesis*, which investigated the relationship between housing and the American Dream in the face of mass foreclosures. The report pronounced a succinct but radical conclusion: change the dream and you change the city. In this scenario the right to the city is not the right to a suburban house, a car and an impossible mortgage; instead we need to redraft the dream: the right to live and have access to the things that make urban life worthwhile: an affordable home, a reasonable wage, freedom from intrusion, harassment or violence. As we consider these questions we must look at the visible and invisible barriers to the city: for the young, the disabled, the disadvantaged and the poor, the old and infirm, the foreign and unfamiliar.

One possible way of engaging with this question was proposed by David Harvey in a lecture given in 2008 at the City University of New York Grad Center. Here, Harvey suggested that the right to the city offers a way to talk about the neighbourhoods and the communities that have been excluded and exploited by inequality. In particular, he stressed that the right to be part of the city should not solely be determined by the ownership of property alone. During the housing boom, he argued, it was only the desires of homeowners that mattered. As a result, those who do not own property, or those who cannot afford a deposit, have no stake in the city.

In response Harvey offered a simple solution that could be found in the ruins of the housing collapse itself. Following the 2008 credit crunch where so many homes were foreclosed because of the owners' inability to pay the mortgage, families lost everything and were forced to move away while the bank got little back on their investment. But this makes little sense – it ruins families, destroys communities and weakens cities. If the banks and municipalities were able to rethink this situation, a more hopeful future was possible. For example, the city could buy the property from the banks at a good price, creating manageable housing cooperatives, guaranteeing that families can stay where they are and maintain their participation in the life of the city.[35]

Consider this scenario in the case of Detroit, which today faces the crisis of 'right-sizing' as a result of the death of communities driven away by foreclosures, leaving large tracts of the city empty and ripe for decay. Mayor Bing now finds himself in a situation where he is forced to spend millions to provide services to neighbourhoods that are barely there, and he is not able to collect civic taxes from the absent citizens who have left. If, at the outset, efforts had been made to socialise housing and keep the community together, the bill would probably have been balanced and the neighbourhood strong enough to face the future. In addition, this would have helped to increase the right to the city and equality, and built a city based on trust. For if the city is not good for all, it is not good at all.

But can we design trust, just as we can design and model other behaviour in the city? I asked this question of urban strategist Scott Burnham as we sat on the fifth floor of the Royal Festival Hall, overlooking the south bank of the Thames. Looking northwards towards the heart of London, the impressive skyline was a reminder of the capital's history, sweeping from the Houses of Parliament in the west towards St Paul's Cathedral and the City in the east. Many of the most prominent buildings were monuments of past glories, imperial grandeur, as well as the capital's continuing economic power. The Royal Festival Hall itself tells another story, for in the aftermath of the Second World War it was decided to stage a festival that would bring hope once again to the nation. Thus, in 1951, the Festival of Britain was held in previously ignored industrial waste-ground on the south bank, to promote a new post-war future rather than a fanfare for previous national superiority and tarnished pomp.

The whole site was transformed in the hands of a fresh generation of modernist architects who wanted the new style to represent an optimistic future, as designer H.T. Coleman noted: 'There was a real sense in which the Festival marked an upturn in people's lives . . . it was an event for a new dawn, for enjoying life on modern terms, with modern technology.'[36] The Festival Hall is all that remains of that event, a reminder of former dreams as well as one of the most popular places in the city today for everyone from classical music fans to skateboarders. Looking across the river, it seemed appropriate to talk about whether ideas and stones can help revive a sense of trust in the city, just as it had done with the nation's sense of hope and renewal five decades ago.

Scott Burnham has travelled around the world working on projects with designers, architects and cities, hoping to make people look at urban spaces differently. In particular he is passionate about exploring ways that city design can enhance and nurture trust. Yet his reading of what trust is is different from that of Uslaner; rather he believes that everyone has a set quantity of trust which is constantly being redistributed according to experience and circumstances. The fact that we no longer trust politicians and the police means not that we have lost trust but that we have placed our trust in other relationships and forms. Rather than signalling the end of trust, instead what we are seeing is its redistribution into other systems such as the proliferation of open source and sharing communities – what Burnham calls a 'sharing economy'. As a result, as hierarchical trust has declined, a belief in the commons has become more important, as we 'discover new values, and new ways of creating and extending trust, outside of existing damaged systems'.[37]

But, I asked, how does this reflect on the way we build cities? He then told me about some of his previous projects. Between 2003 and 2006 he was the creative director of Urbis, the centre of urban and popular culture in Manchester, where he held exhibitions on street art and the work of leading designers such as Peter Saville and architect Will Alsop, which set out a vision of Manchester as a

The *Sculpt Me Point* exhibit by Marti Guixe, Amsterdam, 2008

twenty-first-century mega-city. In 2011 Burnham was also involved in the innovative Urban Guide to Alternative Use project in Berlin that encouraged people to rethink how they used the everyday objects of the city. Therefore, with a simple piece of plywood and some chairs a series of bollards became an outdoor café; a municipal wheelie bin became a pin-hole camera; a rotating billboard transformed into a carnival swing. All these projects reminded the user of the flexible and adaptable nature of the city's fabric for fun or the joys of civic life, reinventing urban spaces as places of play and the unexpected.

In 2008 Burnham created a specific project for the IJ Waterfront neighbourhood in Amsterdam, which at that time was being converted from a run-down industrial sector into a more lively residential and work zone. Part of this transformation was to encourage people to think about the area differently, to visit and enjoy the improved public spaces. Burnham, alongside the leading Dutch design team Droog, developed a series of features and events that encouraged the visitor to interact with the exhibits; as he describes: 'The IJ waterfront area of Amsterdam was transformed into a creative playground where people could interact, alter and rework a series of design installations. To use a software analogy, the designs were installed in version 1.0, and it was up to the public to develop them into version 2.0 through individual and collective creative intervention'.[38]

The variety of events and exhibits came from an international gathering of artists and designers: the Nothing Design group from Korea set a series of fish-shaped wind vanes on poles along the river front. Each pole could be adjusted in height, and turned so that it filled and fluttered in the wind depending on the direction in which it was pointed. The international Office of Subversive Architecture created a sand box so that participants could create their own cities. Ji Lee produced a bubble project allowing users to print off their own blank speech bubbles that they could then fill in and place upon advertisements around the city, thus challenging the corporate message and the commercial dominance of public space. Potentially the most problematic entry in the exhibition was Marti Guixe's *Sculpt Me Point*, which saw a large structure of concrete breeze blocks left in the middle of the street, to be used by passers-by any way they wanted.

As Burnham described, his apartment window stood opposite the exhibit and initially he watched as people started by scratching swearwords and rude symbols into the surface of the concrete, as if the shock of being allowed to do whatever one wished forced one to deface and rebel. This is how we expect everyone to behave if we give them the freedom to do what they want, Burnham explained, but almost immediately, there was another impulse and

Obsessions make my life worse and my work better by Stefan Sagmeister, before it was tidied up

he watched as a group of young skateboarders came along and spent a number of hours working together spontaneously on carving an elegant elephant into one of the faces of the block.

Perhaps one of the most surprising reactions to the exhibition came from the police, a reminder of the difference between authority and trust. One of the main exhibits, devised by the artist Stefan Sagmeister, was a street collage using 250,000 Euro cent coins, which stretched across a street in a swirl that spelt out the phrase 'Obsessions make my life worse and my work better'. Both Sagmeister and Burnham had purposefully left the collage open to the public so that they could interact with it as they wanted; if they lost some coins, they concluded, so be it. The police saw it in a different way and within twelve hours of the opening of the exhibition it was reported that there had been a theft. By the early morning they were sweeping up the coins and putting them in bags, informing the organisers that they had 'secured' the work.

So where was the trust in all this? Clearly people had come to the exhibition and interacted with the objects and perhaps even started to think about public spaces in the city a bit more. Certainly it encouraged people to think about the space – the IJ Waterfront – in different ways. It may have also allowed people to think differently about the potential for spaces within the city, as well as offering a reminder that sharing and finding common spaces helps people to get along. But does this build trust?

According to Burnham, it does. While Putnam put an emphasis on formal participation and association as the bedrock of trust, Burnham suggested that the simpler and less organised interacting on common ground was a powerful enhancer of togetherness. Events that could have incited and encouraged uncivil behaviour in fact nurtured the very opposite. Trust was allowed to express itself spontaneously. Yet more importantly than this, Burnham reminded me that trust was not a building, it was not bricks and stones; instead it was the sharing of the process of building that created and nurtured trust.

That we no longer trust governments, corporations and police does not mean that we have lost the art of trusting. We are already more trusting than we imagine in a new sharing economy that encompasses car clubs, Airbnb; World Book Night; peer-to-peer platforms; Wikipedia; Instagram; open source software such as the Linux operating system and the Firefox browser, as well as the Creative Commons code of practice.

However, we need to be aware of how the uses of urban spaces can impact on this. We need spaces that allow us to be ourselves. We do not necessarily have to build new places in order to create these trusting spaces, we need to have open, public spaces where we can behave and interact in trusting ways. Gates, surveillance cameras and empty condominiums, at a time when there is such a housing need, a problem with access to work and poor infrastructure, stand in opposition to the open city that is the right of everyone.

7

WALKING IN DHARAVI

Sitting in the Saltwater Café in the smart neighbourhood of Bandra with Rahul Srivastava and Matias Echanove, the two founder members of URBZ, a radical design and study activist group, I was starting to feel a little uncomfortable. I had now been in Mumbai for more than a week, walking through the numerous suburbs and neighbourhoods, trekking northwards from Colaba at the tip of the peninsula, attempting to understand this most complex city.

I had already seen much that challenged my assumptions about the Indian metropolis that at once felt so familiar but was also so alien. Rahul, with a sympathetic smile and with the best of intentions, was suggesting that perhaps the title for my book was, well, problematic, and cities were not necessarily good for you. In addition, perhaps I was being too simplistic about my definition of what a city was. From the balcony of this decidedly chic bistro, serving European cuisine as muted electro-Indian pop played through the speakers, life was undisputably fine. This was what the city was so good at providing: the bringing together of the best of things. But Mumbai was an city that was an urgent reminder that the city was also a place of extremes.

Beyond the confines of the café, Mumbai was in a maelstrom of transformation. As I wandered through the crammed, busy streets, walking past exquisitely dilapidated colonial houses, remnants of earlier empires, I was also mapping an ultra-modern city, plastered with Vodafone banners and Bollywood posters.

Vast new tower blocks were rising above the historic city, oblivious to the everyday hustle that swarmed at their base. Old cotton mills had been torn down and replaced by galactic shopping malls. Young men in hard hats and shorts turned concrete that was to be shovelled into baskets and pulleyed far above the cityscape. Walking through ordinary streets I was suddenly assaulted by the empty shell of a twenty-seven-storey tower block, rising into the polluted sky, surrounded by bamboo scaffolding that seemed to be the only things binding the skeleton together. This was not a building boom; this felt like a game of Tetris played on a massive scale. Work had just finished on a sixty-storey tower, proud to be the tallest in the city, and already the first floors of a new ninety-storey structure were soaring into the air.

On one of my walks, I stood and stared in wonder at the most expensive house in the world, Anthilla, the $1 billion home of Anil Ambani, ranged over twenty-seven levels, with enough parking space for 160 cars and three helipads; and living space for 60 servants. With a swimming pool and cinema, it also included a ballroom that was described by the celebrity novelist Shobhaa De as 'one of the wonders of modern India' that would put Versailles to shame.[1] On the other hand, the writer Arundhati Roy interprets the building as a symbol of the ghostly spectre of Indian capitalism:

'Is it a house or a home? A temple to the new India, or a warehouse for its ghosts? . . . Is this the final act of the most successful secessionist movement in India? The secession of the middle and upper classes into outer space?'[2]

On another day, I exited Mahallaxmi train station and walked past the Dhobhi Ghats where the laundry of the city was washed

Anthilla, the most expensive house in the world

within 2,000 soapy concrete pens. I passed a sea of purple hotel towels that billowed in the wind like a field of lavender and walked towards Jacob Circus and then south down Maulana Azad Road. As I meandered down the street, I looked at the stalls and the diurnal theatre of urban life: a shop selling 'Leevee jeans'; a man selling watches from a washing bowl in which the timepieces were immersed in water to prove their water resistance; a sports shop with a canopy fringed with cricket bats; teatime at the Rolex Café; the constant frying of patties and puffs in vast roadside kitchens; red chicken legs rubbed with chilli and charred by the coals standing ready for a hungry buyer. And, above the hubbub, the call to prayer breaking through the sounds of banging and traffic.

The human traffic of Mumbai is overpowering. This is the fourth largest city in the world, with nearly 13 million within the city limits and 20 million people throughout the metropolitan region; it is also the most dense city with an average of over 27,000 people per square kilometre, the most dense neighbourhoods rising to over 100,000 per square kilometre. In comparison, New York averages at 10,000 and London at 4,900 per square kilometre. This population explosion had only occurred in the last decades – rising from 4 million at Independence in 1947 to its current levels, half of these people arriving in the 1960s and 1970s. The pilgrimage continues: 500 families arrive in Mumbai every day to seek their fortune, driven from their rural land, desperate for shelter and work. It is estimated that by 2020 Mumbai will be the most populous city in the world.

On another day, my wanderings took me in a different direction and from Bandra station I walked towards the BKC, the Bandra Kurla Complex, the latest redevelopment project in the city, an ambitious glistening enterprise zone, planned as the home for the latest multinational corporations, banks and the stock exchange. Wandering through the empty streets of the new enclave, I found the avenues lined with grand offices designed in the blandest business-park modernism: steel and glass shapes that could be seen anywhere from Singapore to Helsinki or Houston. This neo-liberal non-space, a corporate wilderness, is the yang of the rest of the metropolis: the new Indian dream of the future.

The BKC is conveniently located within a short distance of the newly rebuilt Chhatrapati Shivaji International Airport that links Mumbai with the rest of the world. As India's business city, the latest hopes for Mumbai are to transform the chaotic mass into an aerotropolis, an urban hub based around the airport, so that international businessmen travel smoothly across the globalised market without having to encounter real life. As the economist John Kasarda notes: 'The aerotropolis represents the logic of globalisation made flesh in the form of cities.'[3] But where are the people in this vision?

The divide between the ambitious dream and the evidence on the ground became clear as soon as I left Bandra station and walked towards the BKC. An elevated walkway – the skywalk – rose from the station concourse above the tracks and then continued to direct me along a lengthy covered pathway. From this height, it soon became apparent that the walkway was not just avoiding the rail lines but also a squatters' colony that stood only a few yards across a rubbish heap from the busy tracks. Here a community had found space to build a collection of huts and stalls, erecting a home within

On the skyride to the Bandra Kurla Complex

the no-man's-land of the city. Children played, women stood at their doorways and gossiped, goats chewed at scraps – this was a well-established community getting on with their everyday life.

The skywalk continued, crossing over a main road which led to another, larger squatters' colony. Here the dwellings were even more established; some constructed with bricks, others even rising over three storeys. At that height one could look into the top rooms from the elevated pathway. On the street level, which had clearly been given a new layer of asphalt recently, there were shops, workrooms and stores. If these were slums they were long-standing, well organised and industrious – a stark contrast to the empty streets of the nearby BKC. Clearly, the skywalk had been created to link Bandra station to the complex without having to cope with the dilemma of the squatters' commune. This seemed like a strange way to build a city.

The development of BKC and the dreams of the Mumbai aerotropolis have made the real estate around the airport extraordinarily valuable. This also happens to be the same land that is home to one of the largest slums in the world, Dharavi. As I walked southwards away from the BKC, within five minutes of following the Bandra Sion Link Road, I was on the edge of the densest slum in Asia, a community now housing up to 1 million people in an area of 590 acres (just over 2.4 square kilometres).

The first studies of slums were conducted in Britain in the 1820s and 1830s, when liberal reformers such as Edwin Chadwick made a connection between poverty, housing and health. London at that time was the greatest city in the world, but between 1800 and 1840 it had almost doubled in size, stretching the old fabric of the capital to its limits. In 1861 journalist John Hollingshead visited a notorious rookery and found:

> The small yard seemed rotting with damp and dirt. The narrow window of the lower back room was too caked with mud to be seen through, and the kitchen was one of those black-holes, filled with untold filth and rubbish, which the inspector had condemned a twelvemonth before. The stench throughout the house, although the front and back doors were wide open, was almost sickening; and when a room-door was opened this stench came out in gusts. In one apartment I found a family of six persons, flanked by another apartment containing five.[4]

Nineteenth-century London was not the only metropolis of extremes. At the same time in Paris, Napoleon III commissioned Baron Haussmann to level to the ground the old medieval housing stock and replace it with sweeping new boulevards. This was the first instance of slum clearance on a grand scale, but rather than eliminating poverty, it simply shifted it to the already-desperate quarters of the city that spiralled further into despair. The poor were considered a waste product, residue from the improvement programme, which could be moved or removed at will.

Similar projects aimed at clearing out the human overspill of industrialisation were conducted across Europe. In most cases the slum regions were created by inadequate housing, where demand outstripped supply. Buildings in the poorer neighbourhoods were therefore divided up and rented out at a pittance. With such a low income, owners saw no advantage in improving their property and so it was left to decay. Hope departed soon afterwards, leaving disease, poverty and desperation to do the rest. The political philosophy of the day adopted the latest science to accuse the poor of genetic degeneration; racial stereotypes were used to label the wretched as 'other'; moral judgement was made from the pulpit, and victims lost their identity and pride.

In 1880s New York, a young journalist, Jacob Riis, visited the warren of tenement houses on the Lower East Side of Manhattan. Riis had arrived in America from Denmark with only $40 borrowed from friends, a gold locket and a letter to the Danish consul, and experienced first-hand life within the slum. He then left the city to seek his fortune working as a carpenter, farm hand and brick maker, which forced him to suffer periods of destitution in which he slept on tombstones and ate only windfall apples. He returned to New York as a successful salesman, only to be cheated out of his profits and his stock by unscrupulous partners, forcing him back to life in the Five Points slums. He then dedicated himself to politics and journalism, gaining a contract at the *New York Tribune* as a police reporter. Thus he set his office up on Mulberry Street and started to record the slum life that surrounded him.

Riis's book *How the Other Half Live*, published in 1889, is a portrait of the Five Points that revealed the horror of poverty within New York, and was a call to action to combat the vicious nature of the slums. The neighbourhood had not always been down at heel, but was once home to the 'knickerbockers', the aristocracy of Manhattan. Yet over time the rich moved out and the development of tenement housing attracted a different kind of resident. Local landlords exploited the itinerant labourers and immigrants who came for work, squeezing six men into a room to maximise profits. Housing conditions and living standards swiftly collapsed, as Riis noted: 'The 15,000 tenant houses that were the despair of the sanitarian in the past generation have swelled into 37,000, and more than 1,200,000 persons call them home.' As immigration continued, the crisis became calamitous and disease frequently ripped through the populous disregarding race, age or gender.

In one notorious corner of the slum, the Bend, Riis revealed the full extent of the problem:

CORBIS

From Jacob Riis's *How the Other Half Live*. A room in a migrants' hostel, Lower East Side

In a room not thirteen feet either-way slept twelve men and women, two or three in bunks set in a sort of alcove, the rest on the floor. A kerosene lamp burned dimly in the fearful atmosphere, probably to guide other and later arrivals to their 'beds,' for it was only just past midnight. A baby's fretful wail came from an adjoining hall-room, where, in the semi-darkness, three recumbent figures could be made out. The 'apartment' was one of three in two adjoining buildings we had found, within half an hour, similarly crowded. Most of the men were lodgers, who slept there for five cents a spot. Another room on the top floor, that had been examined a few nights before, was comparatively empty. There were only four persons in it, two men, an old woman, and a young girl. The landlord opened the door with alacrity, and exhibited with a proud sweep of his hand the sacrifice he had made of his personal interests to satisfy the law.[5]

Looking at Riis's photographs of Mulberry Street in 1888 and walking through Dharavi today, one senses that slums have faced the same challenges across history. Whatever the historic causes of inequality and poverty, the results are similar. Yet what is most strikingly different is the scale of the problem today.

In 2003 the UN-Habitat produced a report, *The Challenge of Slums: Global Report on Human Settlement*, which proposed a new agenda for the twenty-first century on the key issue facing the future of the city. The UN had long predicted that the world was on the verge of becoming urban, reaching 50 per cent by 2007; yet perhaps less obvious to observers from the developed world was where this growth was going to occur, and what it looked like. The 2003 report aimed to set the terms and plan for facing the next human crisis. In 2001, it stated, 924 million people, nearly one in three of the urban population, lived in slums; and this number was increasing.

As journalist Robert Neuwirth calculates, 70 million people arrive at the city somewhere in the world every year, that is to say 1.4 million arrive every week; which is 200,000 every day or 8,000 an hour or 130 every minute.

Yet this single figure – the total sum of 924 million slum dwellers across the globe – does not quite give the full picture, while the median figure, one in three of the world's population, disguises a more stark reality. Within the west, 6 per cent of the urban population live in slums; at the other end of the spectrum a staggering 58 per cent of the urban population of south-central Asia currently live in extreme poverty. In Mumbai this figure is closer to 62 per cent, nearly two out of every three people. If that was not bad enough, it was also calculated that over the next thirty years this total figure will more than double, so the number of slum dwellers in 2050 could exceed 2 billion.

So where do we start? How can we define the nature of the problem: the identity of the slums? Is it a question of corruption, weak government, or complexity itself? Is the slum a universal phenomena or does every neglected neighbourhood have unique causes and histories? Is it an essential part of the developing city, a dialectical moment of transition? Where does the solution lie: is it a problem for the politicians, charity or the slum dwellers themselves?

The 2003 report attempted to define what a slum was, and therefore attempted to measure the dimension of the problem. This, however, begins with the difficulty of language. In 2002 the UN Expert Group Meeting devised a simple five-point definition that offered broad parameters. Every slum is unique, it proposed, facing its own challenges, and the product of a particular set of causes but in each, in varying degrees, one can find inadequate access to safe water, inadequate access to sanitation and other infrastructure, poor structural quality of housing, overcrowding, and insecure residential status.

Both Rahul and Matias told me that they did not like the word 'slum', because this was a pejorative term that connected Dharavi with a long history of condemned places. Indeed, few who actually live there call their home a slum; instead it is more likely to be termed *un bidonville* or *les quartiers irréguliers* in France, *barraca* in Barcelona, *conventillos* in Quito, *colonias populares* in Mexico, *solares* in Lima, *bohios* in Havana, *Elendsviertel* in Germany, *shammasa* in Khartoum, *tanake* in Beirut or an *aashwa'i* in Cairo. In Brazil the favela is a well-known nomenclature but you can also find *morro*, *cortico* or *communidade*; the famous Istanbul slums that have become centres of civic politics are called *gecekondus*. In Mumbai, no one spoke to me of the slums; rather it was divided up into pavement dwellers, *chawls* or *chalis*; elsewhere, such as in Kolkata, it is *bustees*. In Manila there are even more specific terms: the *iskwater* is a run-down collection of shelters made from poor materials; the *estero* are streets narrower than sewers and with a distinct smell; *eskinita* is an alley that fits only one person at a time; and *dagat-dagatan* is a site that is frequently flooded.[6] Can one find a single set of definitions within this array of labels?

Perhaps geography might offer a simpler definition. Many slums are to be found on the edge of the metropolis, places that the rest of the community has disregarded, municipal land that can be populated with few official restrictions or where land ownership is contestable. Other slums are closer to the centre, places that have been evacuated or disregarded by the rich, and exploited by the poor who need cheap shelter and proximity to places of work. Often the slum is in a place that is cut off from the rest of the city infrastructure: water, transport, electricity. Dharavi first emerged in the 1960–80s in a period of extraordinary urban growth, and was developed on land that had been abandoned, despite being owned by various agencies, state government, local municipality and private hands.

Between 1971 and 1981 Mumbai grew by a total of 2.2 million, or 43 per cent. By 1985 it was estimated that half of the 8.2 million population were living in temporary homes or on the pavement. The people who settled there came from across the subcontinent: Maharashtra, Uttar Pradesh, Tamil Nadu and Karnataka. For many Mumbai was the final destination after a long journey, often driven from their rural homes by debt, disaster or drought. Dharavi comprised approximately 75,000 huts and houses constructed on one storey, with plastic sheeting or a tiled roof. The average wage for a new arrival making his way in Dharavi in 1978 was 459 rupees per month.

As I walked around Dharavi, I encountered the different faces of the slum as defined by UN-Habitat, but I also found other things that I was not expecting. Within the area given over to heavy trades I came across ingenuity and a recycling industry that, statistically at least, makes Mumbai the greenest mega-city in the world; in a community centre I found a group of young Muslim women learning English, hoping to gain good jobs in local call centres; every time I looked to the skyline I could spy a mobile-phone mast, while on the central 90Ft Road I found shops and stalls all along the thoroughfare selling the latest smartphones.

This reminded me that the slum was part of the city, not apart. The literature of the slums often treats the squatter camps and temporary shelters as a separate place, detached from the rest. However, throughout history the slum and the city have shared the same story. Perhaps the most pernicious thing that slums have done is not to separate people from the city, but to render them invisible.

In a survey that the sociologist Janice Perlman conducted amongst three generations of Brazilian favela dwellers, each was asked about what it meant to have a successful life, and whether life had got better. In 1969 only 24 per cent of the first generation reported that things were good; when they were asked the same question again in 2001, it elicited a more positive 46 per cent. The next generation, their children, were also optimistic, with 63 per cent agreeing that things were better. Meanwhile 73 per cent of the grandchildren's generation considered that their prospects had improved.

This, however, hid a more invidious truth: while life had got better the sense of belonging, of being a '*gente*' – someone – was still a distant, ungraspable dream. It is as if life in the favela robs the dweller of the usual rights to the city. As one elder community leader admits, despite spending many years campaigning for the rights of slum dwellers: 'I thought I would become *gente* someday, but my time has passed.'[7] A slum is not just a place but also a social status.

In another instance, on the outskirts of Johannesburg, the problems of becoming somebody are more starkly delineated. Diepsloot is a new twenty-first-century settlement that emerged off the William Nichol Highway at the very edge of the city limits, beyond the malls, golf courses and gated communities of the suburban rich. It was assembled in the last days of the apartheid era. In efforts to improve the slums that circled the city in the 1990s, new residency rules were imposed on the community of Zevenfontein; anyone who did not have papers was not invited to share in the 'de-densification' projects and was forced to move on.

Many ended up at Diepsloot, which was set aside by the city government. Local landowners tried to block the government's plans for a 'less formal settlement'; one threatening, 'If they move here, I will be shooting ten or fifteen every season. I'm not scared.'[8] However, when the ANC won the first democratic elections in 1994, there was hope that the new government would fulfil its promises of houses, jobs, services and education.

Instead the crisis got worse. In 2001 the improvements to Diepsloot were no longer a priority, despite the continued trail of new arrivals from the slums at Alexandria. By 2007 it was estimated that there were nearly 200,000 settlers, and that 30,000 more were arriving every year. Whatever housing scheme the government planned and implemented it could never respond to the escalating level of demand. As a result unemployment rose to over 50 per cent and nearly 75 per cent lived beneath the poverty line. In addition, living conditions were also seriously lacking: the waste system was almost five years behind schedule and every street ran with 'daylight sewerage'. In 2009 tension and jealousy over the allocation of the few resources exploded into a series of tribal riots. Yet the local ANC government delegates continued to celebrate how far they had got. As Anton Harber, who has studied the problems within Diepsloot, drily notes: 'After every interview with the leadership, I walk through the area and am struck by the disjuncture between the progress they proclaim and the reality that presents itself.'[9]

If things were not difficult enough, Harber highlights how the attempts to redevelop the community have been obstructed by the plight of local wildlife. When an environmental impact report was commissioned to look at how the development of housing might affect the region, it was stated that part of the plans would cover over breeding grounds for the protected native giant bullfrog. The report caused an outcry amongst environmentalists and scientists, and there was a wide-ranging debate on whether to move the frogs, or to halt the development programme. It was no small irony that a large section of this wetland had already been recently destroyed to make way for the new middle-class suburb of Dainfern; yet when the news was announced that more would be lost to slum redevelopment the condemnation reached fever pitch. It was eventually decided that the bullfrogs could not be moved, and that development would have to go around the breeding wetlands.

The word slum invites us to see a place that deserves demolition. Instead, we should try and rethink the definition of what such a place is, and what it might be. In order to do so we need to make the invisible and the forgotten visible. We need to recognise that the slum, just like the city, is more than its buildings, huts and infrastructure; we must also remember the people who have travelled vast distances to be there, their hopes for a better life, their expertise and their industry that prospers within the chaotic confines. They are as much a part of the life of the city as well as being the source of its future success. To address the problems of the slums we must address the difficult, wider issue of the right to the city for all.

Outside Dharavi, where all the garbage of the city is delivered

On the edge of Dharavi, the road was packed with trucks that were being unloaded by teams of workers. It seemed as if the detritus of the city was being dragged into the narrow alleys that ran from the road into Dharavi: broken machines, heaped rattan sacks of plastic bottles, car parts. This was the rubbish of Mumbai that had already been sorted and was being brought to Dharavi for recycling. As a guide led me through the warren of packed-mud streets, he pointed into the dark doorways of some of the factories and warehouses.

The neighbourhood still has a thriving leather market, though the skins are no longer treated there, but one can visit where the fabric is cut and sewn, buy bags and jackets on Mohandas Gandhi Road for a third of the price on offer on touristy Colaba Causeway. In another room, a length of silk fabric was stretched and pinned to a long table, and on either side two men in vests and caps pressed dye blocks at extraordinary speed, creating exquisite patterns, without error or hesitation. Nearby, the open door revealed a furnace where a man stripped to the waist, wearing goggles and gloves, stirred molten aluminium, melted down from beer and soda cans that had been scavenged by teams of recyclers who wander around the city, picking up the rest of the metropolis's discarded rubbish. This molten metal was next poured into bars which were then moved to another factory a few alleys away where it was melted down again and moulded into machines that would be used to break down recycled plastic in another nearby unit.

In one warehouse I was shown a sack of white plastic pen tops, similar to the type I had used at school. I could not calculate how many there were, which had once filled the city's pencil cases and now filled such a large bag, but each one had been cleaned in preparation for the grinder. In another warehouse the large old cooking-oil cans used by restaurants were stored ready to be cleaned in boiling vats of water and then resold back to the oil manufacturers. There were also stacks of paint pots that were cleaned in an oven, the flames burning off the old paint, then to be reused. Bales of used paper were being sorted, bound together and made ready for shipping. One whole area, populated by recent arrivals from Tamil Nadu, was dedicated to pottery, and in between the houses, flat rectangular kilns were built in which the pots were fired. The fronts of the surrounding houses were blackened with soot.

Moving out of the neighbourhood into another quarter, the work continued. There was a bakery that made snacks, pastry puffs, that would later be transported across the country, and beyond. There were carpenters and woodworkers carving intricately decorated works that would soon be for sale in the best stores in the city centre. Elsewhere, women sat in the shade, ripping handfuls of dough and rubbing it upon a flat plate, making poppadums that were then left to dry in the sun on wicker racks that fanned out like open umbrellas. On the main alleys, there were vegetable sellers with mountains of shiny red tomatoes, mobile-phone shacks, butchers with meat hanging off hooks, juice stalls grinding the pulp out of sugar cane, while a man skinned and carved a pineapple to be sold alongside a slice of melon and papaya.

According to a report by the Centre for Environmental Planning and Technology in Ahmedabad, Dharavi contains 5,000 industrial units producing garments, pottery, leather and steel goods as well as a further 15,000 single-room factories. It is a place of extraordinary industry and produces almost $500 million in revenue every year.

This is proof of the power of the informal economy or what the journalist Robert Neuwirth calls 'System D'. It is economic activity that is rarely recognised by governments, economists or business leaders, but is at the heart of developing communities like Dharavi. As Neuwirth writes, System D is 'the ingenuity economy, the economy of improvisation and self-reliance, the do-it-yourself, or DIY, economy . . . off the books, in jobs that were neither registered nor regulated, getting paid in cash, and more often avoiding income tax.'[10]

It is estimated that today System D includes 1.8 billion people worldwide; and by 2020 will include two-thirds of all workers globally. If it was possible to calculate the total income generated from the informal economy into a single figure it would represent the second-largest nation in the world. With such sums it is foolish to think of what occurs in places such as Dharavi as outside the system. For the vast number of people around the world it is the only system available, as Neuwirth notes: 'It makes no sense to talk of development, growth, sustainability or globalisation without reckoning with System D.'[11] When 65 per cent of all Mumbaikar live their lives within System D it is ludicrous to continue to pretend that this is an invisible marketplace, somehow less important than the business of the neighbouring Bandra Kurla Complex.

Settlements like Dharavi are the essential location for System D economics. They are places of transition, or, as Canadian journalist Doug Saunders calls them, 'arrival cities', places that mark the movement from the countryside into the urban world. The informal economy is the system that accommodates the latest arrivals who are unable to integrate into the urban economy straightaway, and it is also the means through which the refugee gains both economic stability and citizenship. As Saunders says: 'These transitional spaces – arrival cities – are the places where the next great economic cultural boom will be born, or where the next great explosion of violence will occur. The difference depends on our ability to notice, and our willingness to engage.'[12]

Both of these ideas offer some insight into the fraught story of the relationship between Dharavi and Mumbai. Since the 1960s there have been numerous attempts to get to grips with the settlement, to find a solution to the problems of the slums as well as the human question of what to do with the squatters themselves. This sequence of government initiatives, policies and acts of violence are interwoven with the life and struggle of Jockin Arputham, who was born far from Mumbai in the gold fields of Kolar, outside Bangalore. The parallels between the two reflect the two different ways of looking at the slums: a top-down determination to get rid of the unsightly settlements, and the bottom-up, people-centred hopes to improve the lives of those who live there.

Son of a prosperous engineer, the young Arputham enjoyed a comfortable childhood – 'we had a 100-acre farm, a British car (an Aston) and were well off enough for me to have a tea boy to carry my books when I went to school'.[13] However, his father began to drink and the family fell on hard times. He was forced to leave home at sixteen and began a career as a carpenter in Bangalore. In 1963 he moved to Mumbai, then Bombay, persuaded by an uncle that the city was a place for ambitious young men, only to find that his relative lived in a shack by the railway and survived as a smuggler. Arputham was soon forced to live on the streets without shelter. He would not sleep under a roof again until he was married twelve years later in 1975.

In the 1950s and 1960s the state's reaction to the slums was simple: most of the groups had settled on officially owned lands, which were poorly policed, and often the encroachment onto the land was eased with bribes and the turning of a blind eye. Long periods of inactivity were sporadically disrupted by moments of violence as the state and the municipality attempted to demolish the settlements and drive the squatters out of the city. While the state had strict laws about the resettlement of people moved by rural projects, there was no similar obligation to house those displaced in the city and as a result the problem only became more complicated. When people were moved on there was no importance put on the family, work or social network that was being uprooted.

Things changed in the 1970s when the state realised that if slums were to be demolished there needed to be some form of resettlement policy and as a result the Slum Improvement Board was launched. Attempts were made to bring amenities to established settlements. In order to do this, however, the government needed to know the extent of the problem and so the systematic counting of the slums began. The explorations found that 2.8 million dwellers were spread out across 1,680 informal locations. The state then had to decide who was, and was not, to be allocated services. Anyone living on central government or private land was excluded; those who were deserving were given a photopass. A similar accounting was repeated in 1983, revealing that 4.3 million now lived in 1,930 camps around the city. Knowing the extent of the problem at this stage was the first step in confronting it.

Meanwhile, Arputham was still living on the streets near the Janata colony, a camp built out of the mangrove swamps on the eastern suburbs of Mumbai. One afternoon, after talking to a collection of street children, he decided to set up a choir as a community project. The scheme was wildly popular and within a few years had hundreds of participants and a crowd of interested observers. The choir evolved into a street school, attracting over 3,000 pupils in the first month. In the monsoon season Arputham had to find a shed to hold classes, and when that was not big enough, the group built another one on open ground.

At the time one of the problems of the settlement was that no one was coming to collect the garbage, which gathered in piles, rotting on the edge of the community, threatening disease. On one Sunday Arputham organised a picnic where each pupil carried 1 kilo of rubbish and dumped it in front of the municipal offices in the centre of the city. There was an instant response and negotiations started on how to organise regular refuse collection. The activism continued with weekly projects – cleaning a toilet one weekend, collecting rubbish from public spaces the next. Soon the activities gained the attention of the local Tata Institute of Social Services as well as the French NGO Service Civil International, which helped with funding and organisation.

In his campaigns against the authorities Arputham became known as a local community leader and his resolve was tested in 1967 when a serious threat came from the local employer, the Bhabha Atomic Commission, which wanted to build on the settlement land and started a process of eviction with the full compliance of the authorities. The squatters were forced to defend themselves as well as prepare for a legal battle by proving that the settlement was not a temporary colony. After research in the library, talking to old residents as well as numerous 'Parsi Babas', they proved the land belonged to the government, and therefore the redevelopment was illegal.

The case gained such prominence that many high-profile figures joined the campaign and Arputham soon was moving from slum to slum helping them with their own struggles. He calculates that in the 1970s he was arrested and imprisoned at least sixty times, but the fight continued. When experts and foreign campaigners came to aid the campaign they were often given short shrift: 'All these people, these experts, thought that they were coming to teach us – but we already had our own techniques that worked very well.'[14]

In 1976 Indira Gandhi's government imposed the Emergency Laws and, in May that year, the authorities came to shut down the Janata colony. Arputham was arrested, put in front of a judge three times, and three times released, the court refusing to accept the police's allegations. Instead he was commanded to help the authorities with the eviction and displacement of the squatters and the eventual demolition that took place over forty-five days. After that, the police told Arputham to leave the country, forcing him to spend the next eighteen months in exile.

In the 1980s a new wave of slum redevelopment began, funded by the World Bank. At the same time the Indian Supreme Court ruled that 'the eviction of a person from a pavement or a slum will inevitably lead to the deprivation of his livelihood . . . and consequently to the deprivation of life' and so if a person could prove that he had lived in Mumbai since 1976 he was eligible for housing. As a result all projects, funded by World Bank investments, were forced to be concerned with both demolition and rehousing.

The new scheme was called the Bombay Urban Development Project and the money was divided into two areas of investment:

the Slum Upgrading Programme promoted the formation of cooperative housing associations and promised services and infrastructre on a 'cost recovery' basis. As a result new blocks of flats began to sprout up on the edge of Dharavi and other settlements, home for 88,000 families who took out improvement loans that could then be converted into mortgages for leasehold. The second project, the Lower Income Settlement Programme, gave subsidised land to the needy; however, there was no attempt to improve the living conditions or size of dwellings built on the land itself.

While many benefited from both projects, neither scheme attempted to address the needs of the truly desperate at the bottom of the pile. The World Bank expected a return on its investment and therefore the thousands designated as ineligible for any kind of protection – the very poor, those who arrived after 1976, families who had settled on private or non-governmental land – were no better off.

CORBIS

Jockin Arputham, head of the National Slum Dwellers' Federation

Yet politicians were starting to realise that it was upon the poor that their power rested. After all, many of the rich in Mumbai do not bother to vote because they have wealth enough to extricate their families from the parlous state services; therefore elections can be won or lost by garnering support and making promises to the very poor. In turn, the poor were also starting to make their own demands.

Jockin Arputham returned to India after Indira Gandhi lost the 1977 election, having travelled to Japan, the Philippines and Korea where he made contact with other campaigners. Once home Arputham realised there was a gulf of understanding between the streets and the NGOs as well as between the streets and the politicians. As a result he decided that rather than mutual antagonism, there was some ground for conversation: 'I endlessly pawned my typewriter when there was no money ... It was during these years that I saw a need to change the approach. I was doing all agitation, breaking this and that, being completely militant, but the material benefit to the people was zero. I couldn't even build one toilet. I had not even asked the government if it could build the toilet.'[15]

However this conversation would have to be conducted on a new set of terms: it was the slum dwellers themselves who knew best what they needed: 'If we ourselves don't know what we want, lots of people like the NGOs and big project wallahs will be very happy to come and dance on our heads.'[16]

Out of this new engagement, the seeds of the National Slum Dwellers' Federation germinated. In 1984 the Street Dwellers' Federation united with two other locally based groups: SPARC, the Society for the Promotion of Area Resource Centres, founded by Sheela Patel; and the network of women's saving collectives Mahila Milan. SPARC began in 1984 in Byculla, another poor neighbourhood in Mumbai, when Patel noted the need for informal places where women could meet and exchange ideas, as well as find safety. Finally the slum dwellers themselves had groups and organisations that could represent them, and participate in the decision-making that would influence their own destiny.

Today, the current government attempts at slum redevelopment have benefited from many of the disastrous lessons learnt by not listening over the previous decades, but the demands to reinvent 'aerotropolis Mumbai' have placed new pressures on Dharavi based upon the exponential rise in the value of land in the area, the need for new infrastructure and the government's long-term commitment to improvement.

In 2003 the consultancy firm McKinsey was commissioned by a group of booster-ish businessmen, Bombay First, to write a report setting out Mumbai's status as a 'World City'. The plan set out six key areas of investment, the main one being a hyper-scaling of the real-estate market as the means to kick-start the economic boom; as one critic later commented: 'As a report by the builders' lobby, the recommendations scream[ed]: privatisation, corporatisation and build, build, build.' The report particularly recommended developing previously abandoned land, relaxing restrictions on building on coastal zones, and opening up the slum redevelopment authority to the market.

In 2004 the whole scheme was handed over to the developer Murkesh Metha, who had a $3 billion plan in mind and later explained to the *LA Times* his excitement: 'You're talking of a location that's fantastic. This is the only location in Mumbai where I can bulldoze 500 acres of land and redesign.'[17]

On 1 June 2007 global tenders were sent out to builders inviting them to come up with new schemes to redevelop Dharavi. The slum dwellers, on the other hand, would be provided with new seven-storey tower blocks and the promise of 225 square feet of apartment space, as well as all the modern services of water and electricity. For this, the new owners would only have to pay a meagre monthly rent of around 300 rupees (generating a monthly income of nearly $10.8 million for the developers). Of the 40 million square feet that would come available from the rehousing scheme, Dharavi would be replaced by 'a brand-new beautiful suburb' with parks, schools and malls all provided for the pleasure of the burgeoning Mumbai middle class.

In 2009, however, problems began to emerge. A handful of contractors exited the project citing a lack of clarity and a delay in implementation, while an expert committee condemned the scheme as a 'sophisticated land grab'. There was also a complication over how many people needed rehousing and even the number of people in Dharavi itself.

At this moment, Jockin Arputham and SPARC began campaigning for a proper survey of the settlement, as well as publishing an open letter pointedly entitled 'An Offer of Partnership or a Promise of Conflict in Dharavi, Mumbai', asking for recognition of the slum dwellers and their right to be involved in the planning process. The position of the Dharavi residents was clear: include us in the decision making or else.

As I walked around Dharavi, five years after this letter was sent, nothing had yet been done. In the week before I arrived there had been local elections and one of the vote-winning policies that each party was heralding was an ever more generous FSI (floor space index), promising each family as much as 300 square feet. In the newspaper the following week a story claimed that work could start immediately on the redevelopment scheme but nobody I spoke to expected any change to occur in the near future. There were rumours that Mehta might be taken off the project and the whole thing returned into government hands.

In the meantime, new immigrants continue to come to Mumbai every day hoping to be part of the arrival city; a place where child mortality rates are some of the highest in the world, where 6.3 per cent of all children under five are expected to die, where more than 1.2 million earn less than 20 rupees a day (30 pence or 50 US cents), and where over 1,000 people are killed each year because they live close to the railway tracks.

So what is to be done? Will removing 'slum' from our urban vocabulary change the city on the ground? From the many new perspectives on the metropolis, can we find something there that might allow us to look at these settlements differently and allow us to hope that cities might be good for us? This is what I was hoping to hear as I sat at the Saltwater Café in Bandra with Rahul Srivastava and Matias Echanove. Except they were refusing to accept that this was a possible topic for conversation. Not only did they question what I meant by 'the city' – suggesting that I had an overly western idea that did not necessarily fit with the variety of urban experiences in Mumbai – they also told me that the slums will not be changed or improved by people sitting in cafés, committee rooms or government departments. In fact, they would refute the basis of the question altogether, stating that the problem lay with the assumption that 'the debate was about how Dharavi should be redeveloped, never about whether it should be redeveloped at all'.[18]

As an explanation for this seemingly unexpected view, Rahul and Matias consider that the ideas of Jane Jacobs were just as relevant in Dharavi as they were on Hudson Street. Just as Jacobs defended her home from Robert Moses, so there was an argument that Dharavi was just as vital, complex and robust. One should condemn the local authorities for the failure to address the problems of sanitation and health, but the solution was not the destruction of the place. Every redevelopment plan, as they pointed out, was not what it appeared: when politicians and developers claim to be helping Dharavi, they often mean that they want to sell something. Dharavi offers an alternative, a rebuke even, to the mall and the air-conditioned business park beyond. Thus the Slum Rehab Schemes of the government were all market solutions and did not actually address the real needs of the neighbourhood.

In the 1990s the Peruvian economist Hernando de Soto proposed that the slum dwellers' right to the city was linked with access to the formal marketplace. If only the poor could trade with the rest of the city, they would soon integrate. De Soto suggested that each slum dweller should be given land rights over their informal property. This simple act of legal rubber-stamping, legitimising what had already taken place, would release 'trillions of dollars, all ready to put to use . . . transformed into real capital'.[19]

Ironically this policy has already been adopted by the many left-wing parties in Latin America as well as the Indian Communist Party, but de Soto's promise turns out not to be what it seems. The new homeowner can indeed trade and leverage the value of his house, by selling or mortgaging it; yet the gift of ownership comes with strings attached that can jeopardise livelihoods and communities. The recipients are also forced to pay tax, register income and become full-blown actors in the formal market. This is therefore less an offer of rights to the city for slum dwellers and more an invitation for the city to invade the slums. Eventually, it will only lead to increased poverty and inequality. Why would one offer this up as a prize to the poorest as if it were a cherished gift?

Governments should be encouraged to face the problems of the slums, but the solution does not come from the top down alone, and nor does it comes from exposing the most vulnerable of the city to the full power of the marketplace. The solution to the slums is not to force them to engage with the market. The best people to know what the slums need are the slum dwellers themselves; and rather than wholesale removal and redevelopment, the best possible solution for the problem of settlements like Dharavi is to replace the bulldozer with slum upgrading, bringing about improvement from within.

Slums often begin in discarded places: Dharavi was built over a stinking creek in a neighbourhood that already had a bad reputation as a noxious tannery. Many of the favelas are constructed on hillsides that would not pass regular safety inspections and are often victims of dangerous landslides during heavy storms. In Dhakar,

Everyday life in Dharavi

Bangladesh, the slums grew along the river's edge and are annual victims of flooding. It is the precarious nature of such places that makes it possible to build informal settlements: no one else wants to be there. Slums are by their nature victims of geology and geography. They are also losers in terms of civic infrastructure: they are situated far from convenient transit; water, electricity and sanitation are slow to follow the setting up of communities as neither government nor utilities see the value or profit in it.

These neighbourhoods survive on a patchwork of services. Electricity is often pirated from the city grid and alleys are criss-crossed with a web of cables and wires connecting the houses to the outside supply. As Jockin Arputham showed at the Janata colony, it was always possible to connect to the nearby water supply and service illegal taps. Otherwise, there are water trucks run by the local mafia which bring water every day, often costing four times more than the municipal supply. The lack of proper sewerage and latrines can cause severe health problems.

In the 1970s Mumbai borrowed nearly $200 million to improve its sewerage system, but none of these new works had any impact on Dharavi. For a number of reasons, there has been an official reluctance to provide toilets and water to the communities that need them most. For the landowners, the provision of services is an implicit acknowledgement of the slum dwellers' rights to the land. For international agencies and NGOs, who hoped to build new houses with their own toilets, the building of public blocks was never seen as the solution. Government itself was averse to initiate projects that meant they had to negotiate with the slum dwellers. Instead whole communities were forced to queue, and often pay, to use the wholly inadequate toilet blocks that were generally poorly constructed, filthy and controlled by local gangsters.

Sheela Patel, head of SPARC, reports that access to water and toilets were some of the most consistent demands from women who came to the centre in Byculla. While the NGO's dream of an indoor toilet was a noble one, it made more sense, and was more achievable, to campaign for the construction of well-managed communal blocks. At the time it was estimated that there were 1 million people fighting over 3,433 public toilets across Mumbai, of which 80 per cent were not working. When SPARC proposed a scheme in which the World Bank paid for the construction of 320 blocks, after which the alliance would manage and maintain them, the Bank insisted that there should be an internal bidding process, opening the project to speculators; as a result the project faltered and was not revived until 1998.

In the meantime SPARC started to construct a series of toilet blocks in Pune, to the north of Mumbai, developing an alliance between government agencies, NGOs and the communities themselves. In the next two years more money was spent on toilets in the city than ever before, consolidating the relationship between the different groups; as Patel notes: 'The programme helped to reconfigure the relationships between the city government and the civil society; NGOs and communities were no longer "clients" or "supplicants" but partners.'[20] By 2001, 400 blocks were completed with 10,000 seats. Working alongside the community also had an impact on the design of the blocks: attention was paid to how people had to queue to use the seats, the toilet doors swung both ways, each seat was connected to the main sewer to avoid blockages, and needed only half a bucket of water to flush. In addition, special blocks were constructed for children. It was proof that the right to have clean water is a right to the city not a right to the land. The toilet block is not a claim to own property but a claim to be allowed to be part of the civil society.

In 2007 the writer Suketa Mehta was asked by the Urban Age Conference to judge a competition for the best project that could change the living conditions of Mumbai. On the panel alongside the author was a former mayor of Washington DC, and the Bollywood actress and activist Shebana Azmi. There were seventy-four entrants in all, from the World Bank itself to NGOs, individuals and community groups. As Mehta records, the prize went to a more humble project:

> Out of the hundred-odd entries we had received, only one came handwritten in Marathi, the local language. It was a home-grown project from a group of local residents. Hundreds of them shared a public toilet, which was a pretty disgusting place. Because it was everybody's property; it was no one's ... So they came up with a solution: they put a couple of rooms on top of the building housing the toilet, and made it an educational centre. They planted flowers around the toilet. The community centre offered simple English and computer lessons, and became a social centre for the neighbourhood. To get to the community centre you had to pass the toilet, and so people started to take responsibility for the cleanliness of it.[21]

The central role of groups like SPARC in the improvement of the slums should come as no surprise; not that they are community-based activists, but that they are women. At the same time as Sheela Patel was setting up SPARC, its centres were also becoming the places for organising its sister agency, Mahila Milan ('women together' in Hindi), a loose network of saving cooperatives.

Most slum and street dwellers could never conceive of using a standard bank but Jockim Arputham sees the development of savings associations, particularly amongst women, as an essential part of self-help and determination: through savings, he notes, 'we don't have to demand that politicians improve living conditions or economic conditions or homes. We can do what we want to and achieve what we want to. Because of savings, you empower yourself.'[22] Each slum settlement that joins the Street Dwellers' Federation is encouraged to set up a micro-bank, families contributing what they can – as little as 2 rupees a day. Emergency loans can then be applied for at an interest rate of 2 per cent a month, or 24 per cent a year. The results are impressive: as the saving group of Byculla announce on their own website:

> We, the women and men of Mahila Milan-Byculla, have to make our homes on the pavement of Bombay out of necessity, not out of choice. The city wants our labour. But it wants it as cheaply as possible. So we make our homes where we can, to be near our work, to earn enough to feed ourselves and raise our kids . . .
>
> But we know we've done a lot of it ourselves. We've learnt that it doesn't matter how you dress, where you live. It's what is inside you that counts. We've been very lucky. We've been helped to learn to change our minds, to overcome the fear within, to learn to sit across the table from the politician or the policeman or the ration officer and face them as equals.
>
> We've learnt that formal literacy is no bar. That differences of religion or race or ethnicity or gender need not get in the way of coming together to solve common problems. But above all, we've learnt that poor people really can take charge of their own lives and change them. They can't do it alone. They need help. But they can do a lot more than some of you give us credit for. And that's what we try to tell others, in India and in other parts of the South.[23]

According to Slum Dwellers International, women are the engines of development, and schemes such as Mahila Milan are means to challenge the assumptions about gender. Saving is the first step towards self-improvement as well as collective action; it moves women into the public sphere as organisers and decision-makers, and creates a community for women where they are not so isolated. In addition to savings schemes the groups have also developed a social agenda: they have challenged gender abuse, starting workshops on domestic violence, working with the police to set up community stations within the slums as well as campaigning for the closure of illegal drinking dens, where there has been a common link between alcohol and abuse against women.

It is impossible to consider the problems of the slums and not discuss gender issues. Even when thinking about the design of toilets, the privacy of women is an essential component. Where there are too few seats and not enough privacy, many women have to wait until it is dark to ablut, or even the middle of the night when there are no queues. Often they will not eat or drink in the day to avoid embarrassment. It is also common that women in the city suffer from higher levels of sickness and mortality than men as a result of less access to food, increased danger during pregnancy and giving birth.

Yet it is coming to the city that also offers the best hope for women, for as Kavita Ramdas, head of the Global Fund for Women, noted in 2001: 'In the village all there is for a woman is to obey her husband and relatives, pound millet and sing. If she moves to town, she can get a job, start a business, and get education for her children.'[24] The future of the city must address gender as much as it looks for solutions to the problems of inequality and poverty. The provision of toilets and the organising of women's banking groups may seem small compared to grand conferences and the announcements of millennium goals and initiatives but they are created by the people most in need to help themselves.

Another example of women helping themselves was seen in 1997 when SPARC was instrumental in organising protests against the arbitrary relocation of thousands of dwellers who lived on land belonging to the Railroad Transport Authority. SPARC and the National Slum Dwellers' Federation were able to negotiate the process of removal and help the formation of cooperative housing for the displaced families. As a result what could have been a very traumatic and perilous procedure was managed with more consideration than had previously been expected, with local groups working with the railway authorities to decide on issues of eligibility, timing and the needs of low-income families. Over 50,000 families were moved into new housing in the suburbs of Mankhurd while new tenements were constructed. The results were twofold: the railway authorities were able to start their improvement project earlier than anticipated while the community felt that they had shared in the process and were willing participants whose voices were heard.

The role of women in the slums is perhaps the most important pressing question, but it is also – potentially – the solution. As Jockim Aputham noted in an interview with *Forbes* magazine, it is often women who have to face the greatest difficulties as they enter the slum. However:

> When we go to a settlement, we start working with women. We do a survey of the settlement starting with the hut count, the area's boundary, the age of the slum. We ask when did you come, how did you come, who is the landowner, what are the facilities you have, do you have drainage, water – and many other questions like that. Then we call for a meeting. In Mumbai, there are 150 settlements with no toilets. We tell them, write a letter to the corporator and go and demand action. Go and meet the corporator, ask him to come with us, go with him to the municipality and ask them for a toilet. Go and demand from the government.[25]

It is often assumed that the invisible slum dwellers have fallen out of mainstream society, that life within the settlements is intolerable and of last resort. Yet Dharavi is a brimming community of industry and family life: unique in its original, spontaneous use of space; as one journalist has suggested this 'probably qualifies [Dharavi] as the most efficient and productive district in the city'.[26] However, we need to remind ourselves of the human aspects of the community as much as its fabric.

Current government policy plans to demolish all of Dharavi and make it available to developers. There is a pledge to rehouse all those who can prove eligibility and each family will be given a 225 square-foot apartment. Yet will this not destroy the finely balanced complexity of the community?

At URBZ, Rahul Srivastava and Matias Echanove both feel that looking at what is actually happening within the homes and workshops of the community is an essential, but much ignored, practice. Studying the history of the URBZ office itself, off the main Mohandas Gandhi Road, they discovered that it was originally a corrugated-iron shack built by the local government twenty-five years ago for displaced slum dwellers, the Raphaels. Since then:

> It became a tobacco stand, general store, gift shop, ice-cream bar, Chinese takeaway and a mobile-phone shop. About fifteen years since their arrival, the structure transformed into a brick and cement house with a little toilet attached. Three years on, it sprouted two more floors. The space now includes three businesses, four families, a few seasonal workers, an embroidery workshop and our office – a little rectangular room with whitewashed walls and windows that stares into a low-rise roof-leaden landscape of corrugated cement sheets, blue plastic sheets and tiles.[27]

The URBZ office

It is easy to judge this as outmoded, pre-industrial and un-modern; is this why the government wants to demolish it? Surely the city of the future is big enough to accommodate both the factory and the 'tool house', the informal workshop that can be found throughout Dharavi. As they continue:

> It might be time to acknowledge that for all its lack of infrastructure and overcrowding, several informal settlements reveal a trend that can be well integrated into a post-industrial landscape. They will then emerge not as much as slums in dire need for redevelopment but as a highly successful model of bottom-up development, with the tool house being at the core of its system.[28]

The slums do not need to be redeveloped in order to integrate the informal economy into the mainstream. Rather, the city needs to make itself more open to other ways of working and living. The ordinary city has much to learn from the slums about the urban future.

It was this simple truth that Rahul and Matias were politely attempting to reveal to me as we sat together on the balcony of the Saltwater Café in Bandra. It was not necessarily that they did not agree with my title, they were just sure that the idea of the city – what it was, how it worked, who was there – had to change. Nonetheless, when I asked them at the end of our interview whether they were hopeful for the future, they both smiled.

8

MAXIMUM CITY

When the Exhibition of the Industry of All Nations opened in May 1853, on Reservoir Square in New York, it caused a tourist boom: over 1 million visitors paid the 50 cents entry fee to wander the crystal halls in which the varied goods and wealth of the modern world were displayed. Inspired by the 1851 Great Exhibition in London, the Palace glistened in the Manhattan sunlight, constructed from 15,000 panes of glass and 1,800 tons of cast iron, and topped by a 100-foot-wide dome which rose 123 feet above the city. Nearby stood the 315-foot-tall tall Latting Observatory from where the crowds could look out across the skyline as far as Staten Island and New Jersey. The whole exhibition showcased the many wonders of the thrusting modern city to awesome effect.

Each day a crowd gathered in one of the main halls, huddling in front of a stage upon which stood a structure that appeared at first glance like a gallows. As workmen took the strain, pulling the ropes taut, a platform rose bearing aloft the inventor Elisha Otis, accompanied by several barrels and heavy boxes, until it reached 30 feet above the heads of the throng. After a dramatic pause an assistant cut the hoists with an axe and the crowds gasped as they anticipated seeing the engineer crash to the floor. But the platform only dropped a few inches and remained there, suspended in the air. It was held by Otis's patented device, the 'safety hoister', a serrated brake that activated in emergencies by gripping the toothed guide rails running the length of the lift shaft. Above the murmur of astonishment, Otis announced to his stunned audience, 'All safe, gentlemen, all safe.' It was a spectacle that heralded a new age in the history of the city.

Otis's story is a forceful reminder of the connection between creativity and the city. He had been born on a farm in Halifax, Vermont, in 1811 and, after leaving home without qualifications at nineteen, had turned his hand to numerous ventures: he had worked as a builder in Troy, he built a gristmill on the Green River, constructed carriages and wagons, but nothing seemed to bear fruit. After a bout of illness he then moved to Albany where he found employment at the Tingley Bedstead Factory as a mechanic and rail turner. It was there that he developed his idea of a ratchet device that could hold a platform in place if the pulley system broke. His new invention made safe the raising of heavy machinery on the workshop floor. After setting up his own office, a few orders started to trickle in, enough to persuade Otis not to leave the east coast and join the Californian gold trail. But his fortunes really changed in 1854, when the impresario P.T. Barnum paid Otis $100 to display his latest invention at the Exhibition in New York.

The elevator was nothing new: it had been in use since the days of the Romans, but what Otis had done was to make it safe. Within a year of the Exhibition, Otis was swamped with orders; in 1854 he turned over $2,975, only to double his profits the following year. It was not until 1857, however, when an elevator was installed in the 'the greatest china and porcelain house in the city' – E.V. Haughwout and Co. on Broome Street and Broadway – that the Otis Automatic Safety Device was used for human passengers. As Elisha developed his company with his two sons, Charles and Norton, they continued to improve the design, soon offering a steam-powered lift that rose at a steady 0.2 metres a second (today, the fastest elevator in the world in the Taipei 101 Building travels at 1,010 metres per minute, rising 101 floors in thirty-nine seconds).

Despite Elisha's death in 1862, the Otis Elevator Company flourished and by 1870 there were 2,000 steam-powered contraptions in operation. That same year it was calculated that the new lifts installed at Lords & Taylor on Broadway had carried over 10,000 shoppers up and down five floors within the first three days of operation. By 1884 the company had opened an office in Europe and was providing elevators for the Eiffel Tower, London's underground stations, Glasgow Harbour, the Kremlin and even Balmoral Castle. Today, more people in New York travel via an Otis elevator than by any other form of public transport.

CORBIS

A reimagining of Otis's performance: 'All safe, gentlemen, all safe'

Before Otis, there were few places where buildings were constructed taller than five storeys. It was as if the world had heard Julius Caesar's edict that no building in first-century Rome should rise higher than 70 Roman feet (later reduced to 50 feet by the Emperor Nero) and had never wondered what it would be like to build upwards into the air. Only in Sana'a, the capital of the Yemen, did some of the traditional mud tower houses teeter precipitously up to eight or nine storeys.

All that changed in the 1870s, when a combination of steel-frame buildings, stronger than brick or stone, and Otis's elevators allowed architects to dream of new kinds of cities. So in 1885, the ten-storey Home Insurance Building was opened in Chicago and named the world's first skyscraper, with its architect, William Le Baron Jenny, proclaiming that 'we are building to a height to rival the Tower of Babel'. Then, in 1902, the Flatiron Building was opened in New York, containing an Otis steam-powered elevator rising to all twelve floors. Within a decade, the Woolworth Building had scaled fifty-seven storeys; and in 1930 the Chrysler Building topped out at seventy-seven floors. Currently, the tallest building in the world is the Burj Khalifa in Dubai, which rises to 160 levels.

New technology, such as Otis's elevator, offers us the tools to transform the city. Technology drives the way a city works, and the way a city is built; it determines the maximum size that a city can grow and who lives there, the complexion of its human capital. Friedrich Engels gives a vivid portrait of the industrial city, Manchester in the 1840s: 'The degradation to which the application of steam-power, machinery and the division of labour reduce the working-man, and the attempts of the proletariat to rise above this abasement, must likewise be carried to the highest point and with the fullest consciousness.'[1] This was the diagnosis of the city driven by the steam engine; the industrial metropolis of the age of coal that forced workers into factories, and reduced men into mechanical parts.

In a similar fashion the post-war era was an age propelled by the technology of the automobile that delivered a new kind of city, pushing its outer limits ever further, continuing the trends first set by the trains and tramways of the Victorian metropolis. The city had already been divided; the city centre had become the public sphere in opposition to the domestic bliss of the suburbs, and was further divided into business districts, industrial zones and business parks all linked by asphalt so that one could avoid experiencing the city at all. This was the city dreamed by Le Corbusier and Robert Moses: an efficient, rational machine. Today, we are living in the consequences of this vision: empty streets, congestion, obesity and disconnected neighbourhoods.

While the industrial age was transformed by factories and trains, today's city is redrawn by the mobile phone. Modern technology offers an alternative way to rethink the city where the internet, computing and ubiquitous data transform the places where we live as well as how we work. How can the phone in your pocket improve the world? How have the things that we now take for granted – text messaging, social networks, sat nav – changed the lives of millions? We are at the beginning of a new urban era in which technology can create smart cities, where information can regulate the metropolis. Perhaps this latest era of technology offers the key to the true potential of the city.

In parts of Nigeria, the mobile phone is called *oku na iri*, 'the fire that consumes money'; nevertheless this simple piece of equipment has had a huge impact on the developing nations of Africa.[2] Since 2000, the rapid escalation of mobile technology across the continent has been extraordinary: in 1999 only 2 per cent of the total population had access to mobile phones; by 2010 this had risen to 28 per cent; adoption has been at twice the speed found elsewhere in the world, growing at approximately 45 per cent a year. For many in sub-Saharan Africa where there is less than one fixed phone line for every 1,000 people, this does not mean that people are choosing one form of technology over another; for some, this is the first time they have ever had access to a phone at all. As a result:

> In Mali, residents in Timbuktu are able to call relatives living in the capital city of Bamako – or relatives in France. In Ghana, farmers in Tamales are able to send a text message to learn corn prices and tomato prices in Accra, over 100 kilometres away. In Niger, day labourers are able to call acquaintances in Benin to find out about job opportunities without making the US $40 trip. In Malawi, those affected with HIV and AIDS can receive text messages daily, reminding them to take their medicines on schedule.[3]

In 1999 there was only mobile coverage for approximately 10 per cent of the continental population, and most of these were in the main cities of the northern African nations and South Africa; by 2008 this had increased to over 60 per cent (95 per cent in north Africa, 60 per cent in the sub-Saharan region), a total area of 11.2 million square kilometres, the combined size of the US and Argentina. Coverage was first rolled out within the major city centres but quickly included many rural regions, connecting the villages with the main regional markets and beyond. In villages in Uganda researchers found that even in places without electricity, many people had fully charged handsets, and had used their phones in the past two days; this revolution encouraged the president of Rwanda, Paul Kagame, to comment that: 'In ten short years, what was once an object of luxury and privilege, the mobile phone has become a basic necessity in Africa.'[4] It has also proved to have an impact on economic growth; in a study of twenty-one OECD nations, a 10 per cent rise in telecommunications penetration resulted in a 1.5 per cent rise in productivity.

This productivity comes in many different forms. The business of telephony itself creates a market in handsets and a network of sales agents, from official outlets to the informal economy where card shops and repair workshops proliferate; it also offers new opportunities to the ordinary worker: the connected network saves money and reduces transportation costs, particularly saving the money and time expended searching for employment. It allows for the exchange of market information so that consumer prices are regulated. Within companies information can also be used to coordinate the supply chain, avoiding shortages or overstocks. In certain markets this has clear benefits: in the grain markets of Niger, being connected can have a nearly 29 per cent impact on profits over a year.

Kenya offers an example of how the mobile phone has been transformed from status symbol to vital economic tool. In 1999 Safaricom, the nation's leading mobile operator, estimated that by 2020 there would be a total of 3 million handset users; by 2009 they were coping with 14 million on their network alone. At first the swift adoption of mobile telephony was a reaction against the old ways of doing things. When many firms could expect an average of thirty-six days a year of interrupted fixed-phone network, often down for more than a day at a time, and when a landline connection could take over a hundred days to arrange and come with a heavy bribe attached, opting for mobile telephony made sense. Because of the initial expense of the handsets, mobiles started as office technology in the hands of the rich, educated and employed. Yet by 2009, the lower prices for handsets and cheaper pay-as-you-go 'airtime' tariffs allowed 17 million – 47 per cent of the total population – to own their own private phone.

This is in sharp contrast to access to the internet or banking. In

1999 there were less than 50,000 internet users in Kenya, rising at a rate of about 300 a month; by 2011 this had reached just under 9 million, but with only 85,000 of those users having access to broadband. Some 99 per cent of all this internet traffic actually comes from mobile devices, and as a result Safaricom controls 92 per cent of the market.

There is also limited access to banking: in eastern and southern Africa overall, less than 30 per cent of the population has a formal bank account (ranging from 63 per cent in South Africa to only 9 per cent in Tanzania). In Kenya, as elsewhere, access to services is the main problem: in 2006 there were only 860 bank branches throughout the whole nation, and 600 ATMs. The transfer of money, therefore, is rarely conducted through a traditional bank; instead, the post office or Western Union office is used as an official courier at a price; bus drivers or taxis are also often used to carry money from one location to another with the high risk of theft.

As a result of these two problems, one of the key innovations that has occurred in Kenya is the exponential rise of M-banking: using the mobile phone to transfer money. In 2006 the London-based team within Vodafone UK, led by Nick Hughes and Susie Lonie, and sponsored by the Department for International Development, developed M-Pesa ('M' – '*mobile*', '*pesa*' – Swahili for money), a micro-banking facility employing the mobile network to transfer funds, pay bills and deposit and withdraw money. The operation, which was then adopted by Safaricom, was intended to be simple: there are no costs to signing up or making a deposit. Once you're signed in, the facility is also easy to use and launches from the phone's main menu, asking the user for identification and validation before offering a selection of services; for a money transfer, the user is asked to identify the recipient's phone number and the sum to be sent, and then to confirm the whole transaction.

M-Pesa offers a new access to banking, but also has an impact on the real economy. In comparison to the sparse distribution of banks, Safaricom now offers M-Pesa from over 23,000 authorised outlets, ranging from dedicated booths painted in the distinct green of the network's logo to supermarkets, phone shops, petrol stations and other banks.

The other thing to note is the sums of money that are being distributed through the network. In 2010 there was a monthly gross transfer of funds of US $320 million, a factor of approximately 10 per cent of Kenya's GDP as well as $650 million in deposits and withdrawals. That year seventy-five companies also moved their payment systems onto M-Pesa, including the largest electricity utility company, which now services 20 per cent of its 1 million customers through the network.

Yet the average M-Pesa user has only $2.30 in their account; only 1 per cent of account holders have more than $13 in total. Despite the fact that the network handles a vast number of transactions, they are usually very small. As well as convenience, therefore, the service offers banking to the 'unbanked', those who previously

CREATIVE COMMONS

An advertisement for M-Pesa

have not had access to saving and deposit facilities. In particular, it is noticeable how many are using the system to send money home. M-Pesa provides the connection for money to pass from the city to the family back in the village; it offers security within a turbulent and precarious economy. It guarantees a simple solution for the poor to save and manage their money, promoting financial inclusion which is, for some, the first foothold in the urban economy.

There are now schemes for even the poorest to get connected. In August 2011 the UN announced a new initiative to help the billion worldwide who live on under $1 a day to have access to telecommunications. Under the Movirtu scheme, communities can share a phone; however, each person is to be given a unique number to make and receive individual calls. Therefore a community can come together to purchase a phone yet with a guarantee of privacy for each individual.

It has often been suggested that the latest technology threatens the city. For the bestselling futurologist Alvin Toffler technology allows one to be connected anywhere in the world and thus we will all live and work remotely in 'electronic cottages', far from the city limits. Why tolerate the problems of the city when we no longer have to live on top of one another?

But strangely enough, thanks to new technology – mobiles, the internet, Web 2.0 – we are now more and more likely to embrace the complex density of the city than ever before. For whilst technology makes communication easier, it does not stop us desiring the closeness of other people. In addition, as communication becomes cheaper, the value of human contact rises. Technology does not supersede the things that make the city so unique – creativity, community and diversity – but it can increase the complexity and depth of our connections.

In a 2011 study of Twitter users, the figures showed that, despite the global nature of the social network, usage was predominantly urban, and local. Painstakingly calculating the geography of over 500,000 messages, the results show that while social media is extremely good at collating weak ties, it was also used to enhance real-world connections rather than replace them.[5] In effect, technology makes us more social, desiring closer real connections, not less.

This may seem counterintuitive but it has a big impact on making our cities more important as places where we come together. The results, however, are not without consequences. Social media can start a revolution, but it can also drive a riot or reinforce the violence of a brutal regime. Bandwidth is not a panacea that will change the world by itself. Three examples from London, Cairo and Nairobi show the different ways social media can transform a city.

On the night of 6 August 2011, when the riots started in Tottenham, north London, #TottenhamRiots started to be passed around on Twitter. The following morning, a 'ping' appeared on the BlackBerry messenger service: 'Start leaving ur yards n linking up with your niggas. Fuck da feds, bring your ballys and your bags trollys, cars vans, hammers the lot!' It was then forwarded and spread across the network. Secure, only available to users with a BlackBerry handset and a PIN, the message was a call to arms. Over the next three days, the network became the nervous system of the mob, connecting rioters and looters, sharing images and coordinating the rampage.[6]

Six months before that, on 8 February, protesters filled Tahrir Square and Twitter began to generate another wave of messages linked by the hashtags #jan25; #tahrir; #egypt. Since 14 January, when the Tunisian president Ben Ali stepped down in the face of widespread anger, people had been using social-media technology to discuss and organise protests against the Mubarak regime.

Tuesday 25 January was decided as the 'Day of Revolts' and in preparation postings were put up on Facebook; Asmaa Mahfouz placed a video on her page calling for everyone to march: 'I, a girl, am going down to Tahrir Square, and I will stand alone . . .'[7] Her challenge spread like a virus.

Elsewhere, Wael Ghonim, head of marketing for Google in Dubai, returned home and started to coordinate protests through the 'We Are All Khaled Said' Facebook page, a site he had created in memory of a young Alexandrian who had been beaten to death by the police the previous year. The day after the first protest, the authorities were so taken aback by the size of the march that the internet was switched off; on 27 February Ghonim was arrested and was not seen for the next twelve days until the Mubarak government was eventually closed down. In later interviews, Wael Ghonim personally thanked Mark Zuckerberg, CEO of Facebook, for his role in bringing down the government.

On the morning of Friday, 11 February, the atmosphere in Tahrir Square was tense; during the night the Supreme Council of the Armed Forces issued a second communiqué, but no one really understood what they had said. After morning prayers, the crowds began to swell. At 5.20 am nearby Ashraf Khalili tweeted: 'I can still hear the drumming and chants from tahrir from my balcony. "Not afraid. Not afraid". You gotta love these guys.'[8] As the day continued, social media was used to encourage people to stay strong, to coordinate marches to the TV station and the presidential palace; to circulate information and news; rumours churned through the network but were quickly scorched. There was even time for humour, Sultan Al Qasssemi joking: 'You know you're in trouble when: Iraq embassy in Cairo urges Iraqis to return home.'[9]

At 18.02 Amr El Beleidy announced 'Omar Suleiman speaking now!' Just twenty seconds later 3arabawy updates 'Mubarak has stepped down, says Omar Suleiman'. Two seconds later MennaAmr reacted with 'WHAT THE FUCK!' and over the next few minutes the message stream was filled with celebrations. ManarMohsen wrote: 'Who did this? WE did, the people. Without guns. Without violence. Rather, with principles and persistence. Mabrouk, everyone!'[10]

In Kenya, three years earlier, people were also in the streets. In December 2007, following the contested elections, violence broke out across the country as Mwai Kibaki was named president for a second term. Many of the opposition, as well as official observers, accused the president of corruption and manipulating the polls. Nonetheless he was sworn in three days later in the face of a number of non-violent protests, urging peace in his New Year's message. The peace did not last long and the following day the BBC recorded that they had seen forty bodies belonging to demonstrators in the Kisumu mortuary; later, images of police shooting unarmed protesters appeared on YouTube, while stories began to circulate that some thirty people had been herded into a chapel and the building then set alight.

By 2 January the death toll had escalated to 300 and was gaining international attention. This only led to more recriminations, failed mediations between the parties and clashes between protesters and police on the streets; by 28 January the toll had risen to 800.

Ory Okollah had returned home to Kenya from Johannesburg to vote but found herself stuck in the family home with a child and a laptop. While she ran out of supplies, she maintained her blog on Kenya politics until she decided she was no longer safe and left for South Africa. There, she posted updates and blogged on the possibilities of using Google Earth satellite imaging as a means to crowd-source stories. Within days, she had responses from other bloggers and engineers including Erik Hersman, David Kobia and Juliana Rotich and within weeks they had created the Ushahidi

(Swahili for testament), and were coordinating reports of violence sent in by text or phone and then mapping them on an interactive Google Earth map.

Ushahidi used the same complex network of telecommunications as the rioters in London and the protesters in Cairo to gather together real-time information. Where it was different was that it used mapping and location in order to bring help and also to act as a witness to events. When the UN Commission on Human Rights visited Kenya in February following the resolution of the crisis, they concluded that 'greater accountability and an end to impunity will be key to addressing the underlying problems and preventing further outbreaks'.[11] Ushahidi, despite being a non-governmental group, set up by passionate bloggers, offers a software platform that can be used in any kind of crisis.

Since 2008, the platform has been improved and made freely available for anyone who wishes to download the tools from the Ushahidi website. It has been utilised to collate election data in Liberia, Morocco, Nigeria, Egypt, Tanzania, Brazil, Sudan and the Philippines. In addition, the crowd-map software has been adopted in any number of ways: in Belarus, it is being used on www.crisisby.net to monitor human-rights violations by the regime of the last dictator in Europe. Women Under Siege collects data about atrocities and sexual violence against women in Syria during the uprising.

The applications for crowd-sourcing maps can be almost endless. In Taiwan, Angry Map records reports of bad behaviour in the hope of naming and shaming people into civility. [Im]possible living is a site in Milan, Italy, that discovers abandoned buildings and hopes to connect them with schemes for potential reuse. In New York, crowd-sourcing maps software drives the Future Now NYC programme, which gathers together ideas from local schoolchildren about ways to improve their community, from more trees and a football field to

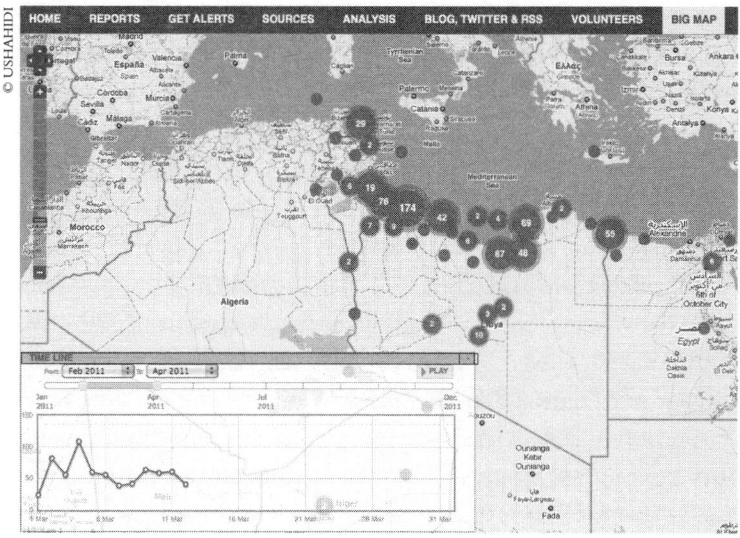

A website using Ushahidi software showing reports of human rights violations in Libya during the uprising in 2011

'gun free' teen clubs. The CUNY Grad School of Journalism has also collected data to create a map of danger spots in the Brooklyn neighbourhood of Fort Greene, adding both traffic accidents and street thefts to show how users can avoid them.

One of the most extraordinary uses of the Ushahidi platform is at moments of natural disaster when infrastructure is often at its most fragile and real-time information from people on the ground, NGOs and emergency services really does mean the difference between life and death. On 12 January 2010, Port au Prince, the capital of Haiti, was hit by a devastating earthquake. Within hours the city was reduced to rubble: hospitals collapsed, infrastructure was torn out at the roots, radios went silent as there was no electricity or broadcasts, while the streets were so strewn with debris that it was difficult to travel anywhere.

There was no way anyone could calculate the level of the damage, the number of people lost or dead, the families torn apart. Within twelve hours a dedicated Ushahidi website had been launched, first reporting on problems at the airport. This was followed by notices of a building collapsed at Delmas 19, Rue Mackendal, and the destruction of the national palace; the next morning, it was announced that a hospital to the north-west of the city was still in operation, fully staffed, while there were calls for food in the Bel Air neighbourhood. Soon there were requests to find lost people, friends, family, a doctor. All the messages were catalogued and then placed on the map to give location, time and specific need.

At the same time, techies, cartography fans and NGOs were looking at other means to help on the ground. Even before the quake, Port au Prince had been a chaotic city; beyond the central neighbourhoods there had been few attempts to map the slums, shanties and informal streets. Many of these were out of bounds to officials; others were in such a state of flux that no map could reasonably keep up to date. However, in this time of desperation, there was a need for accurate maps so that aid could be delivered where necessary. Using Openstreetmap, volunteers pored over Google Earth satellite maps tracing primary and secondary streets, damaged buildings and, as they emerged, refugee camps.[12] Within forty-eight hours, volunteers working independently around the world were changing the way aid workers were operating on the ground, giving them accurate locations and data.

Sitting beside my son on the sofa, we often set off around the world. Our journey usually starts at home: we find our street and then our house and imagine that the satellite is picturing us at that very moment. We then decide where to go: this time – the Pyramids. The image zooms outwards; our street becomes part of the cross-hatched urban fabric; then the city fills the screen, then the outline of Great Britain dusted with clouds and encircled by sea. The camera seems to halt, momentarily standing still in space, then begins to swerve right, and down, south-eastwards, across Europe, over mountains, along the length of Italy, skimming the Mediterranean until the screen becomes dusty brown and burnt red as we reach north Africa. Finally, the focus begins to zoom inwards even as we continue to travel: Cairo, indicated by a small yellow star, begins to expand and grow into a city. We are destined for the edge of the metropolis, a place where the desert meets the suburbs: Giza.

And there they are. Initially, the Pyramid of Khafre is almost impossible to see, the stone the same russet colour as the surrounding landscape; only the shadow of the east face makes it clear that this is a vast structure. My son clicks to get a better look and then uses his finger to move around the site. He tells me all that he has learnt in his recent lessons on Ancient Egypt. He finds the Sphinx, close by the Valley Temple of Khafre, and is almost speechless with excitement. He tells me the whole story of the riddle of the Sphinx and how Oedipus was able to outwit the mythic monster. He then wanders through the Eastern Cemetery and goes in search of the Tombs of the Queens.

Later, I return to Google Earth and move from Giza and the historic site of the Pyramids, to go in search of Tahrir Square; and because it does not appear in the search facility, I try to work out from the city plan where it might be. Cairo is so vast and chaotic, even from the air, that it is difficult to tell where the city centre might be. The map is studded with miniature tags that link to Wikipedia, and so I can find information on Boulaq, the Coptic Museum, the 6th October Bridge built in memory of the Yom Kippur War of 1993; I can also find where the metro stations are. From the east side of the bridge I find the Egyptian Museum and then the square. There is little evidence of the crowds from February 2011.

I also look at other cities that have been in the news recently: the Fukushima nuclear plant that was damaged by the earthquake in March 2011; or I peer over Kabira, the slums outside Nairobi, where the shacks are so closely packed together that it is impossible to see where the streets and alleys wind through the neighbourhoods; finally, I click to the High Line in New York, and watch in wonder at how a channel of verdant green snakes through the city.

Google Earth brings joy and fascination, but it can also be used to make a difference. In 2008 Clean Up The World started to use it to highlight places of particular crisis as well as show the impact of the International Clean Up Weekend. It is also being used to track the loss of the Antarctica ice cap, the depletion of the rainforest in Amazonia, measuring the largest oil spills in the world's oceans[13] as well as the extent of urban sprawl in cities like Houston and Phoenix.

Google Earth is already having an unexpected impact on urbanism. In Dubai, islands are being designed to be seen from the air. Palm Jumeirah is a man-made island that spans out into the Gulf in the shape of a palm leaf that can be seen by satellite or aeroplane. Elsewhere the availability of aerial images has changed the way a city is run. In Athens, in the aftermath of the Euro crisis, the Greek government has been using Google Earth to find out who has a swimming pool in their gardens and then checking this apparent wealth with their tax returns. This has resulted in a number of gardens being covered over in the city. During the Olympics, 'Adizones', 'giant multisport outdoor zones' sponsored by Adidas and offering a selection of gym equipment as well as dance and gymnastics, were built in public parks around London. From the air these projects clearly marked out the shape of the 2012 Games logo.[14]

The Palm Jumeirah, Dubai – the city designed to be seen from Google Earth

Finally, in my laptop tour of the world, I type in the name of a city that does not even exist yet – Songdo – and am taken to a patch of bare ground to the west of Seoul, South Korea. This new city is to be built on land that has been reclaimed from the Yellow Sea, and is planned to be the most advanced technological city in the world. Songdo has been designed with the network in mind, working alongside the Silicon Valley software giant Cisco's Smart+Connected systems, which converge technology, architecture, people and urban life into seamless unity.

This is a new generation of metropolis: the smart city, built according to the new rules of the Information Age. It is a connected city in which real-time information monitors and regulates the urban fabric; buildings, objects, traffic lights are both sensors and activators. The new city is no longer a static collection of places but 'a computer in open air'. It is a sentient place, which can gather information, change, and react to the feedback; in the words of

Assaf Biderman, associate director of the SENSEable City Lab at MIT, smart technologies can make 'cities more human'.[15]

But how can technology possibly make our cities more 'human'? One is right be to suspicious of such techno-utopianism; wasn't Le Corbusier's dream of the autopia a similar fantasy? What can machines do that people can't?

The first noticeable change in the smart city is that everything is connected. The first mobile-phone network, NTT, was set up in Japan in 1977; since then handsets and networks have spread across the world. By 2002 there were 1 billion connections, rising to 5 billion within eight years. With a total world population of over 7 billion, even with some people having two mobile phones, this seems an unexpectedly high number. Clearly the figure includes more than the connections between people with mobile phones, ringing and texting each other. In the last few years, there has been a proliferation of machines connecting to each other rather than human connections: the dial-up desktop computer, superseded by broadband, and now by wireless bandwidth, 3 and 4G, tablet technology, and other mobile computing devices. At the same time cloud computing widens the connexity of things, making it easier to access our data from any place.

However, it is not just our phones and computers that are now connected, we will soon live in the 'Internet of Things' where the internet enters the real world and collects data from every object around us, so that every aspect of our lives interacts. Data will be collected every time we use the public-transport system, our cars can be connected to the garage to tell them when there has been a fault, traffic lights and road signs will contain sensors that detect congestion and traffic flow, smart buildings will regulate internal temperature or lighting, face-recognition software might be used for everything from banking to security.

The city is becoming not just a collection of places and bodies but a living and connected network in which buildings, signs, users and vehicles communicate with each other in real time. This may sound like science fiction but there is no HAL 2000-style mainframe taking control over the city, nor is this *Metropolis*, Fritz Lang's dystopian image of the late-industrial world. The smart city uses technology as a tool to collect vast amounts of information which we can then employ to improve the way things work around us. It is a means of informing the real world, not replacing it, creating what Anthony Townsend of the California-based Institute of the Future calls a 'blended urban reality'.[16]

Songdo is a new city being built from the top down. In the 1990s Korea had been hit hard by the global recession and was forced to accept IMF backing, which included as one of its stipulations that the local market had to be opened up to international trade and foreign investment. Initially, there was little interest and as a result the government developed a series of free enterprise zones, FEZs, to tempt new sectors like logistics, financial services and IT. This coincided with a reclamation project on the land near Incheon International Airport which included three small islands, one named Songdo, the Isle of Pines. Most of this work had been contracted by Daewoo, which hoped to create a 'media city' to compare with Silicon Valley, but when the corporation got into financial trouble, Songdo was abandoned and the city authorities contacted the Korean-born American businessman Jay Kim, who had previous experience of working on big projects as well as having strong US contacts. From his office in Pasadena, California, Kim started to make enquiries amongst the major American developers.

Over the next few years a team was put together, including John B. Hynes III of Boston-based Gale & Wentworth, and Stan Gale, who quickly started to negotiate with the city office, as well as the

Korean steel giants POSCO, and leading urban architects Kohn Pedersen Fox, who developed a plan for what was now being called Songdo International Business District (IBD). By 2002 the masterplan had been formed to include a community of 100,000 residents and workspace for another 300,000. The city was to be broken down into zones: 50 million square feet of office space; 30 million square feet for residential; 10 million square feet for retail; 5 million square feet for hotels.

There was also to be a convention centre, a golf course designed by Jack Nicklaus, a mall, an iconic skyscraper, schools, a central park and water features. It would all be built to the highest sustainability standards and be linked to the international airport by a bridge that ran 7.6 miles across the Yellow Sea to Incheon. As one marketing brochure points out, Songdo takes the best of the world and makes it even better:

> Canals were modelled after Venice's Grand Canal; its skyline after Hong Kong; the cultural centres after Sydney's Opera House; and the pocket parks in residential areas mimic Savannah, Georgia. Songdo IBD's Park Avenue and Central Park will create a mix of relaxation and urban sophistication like their namesakes in New York. Finally, the government center's location at the axis of a hub of spokes draws upon Paris's Arc de Triomphe.[17]

Yet it is the technology at the heart of the city that makes it more than the Las Vegas of Asia. By January 2012 it was already home to 22,000 residents, a number expected to rise to 65,000 on completion, in addition to a commuting population of 300,000 who will arrive by transit or from the nearby airport in Incheon for business. The skyscrapers, public spaces and gardens, impressive plazas and feats of engineering herald a bold and confident metropolis, the compliance of the whole city to the highest Leadership in Energy and Environmental Design (LEED) standards make it one of the most sustainable environments imaginable, but it is the invisible connections, the city as Internet of Things, that is truly impressive. Songdo is more than the people or the buildings within it, and even more than the infrastructure of roads, water, waste, transit and energy; it is U.Life. As Tom Murcott, executive president of Gale International noted: 'The enabling technologies need to be baked into the masterplan and initial design and development from the get-go, rather than a follow.'[18]

U.Life puts new technology at the centre of the city, and since 2008 Gale has been working with Cisco to deliver the intelligence to run the smart metropolis. The whole city will operate from a hub that functions as Songdo's 'brain stem'.[19] Here, for example, cameras will report on the flow of pedestrians on the street, and brighten or dim the pavement lamps accordingly; 'radio frequency identification tags' will be attached to car number plates to watch traffic and reaction to congestion; monitors on buildings and roads will report on conditions to avoid costly works or unnecessary delays; there will be real-time weather forecasts that can prepare the power grid for surges in demand when it gets suddenly cold; at other times, the smart energy grid will monitor usage and flows and predict demand as well as search for efficiencies; there will also be a smart grid for water and waste.

Each home will also become smarter: there will be touchpads in each apartment so that one can control temperature and lighting and track energy use. Smart architecture will help the sustainable city – there will be roof gardens planted with vegetation to reduce the 'heat island' effect, and reduce storm-water run-off. There will be no waste collection as everything will be processed by a centralised system that sucks all the rubbish away.

This appears to promise the best of all possible places, inspired by the finest examples of architecture from around the world, smarter than any previous city in order to make the mundane moments of urban living run smoothly: improving traffic congestion; energy efficiency and smart buildings; enhanced security and surveillance. The instant city, super-smart, built from the ground up from a masterplan is, for many, the vision of the future, the latest version of a hi-tech Utopia, and it can be found across Asia.

Songdo is not alone in attempting to find a new urban order, and many of the latest cities sound more like aisles in an electronic store than metropolitan areas: Putrajaya and Cyberjaya form part of the Multimedia Super Corridor in Malaysia, built in the last decade out of land previously covered by rubber plantations. Mentougou Eco Valley has been designed west of Beijing by the Finnish architect Eriksson as a beacon of what a city could be. Elsewhere in southern China there are plans for the self-styled Sino-Singapore Guangzhou Knowledge City. Outside Abu Dhabi, an ambitious new city, Masdar, is being designed by Foster + Partners, which promises to be the smartest zero-carbon city on the planet.

But this vision of the smart city raises many questions and concerns. What happens when the whole city runs on one type of software and you want to use another – will you be thrown off the grid? What if you want to develop your own code, adapting some of the city's software – will you end up in court for hacking? Who owns the city when it runs on someone else's software? Can it continue to develop and change when the digital infrastructure is copyrighted? What if, as Anthony Townsend warns, 'one company comes out on top, cities could see infrastructure end up in the control of a monopoly whose interests are not aligned with the city or its residents.'[20]

There is lots of money to be made from talking about the smart city. From theorists prophesying their visions, architects with their design innovations, management consultants who wish to sell their solutions, software companies who have developed the proprietary code to run the new world, making and marketing the smart city is big business. Big players such as IBM, Cisco, Siemans, Accenture, McKinsey and BoozAllen are all entering the debate on the intelligent city, the smart-grid, next-generation buildings, developing the tools to bring efficiency, sustainability and a connected metropolis. These big companies are talking to city halls, offering end-to-end solutions, the complete package to retrofit the everyday city for the twenty-first century with a very hard sell.

How Smart Is Your City, produced by the IBM Institute of Business Value, supplies tools for assessing the connectedness of any city and offers a road map:

Develop your city's long-term strategy and short-term goals
Prioritise and invest in a few select systems that will have the greatest impact
Integrate across systems to improve citizen experiences and efficiencies
Optimise your services and operations
Discover new opportunities for growth and optimisation.[21]

In a corresponding document from the same team, *A Vision of Smarter Cities*, the researchers go into more detail on how 'smartness' can be achieved. What is clear from this big-business perspective is that change must come from the top down: 'city administrators should develop an integrated city-planning framework'.[22]

IBM's command to 'think revolution, not evolution'[23] needs to be taken with a pinch of salt. Despite the maverick rhetoric, we need to be cautious of these digital Baron Haussmanns of the future. Can there be a more bottom-up solution that offers some form of 'open-source' city, where information and knowledge is freely distributed rather than proprietorial, and is developed by those who use it rather than those looking for something to sell? This kind of 'open-source' city can adapt and transform as times and demands change; it responds to and reflects the street as much as it does city hall or the marketplace.

Perhaps it is the bottom-up development of technology that is best suited for retrofitting existing cities. Without pulling the whole edifice down and starting again, the cities we live in today need to embrace the latest ways to make them more efficient and sustainable. Technology can be used for inclusion with great impact: M-Pesa offers banking services for the first time to millions who never had an account in Kenya; it is also very good at collecting and gathering data. The smart city is one that integrates the big city-hall projects but allows more open-source involvement to continue. If not, there is every chance that it will be proven once again that we learn nothing from history and the two sides of the digital divide – the cyber Robert Moses and Jane Jacobs – will clash, just as they did in 1961.

The bottom-up 'info-structure' will not by its nature be an 'end-to-end solution'. It will combine a number of devices and platforms, from electronic road signage, mobile phones and GPS, to bikes and maps. It will undoubtedly exhibit some of the most creative and innovative thinking about the metropolis, opening up new ways of navigating our cities, making urban life easier and more diverse. It will integrate the old and the new, weaving together the physical city with the digital grid, offering information as well as the tools for change.

The SENSEable City Lab at MIT, outside Boston, is one of the leading research centres into this potential future of the smart city. In 2009 the director of the lab, the architect and civil engineer Carlo Ratti, proposed that the 2012 London Olympics should be celebrated with the creation of a cloud, a transparent observation deck high above the stadia of Stratford. The floating world would be accessed by a circling ramp that rose from the ground into the air, spiralling for 1 kilometre. The structure was alive 'with an LED information system which densifies locally into lightweight info-screen hotspots where visitors can navigate information about the immediate surroundings';[24] in effect transforming ordinary citizens into true Olympians, and turning the traditional Olympic monument on its head. It was clearly a dream unlikely to see the light of day; but it is this kind of rethinking the relationship between the city and place that excites Carlo Ratti and informs the work at the SENSEable City Lab.

Cities are vast networks of information, but thus far gathering the data at the levels that make a difference has been very difficult; this is now changing. The smart city is a sensor. Ratti's team at MIT have looked at a number of projects that help the gathering together of huge sources of information that allow us to understand the city – not how we think it might work but how it actually, empirically, functions. The Lab has invented a number of exciting devices that help this gathering of data.

'Trash/Track' are small sensors that the Lab tested to uncover the waste chain, what really happens to our garbage. In an experiment conducted in 2009 in New York, Seattle and London, 3,000 electronic tags were attached to different types of rubbish, and their movements were then mapped, revealing just how far our waste travels, questioning the sustainability of our recycling policies.

The Copenhagen Wheel is one of Ratti's most ingenious data sensors. Encased in a red plastic disk, it sits on the back wheel of a bicycle and was first used in the Danish capital in 2009. The device is a miniature engine that stores up energy from the bike when it is moving for those moments when you need a little extra push. The shiny red disc also hides sophisticated sensors that help the rider in a number of scenarios: connected to the iPhone via an app, the wheel collects the data for your fitness regime: distance, time, calories. It can also help navigating the city and monitoring levels of congestion and pollution. Thus it can tell you in advance whether there is traffic ahead, the condition of the roads, the best diversion. This information can also then be shared with friends or others in the neighbourhood.

The SENSEable City Lab is also looking at experiments on a city-wide scale. LIVE Singapore is an on-going project to connect all the data from various government departments to offer a real-time data feed of everything that is going on in the city. While developing an open digital platform that can absorb data coming in from every point in the city as well as an interface that can be accessed by everyone from politicians, traffic police and ordinary citizens on multiple devices, the project has already been collecting data on how Singapore works. It now includes an isochronic map, showing the time it takes to move about the city at various times of the day and where the problems occur. There is also a way of improving the distribution of taxis around the city, how big events like the Singapore Formula 1 Grand Prix disrupts the infrastructure, what the measurement of mobile-phone usage reveals about the way people go about their lives.

As the LIVE Singapore research shows, valuable data can be found in the most unusual places. Eric Fischer is a self-confessed map geek from the Bay Area and loves to rebuild maps of the city through unexpected data sets to show more than just the geographical or the street plan, but the topography of human activity. For example, in his series of Geotagger's maps he set integrated maps of the great cities of the world with tagging information from the vast photo-sharing website Flickr. Thus the map of London became a graph of the most photographed places. Fischer was then able to break down the data to show how differently tourists and locals use the city. This type of info-mapping changes the way we look and understand the city, not just as geography but as a living, transforming human landscape.

This real-time data can empower the city. The smart city offers the kind of data that helps us make better decisions about our urban lives; it can also create feedback loops that make the running of the city more efficient. Driving too fast down a city street, often a sign with the number 20 surrounded by a red ring is not enough to make one put on the brakes. Does your behaviour change when a digital sign flashes your speed on a board? This is a very simple example of how feedback loops of real-time information can influence behaviour; what happens if we can integrate feedback loops into every part of the city?

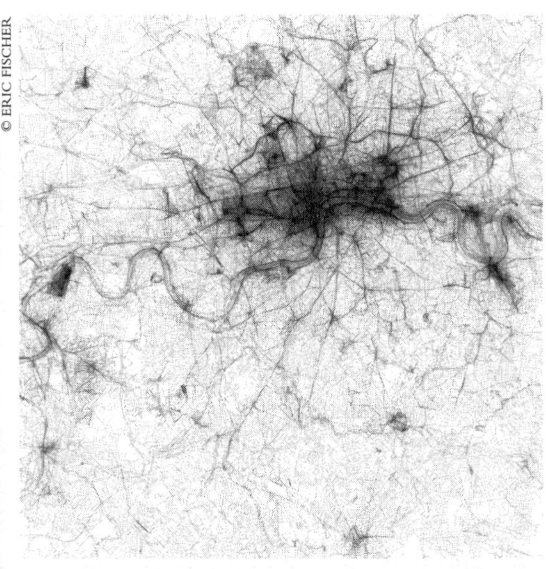

Eric Fischer's geotagged map of Flickr images of London

Like the Copenhagen bikes, a number of researchers have done similar studies with taxi drivers in Beijing, such as the T-Drive initiative shared between the University of Science and Technology and Microsoft. Today in the capital of China the rapidly expanding population of nearly 20 million makes for congested, polluted roads; amongst the traffic of cars, trucks and carts are 90,000 taxi drivers who have a reputation for being surly and uncommunicative, and often new to the city. For them, the meter continues to run whether they are at a standstill or buzzing down the highway. However, a group of researchers decided to work with 33,000 drivers and, using a combination of dashboard-mounted GPS monitors and cloud-computing technology, were able to create an intelligent, real-time traffic service.

Studying congestion on all 106,579 roads within the city, a distance of over 5,500 kilometres, they created a smart grid forming a digital map of the city. This was also integrated with weather and public-transit information. As a result, in testing, the new smart grid improved 60–70 per cent of all taxi trips and made them significantly faster.

The smart city is being built from a combination of big city-hall projects alongside major software companies as well as more humble schemes that can be found on the 3 or 4G mobile in your pocket or the sat nav on the dashboard. Yet the city of the future, however connected it may be, is only ever going to be as smart as the people who use it. Information is not an end in itself, it is a means to come up with better solutions to the problems of urban life. Yet it is surprising how thinking about the smart city forces us to reconsider other aspects of the city. Does technology help us face the problems of congestion? Can smart building make the city of the future more sustainable?

9

MOVING AROUND

On our first night in Marrakesh my wife and I took our two-year-old son to the central square, the Jemaa el Fna, the largest public square in Africa, famed for its food stalls and entertainments. As the sun began to descend behind the Medina, the orange-juice sellers packed up their wares and the strings of lights that ran around the rickety kitchens of the street canteens flickered into life. Massive vats of stew, steaming soups and grills began to bubble and sizzle in preparation for the evening.

The square itself began to fill as leather sellers touted their goods from outstretched arms; snake charmers found their spots, settling down upon carpets, placing a wicker basket in front of them, encouraging the clusters of watchers to speculate what was inside; storytellers cleared their throats as the hypnotic Sufi rhythms of the Gnawa players provided a throbbing soundscape to the proceedings. We wove through the milling crowds, intoxicated by the warm smells of the food, stopping at various points to get our bearings, but allowing ourselves to become lost amongst the throng.

After steaming bowls of delicious harira soup, tumblers of freshly squeezed juices, encounters with Barbary monkeys and de-fanged cobras, it was time to make our way back to the hotel, leaving the nightly carnival to run its course. Walking away from the square we found the main road where our taxi was parked, patiently waiting on the far side of the street. Despite having navigated the crowded square for the past three hours with some ease, crossing the road was a different matter altogether. Looking in both directions, there were neither traffic lights nor a pedestrian crossing to help us.

Between us and the taxi the road was crammed with cars and it took us over twenty minutes of watching how the locals weaved amongst the slowly moving vehicles until we gained enough courage to launch ourselves out. Our child was clasped tightly in our arms as we forced the traffic to stop, signalling desperately to the drivers in our path, ignoring the klaxon of car horns which we soon came to learn are used in Morocco not as a warning of last resort, but as a universal communication system. The whole experience was a stark reminder, if we needed one, that we were not at home.

So what does traffic tell us about the city?

Congestion is the Faustian bargain that we have negotiated for our urban freedoms. It is also a significant source of pollution within the city and a major threat to the environment. In 2005 the average American spent over thirty-eight hours stuck in traffic, though this is by no means the worst example. Gridlock can damage a city – it is estimated that traffic in New York adds $1.9 billion to the cost of doing business, a loss of $4.6 billion in unrealised business, and nearly $6 billion in lost time and productivity – but the solutions are not as straightforward as one might assume. The irony is that the more we want to be free, the more we sit in traffic jams.

Lagos, Nigeria, has some of the worst traffic problems in the world. In a recent report this congestion was caused by a 'perfect storm' of converging factors: a poor level of urban planning unable to cope with the rapidly rising urban population (Lagos is considered the fastest-growing mega-city in the world) and insufficient public-transport schemes. That the roads are of poor quality forces cars to move slowly while the lack of pavements and parking regulations, and the addition of cattle on the highway are further causes of gridlock. Accidents are frequent and there are insufficient services to respond in a timely fashion. As a result many people find it impossible to live and work in the city.

When American journalist Joshua Hammer took a 40-mile drive around Lagos, he did not expect that it would take him twelve hours. In addition, he was surprised when finding himself stuck in one jam to hear a terrible banging: 'These crazy men – they steal the headlights!' my driver exclaimed. Crowbar-wielding thieves were prowling the traffic jam, preying on captive motorists. "Don't get out the car," the driver warned.'[1] As Hammer notes, there is a direct correlation between the level of corruption within a state and the number of accidents on the nation's roadways. Drivers themselves are the problem, for as one tourist website reports: 'much of the traffic madness is caused by drivers' refusal to obey simple traffic rules'; instead they overtake in the wrong lane, drive up one-way streets in the wrong direction, park in congested areas and disobey traffic signals as well as parking wardens.

On the other hand, traffic can be a sign of a city's success. I was reminded of the dictum 'You are not in a traffic jam, you are the traffic' as I sat in the back of the autorickshaw in Bangalore, moving from my hotel for a meeting in a neighbourhood I did not know. I could make no suggestion, nor offer my own special short cut, or even get out and walk, as I was a stranger in an unfamiliar city; I was stuck. This congestion is another result of the city's rapid expansion as it became Asia's Silicon Valley; restricted by its original form as a colonial capital, a garden city for retiring officers, it has found it very difficult to cope with the pressure of growth and the traffic infrastructure is beyond breaking point.

The roads in Bangalore are at gridlock, to the extent that many IT moguls have threatened to move away unless something is done. Yet in spite of tax schemes and congestion controls to regulate the 5 million cars, trucks and motorbikes, the number of vehicles on the road has risen. There have been attempts to get people to walk or take public transit and a new light rail system was announced in 2011, hoping to serve 500,000 workers a day. For the busy engineer, however, the problem of congestion is a waste of time as much as it is an ecological disaster and so in 2010 it was decided to make it easier to reach Electronic City via an elevated highway, reducing driving time from the centre to fifteen minutes. It is a solution for the few, and in time most likely will become as congested as the problem it was created to solve.

The contrast between Lagos and Bangalore illustrates the extremes of the problem of congestion in the city. The most straightforward response to congestion must surely be to build more roads, or to find a way for the traffic to move more efficiently. But although redesigning the city to accommodate the needs of

The Bangalore overpass, riding above the city to high tech suburbs

the citizens who live there sounds a very smart thing to do, it is not as simple as one might imagine.

The history of the city can be charted by its road schemes. Today, archaeologists map out the ancient outlines of the Roman London street plan through the discovery of ancient coins that were haphazardly dropped by travellers. From the air one can see how the London streets still radiate from the point where the first London Bridge once stood on Fish Hill, leading in all directions to the other Roman settlements beyond Londinium. This shows that the growth of the city can be measured by the arteries and capillaries of avenues, streets and alleys. It is often easy to believe that a city is made up of its roads; but congestion itself was not created by cars. Throughout history, traffic has been an urban problem. In ancient Rome, Julius Caesar issued laws banning all wheeled traffic in the city centre during the day, and he also incorporated the *vigiles*, a protean traffic police. Our contemporary cities, as we have seen, have been built around the automobile, and now we are starting to count the costs. What to do? In the future do we change our cities or do we change our behaviour?

First we need to understand traffic itself. On the one hand traffic can be defined by individual behaviour, sitting behind the wheel, sealed off from the rest of the world, avoiding human contact. However, once you add a number of drivers in their cars, all behaving in their own interests, forced to react to each other, this collection of singular elements transforms into a unified flow, showing all the personality of a stream of liquid. Traffic is not a rational, ordered problem. It is not a simple equation between the numbers of cars and the quantity of asphalt available. Rather it displays the same characteristics of complexity as the city itself. The river of traffic is influenced as the roadway widens or slows as it merges into a bottleneck; traffic lights or signposts bring the flow to a stop like a closed tap and then opens, releasing the stream; changing lanes without indicating can often cause a disruption that disturbs the hydrodynamics of movement, sudden braking ricocheting backwards. It makes sense therefore that if we reduce the friction of stoppages and flows, the traffic will move faster.

Perhaps the shape of the city itself is to blame and, therefore, in order to address these grave problems in the future we have to start again from scratch. For many the ordered regularity of the grid system offers the ideal form. This organised, rational system has ancient origins, reaching back further than Athens or Rome, to the first cities of the Indus Valley. Centuries later New York gained its formal networks of streets with the Commissioners' Plan of 1811. The grid itself was decided on when the commissioners put a sieve on top of the masterplan and copied out the regular patterns. Yet Manhattan still suffers from congestion, so clearly a rational street plan is not enough. The complex question of congestion deserves a complex answer, rather than a logical one. If we are looking for the most efficient flow of traffic through the city, perhaps we are looking in the wrong place for an answer.

The Prussian city of Königsberg has an unexpected place in the history of walking. In the early nineeenth century it was said that the locals could set their pocket watches by the sight of the philosopher Emmanuel Kant, who would take his daily perambulation of the city at five o'clock sharp every day without fail. On these walks he would allow himself a brief respite from his deep philosophical musings. Seven decades earlier, Königsberg mathematician Leonhard Euler also took to the streets to solve a very different kind of problem. In 1735 he was given the challenge of finding the quickest route through the city over all seven bridges that crossed the river but without ever using one more than once. Euler had to invent a whole new area of mathematics, graph theory, in order to find the solution.

Euler's challenge has evolved into a famous thought-experiment called the Travelling Salesman Problem. A door-to-door merchant must find the shortest and quickest route between various points in order to maximise his time and profits. As the number of stop-offs increases the variable of potential routes rises exponentially: between two points, the variation of journey is simple; between four points, the variables increase to twenty-four; soon, however, you start to get very large numbers, and finding the quickest route between ten points means checking 3.6 million options. Many scientists have used huge computers to crack this solution: in May 2004, a team of mathematicians found the shortest route between the 24,978 points charted on a map of Sweden using 96 Intel Xeon 2.8 Ghz processors running concurrently, taking a total of 84.8 years of computing time.[2]

But rather than using complex mathematics there is another way that will show us how best to design the most efficient route between a series of random destinations: ants. The common black ant is in constant pursuit of the shortest route between points, but rather than expecting to find the solution individually, the whole colony works together. Each ant lays a pheromone trail and as each ant finds the shortest route, collectively the best trails begin to be identified by the strongest scent. In 1997 Marco Dorigo and Luca Maria Gambardella created a colony of virtual ants to simulate a possible solution for the travelling salesman's problem. The experiments showed that the shortest route is not always the most obvious. The ants were faster than the computers, and collectively made calculations that no individual planner could make in a lifetime.

Even more improbably, slime mould also has a lot to tell us about the best way to design our road systems. In October 2010 a group of Mexican scientists alongside Andrew Adamatzky, of the Unconventional Computing Department of the University of the

West of England, reported the results of their study, with the astonishing title 'Approximating Mexican Highways with Slime Mould' in which they set up an experiment 'to approximate, or rather re-construct, development of transport networks in Mexico'. They did this by replicating the Mexican highway system in a Petri dish, cutting a 'Mexico-shaped plate of agar [jelly], represent[ing] nineteen major urban regions by oat flakes and plac[ing] a plasmodium of *Physarum polycephalum* [slime mould] in place of Mexico City'. By recording how the mould moved across the Petri dish towards the oat flakes, creating connections and routes between the locations, the scientists mapped out the shortest and most efficient routes between the many different destinations.

The experiment was then repeated with similar samples representing Australia, Africa, Belgium, Brazil, Canada, China, Germany, Iberia [Spain and Portugal], Italy and Malaysia. What it proved was that slime mould is naturally better than the official planning brains in creating an efficient transport network, but that some nations were better than others: Malaysia, Italy and Canada planned the most efficient highway systems in parallel with the slime-mould patterns.[3]

Our current road system is thus hindered by a number of factors that make it slower and less efficient than we imagine, and yet we cannot rip it up and start again. But rather than building more roads, or a new road system, another group of planners believes that making drivers more responsible can improve safety and reduce congestion. In a Swiss/German paper published in 2008 by Stefan Lammer and Dirk Helbing it was suggested that the traffic-control system should be liberated from all human influence and be allowed to self-organise. In effect, traffic lights should decide themselves when to go green or red.

Alternatively, the Belgian traffic engineer Hans Monderman has suggested that we should do away with traffic lights altogether. In a 2005 exercise, which has become known as the 'Shared Space' experiment, Monderman turned out all the traffic lights and most of the signposts in the central square of the Dutch town of Makkinga, through which 22,000 cars passed a day. When a *New York Times* journalist visited the site with Monderman he was surprised to find: 'It was virtually naked, stripped of all lights, signs and road markings, there was no division between the road and sidewalk. It was basically a bare brick square.' However, when Monderman attempted to cross the road he 'deliberately failed to check for oncoming traffic before crossing the street, [but] the drivers slowed for him. No one honked or shouted rude words out of the window.'[4]

Monderman's dangerous idea was counterintuitive: by creating a shared space between cars and pedestrians, risk is reduced rather than increased, forcing drivers to be more aware of their surroundings. On the junction in Makkinga that had seen thirty-six accidents in the four years leading up to the trial, there were only two between 2006 and 2008. Such responsibility might force the common commuter to drive more slowly through the centre of town but, in the end, they might arrive at their destination quicker; as one citizen reported: 'I am used to it now. You drive more slowly and carefully, but somehow you seem to get around town quicker.'

In 2012 Exhibition Road was re-opened as a 'shared space', a broad Victorian thoroughfare lined with the major museums of London – the Natural History Museum, the Victoria and Albert, the Science Museum, plus Imperial College and the Royal Geographical Society – linking South Kensington to Hyde Park. This is one of the main tourist areas of the city, attracting foreigners, families and children. Monderman's Makkinga experiment was conducted in a small town where one is more likely to recognise the people crossing the street, and therefore have a stronger connection. Does the rule remain the same in a city?

Witnessing this latest upgrade is a disconcerting experience. I have visited the museums here my whole life, as a child wondering at the dinosaurs in the NHM, pushing the buttons that make the engines work at the Science Museum, marvelling at the Renaissance Court in the V&A. I now go there with my own children hoping to pass on some of the joys of discovery that I once felt. Now there are no stone flags to define the edge between road and pavement, only a shallow brick lip. The painted lines of the centre of the road and the parking spaces have disappeared, replaced by subtle steel studs. Bricks in a criss-cross pattern traverse the roads and ride up onto what was once pavement.

'Shared space' in Exhibition Road, London

Walking along this once familiar road, I now feel more unsure than I used to; I am more aware of the traffic, hoping that it will notice me and my children as it cruises by. I try to suppress the fear that this is an accident waiting to happen, but that is the point. Safety comes from making sure one behaves safely, not by copious restrictions and barriers.

The results from the Exhibition Road experiment are still coming in but in a more thorough study of a similar project, on New Road in Brighton, 92.9 per cent of all people interviewed considered the 'shared space' an improvement; many felt that the design had increased a sense of empowerment, encouraging a sense of ownership amongst the local businesses, as well as a desire for shoppers to spend time there. As a result, 80 per cent of shops saw a marked increase in takings.[5] The solution to the congestion problem therefore lies not in building more but getting people to change the way they behave. 'Shared space' seems to offer an answer to congestion; it does not necessarily reduce the number of cars on the road.

According to the US Environmental Protection Agency, transport is the second-largest source of carbon emissions in America; while electricity generation produces a third of all greenhouse gases, transportation takes up 28 per cent – of which 34 per cent includes private cars, while trucks, SUVs and minivans represent the next 28 per cent. Traffic has been on the increase since the 1990s, accounting for nearly 50 per cent of the rise in all carbon emissions. In the UK, cars and all road transport account for approximately 20 per cent of all pollution. Globally, the figure falls slightly to 15 per cent; however this was partially affected by the economic downturn as the distribution of exports declined. Much of this traffic occurs in the city and it is a crisis that we can all individually do something about.

Will greener cars, with more efficient energy usage, allow us to cut down emissions? Certainly we have the technology to be able to do this, and if there is demand for electric cars or cleaner engines, the big manufacturers will see there is a market for these new vehicles. However, this does not offer the solution one might hope for. Since 2008, Sweden has led the world in purchasing green cars, but car emissions have steadily increased. It appears that while the newer, more efficient cars produce less carbon emissions, the drivers have increased the amount of time they spend in their cars. Why this might be is a cause of some controversy.

For some, such as New Yorker and writer David Owen, this is an example of the Jevon Paradox, named after the Victorian English economist William Stanley Jevon, who proposed that as technology makes energy use more efficient, we are likely to use more of it, rather than less. Cleaner engines, therefore, might reduce emissions; they also encourage us to increase car usage. This, in the end, will more than likely result in still too many cars in the gridlock. A change in engine technology does not, therefore, reduce the number of vehicles bumper to bumper on the road; what is needed is a strategy to get people out of their cars altogether.

Driving around the city, one of the main problems often faced by everyone is the search for a free parking space. In Park Slope, Brooklyn, 45 per cent of all traffic is created by cars circling the block. The situation is even worse in China, where traditional cities cannot cope with the rapid rise in car ownership. Today, there is a desperate lack of parking spaces in the major cities: at the beginning of 2011 it was calculated that in the Shijingshan neighbourhood of Beijing, which is home to 110,000 cars, 11,000 are without parking spaces; the city of Chongqing lacks a total of 190,000 spaces, and this deficit is growing by 400 cars a day. In Xi'an, only 600,000 of the total 1.1 million cars have a parking bay. In addition, private parking can amount to a third of the annual costs of running a car. In 2012 the Shanghai city authorities therefore imposed a new rule making it impossible to buy a new car without first securing a parking place.

The problem in Chinese cities is now so great that even the former president, Hu Jintao, stepped in, commanding that parking be integrated into all new developments.[6] The future of the Chinese city depends on estimating the highest number of parking facilities that the city can tolerate; already, pollution and congestion makes life in Beijing difficult. Failure to prepare the Chinese cities that are currently growing faster than any other urban region in history could be an environmental and economic disaster.

But the cost of parking could be one way to dissuade people from using their cars in the city, and the reduction of parking bays and the high price for leaving one's car in the city centre can have very positive effects on congestion. In 2009 the San Francisco Metropolitan Transportation Agency produced a report on parking restrictions following the idea of 'Parking Guru' Donald Shoup. In his book *The High Price of Free Parking*, Shoup had shown how inefficient free parking could be and how much energy was used searching for a space in a popular neighbourhood. Shoup advises that parking, because it is a fixed supply, should be priced according to demand. In addition, information on where parking is available needs to be displayed on roadside boards, so that drivers know where to go to rather than waste time on a random search for free spaces. The end report also recommended extending meter hours, and only allowing cars to park for four hours. This would bring new revenue to the city, reduce congestion and pollution, and force cars to move on faster.

The San Francisco parking scheme aims to have 85 per cent of all parking bays occupied at any given time, and clear real-time information to allow drivers to find their spot without inconvenience. This will certainly clear some of the congestion, yet it is the cost of driving itself that will dissuade people from bringing their cars into the city in the first place. Congestion charging is also a way of hitting drivers where it most hurts. The first such urban scheme was in Singapore in 1975 and was one of the first policies used to develop the city state as the business capital of the Far East. The effects were dramatic. Before the scheme, in June 1975, 32,000 vehicles were registered as entering the city each day, a figure which dropped to 7,700 as soon as the congestion charge was imposed. Similar schemes have been introduced into other cities including Rome, Stockholm, Milan and, in 2003, London.

The scheme was first introduced in Stockholm in 2007 and it was calculated that within three years inner-city traffic volume had reduced by 20 per cent and traffic jams by 30 per cent. London is the most congested city in Europe, and contains five of the top ten traffic hotspots in the UK. Even worse, most of the congestion can be found on the city's main roads so that 30 per cent of traffic clogs up only 5 per cent of the city's network. On the first day of the scheme in London, 17 February 2003, a total of 190,000 vehicles entered the congestion zone, an instant 25 per cent drop in car numbers.

But over time the results have been less conclusive. Whilst having fewer cars in the centre of the city reduces pollution, by 2008 congestion levels had returned to the 2002 gridlock, and is set to increase another 15 per cent over the next five years. So congestion continues to be a big problem in the city and traffic speeds continue to fall. In 2011 it was estimated that £2–4 billion in revenue was being lost every year because of traffic. In addition, air pollution was getting worse. At least 4,000 deaths a year are said to be attributable, at least in part, to the city's poor air quality.

Congestion charging cannot work by itself, for while cost might dissuade some drivers from getting into their cars, the city cannot function unless people can travel freely, get to work or home at every time of the day. As a strategy for getting cars off the road, the congestion charge affects the poor more than the rich, and becomes an issue about the right to the city. As a green policy, for improving air quality and pollution levels, the jury is still out. However, in some circumstances, no traffic is even worse for the city than grid-lock. For writers such as David Owen, author of *Green Metropolis*, traffic jams might just be good for the city, for as he notes: 'Traffic jams are actually beneficial, environmentally, if they reduce the willingness of drivers to drive and, in doing so, turn car pool, buses, trains, bicycles, walking and urban apartments into attractive options.'[7] So what is the right kind of traffic?

It is hard to forget the experience of standing in the centre of the Santiago de Chile bus terminal. I had never seen so many buses, each with a name in the front window, telling passengers where they were going: southwards along the length of the country to Punta Arenas, northwards across the Atacama Desert and Peru, up to the mountains and westwards to the ports and cities along the coast. It was my second day in the city and I was still attempting to make sense of the place.

If you want to understand how Latin America works, visit the bus station. After buying my tickets, I went to the café and ordered coffee and my first *empanada*, a small pasty filled with meat and potato. As I waited for my bus I watched queues of people snaking around the vehicles, cramming their goods and bags, livestock even, into the storage compartments. My first journey, an eighteen-hour trip to Puerto Montt, only a third of the way down the country, made me realise how small Britain was. On another occasion, I took a twelve-hour bus trip to Entre Lagos in the south, which had a dinner service, waitress and a bar.

In a city where the majority of the population do not have cars, an efficient public-transit system is vital. Transport is any mayor's most pressing priority, and the scale of such projects are mind-boggling. In 2010 it was estimated that the New York subway system alone used as much electricity as the entire city of Buffalo. On an average day in London, at least 24 million journeys are taken. The bus, tube and light-railway network cover a total sum of 3.5 billion miles in a year – approximately forty times the distance between the earth and the sun.[8] This is what we experience every morning as we move from home to work and back again, get the children to school and make sure we reach the hospital in time for the appointment. We take public transport for granted and complain when there are delays or overcrowding. It is the single main cause of complaints to the 311 phone line in New York; the cost of tube tickets was one of the key issues during the 2012 London mayoral contest. More importantly, transit can transform a city.

In his book, *Human Transit*, Jarrett Walker questions whether we have the right priorities when it comes to transport policy: public transit is by far the most efficient way of transporting large numbers of people around a dense urban space, but not everyone can agree on what that actually entails. When we think about transit we often consider it as a secondary alternative to driving ourselves and therefore ask questions like 'Do the buses go where you want them to?' 'Do you want them to be faster or cheaper?' 'Do we want a more frequent service or one that prioritises rush hour?' 'Should public transit focus its attention on servicing the poor and non car owners, or everyone?' Walker makes a clear distinction between what one wants and what is possible. There are many different types of transit to fit all forms of city, he concludes, and the provision of buses and railways is more than a purely functional or financial question; it is a debate about what kind of city you want to live in.[9]

An example of this debate can be found in Curitiba, the capital of the Brazilian province of Parana. It was no accident that in 2001, when UNESCO was searching for a city on which to model the rebuilding of post-invasion Kabul, the ravaged capital of Afghanistan, it chose Curitiba. It is a curious story: until the 1960s the city – in which the population had leapt from 180,000 to 360,000 in just ten years – had been designed around the automobile, with wide boulevards radiating out of the centre. In the 1980s there had been concerns that rapid urbanisation would make expansion unmanageable, the centre gridlocked with traffic, the air thick with exhaust fumes. So the idea of a new masterplan was born with the philosophy: 'a city is not a problem but the solution'. The initial plan was to knock down some of the more elegant turn-of-the-century houses in order to widen the main routes in the centre, as well as force an ugly overpass through the middle.

However, these proposals met with unexpected opposition, led by Jaime Lerner from the architecture and planning school of the Federal University, who complained that 'they were trying to throw away the story of the city'.[10] Thus in 1988, almost by chance, the 33-year-old Lerner found himself named mayor. The first thing he did was to transform the central road, the Rua Quinze de Novembro; but instead of attempting to manage traffic through the middle of the city, he pedestrianised the thoroughfare. Lerner was so concerned about the level of opposition to the scheme that he completed the whole operation in a weekend; closing the road on a Friday night, workmen planting over 10,000 flowers over the next forty-eight hours, and opening again on Monday morning. Beforehand, local shopkeepers had threatened to sue for lost earnings; by Monday lunchtime there were petitions for other areas of the city to be made car-free.

However, Lerner also knew that public transport had to be at the heart of the new masterplan. The project began by devising a transit system running from the centre along the five main corridors into the suburbs. It was designed to connect all the neighbourhoods, and in response zoning laws were used to build neighbourhoods integrated around the network, so that a shiny new bus stop was one of the first things to be constructed when new housing was created. In addition, the system needed to be efficient, fast and well designed to ensure that people got out of their cars and used it, so the BRT Express Buses were given their own exclusive lane running alongside the car.

Yet perhaps the most surprising innovation occurred as Lerner stood at one bus stop and watched how people took so long to get on and off the bus. He noted that it took time for everyone to climb the steps and then pay the driver as they embarked. Instead he sketched an idea for a glass 'tube station', a bus shelter raised up from the pavement to the height of the bus door. A new payment

CORBIS

Lerner's brilliant design for bus stops in Curitiba

scheme was devised, so there was no waiting at the bus door, and a single flat fee, originally priced at approximately £0.20. As a result, every time a bus drove up to the platform passengers could alight at all five doors, allowing a maximum of 300 travellers to get on and off in under fifteen seconds. Frequency of buses was also increased so that there was never a long wait during peak hours.

Whenever possible the new system was developed with the participation of users and locals rather than bringing in experts and adopting expensive innovations. So when the bus manufacturers Volvo suggested that they could devise a sophisticated door system to line up the vehicle with the station platform, an experienced bus driver suggested to the committee that a simple painted line on the platform floor would suffice. Such common sense has meant that the network has never needed city subsidies but has paid its own way since opening. Despite Curitiba having the highest ratio of car owners in the whole of Brazil, the buses have changed people's lives. In 1974 the system serviced only 25,000 passengers a day; today, this has risen to 2 million. At the same time it is calculated that the programme has replaced 27 million car journeys a year, and as a result Curitiba uses 30 per cent less petrol than any other Brazilian city and enjoys the lowest air pollution. As the city prospered during the 1990s, new neighbourhoods were designed with the transport system in mind in order to cope with growth as the suburbs grow.

The social impact of a smart transit policy is made even clearer in the example of Bogotá, Colombia, and the story of another series of visionary mayors – Antanas Mockus and Enrique Peñalosa – who saw the importance of using public transport to ensure access to the city for all. Mockus first came to prominence when he was forced to resign from his position as Rector of the National University, having mooned his students in order to get their attention. The act of 'symbolic violence' encouraged him to stand for mayor, refusing to join any party but rather to stand on a policy of 'No Ps': no publicity, no politics, no party and no *plata* (money), pronouncing, 'You can't fix Bogotá by putting "I love Bogotá" stickers on your car. Instead, say "I hate it but I'll do something to improve it".'[11] At the time, Bogotá was at the point of crisis: growing at 4.5 per cent every year, it was beyond control; at least 40 per cent of the population lived outside the governance of the city, below the poverty line, without basic services such as water, sewerage, transit, education and health. City hall was effectively insolvent. The streets were lawless, with a corrupt police force, an average of 250 murders each month and 95 per cent of all crimes going unpunished. Mockus had no money to make change so he had to persuade people to rethink their behaviour.

In 1993 he launched the non-political programme 'Cultura Ciudadana', making the city its own government: 'The crucial part of a citizen's culture is learning to correct others without mistreating them or generating aggression. We need to create a society where civility rules over cynicism and apathy.'[12] He led the campaign by example and dressed in a Superman costume to encourage others to be 'super citizens'. He printed 350,000 cards with thumbs-up and thumbs-down icons, which people could use to give to pedestrians or drivers who were behaving well or badly. He hired 220 actors to wander through the streets, mimic and shame people who were jaywalking, disrupting neighbourhoods or causing offence. At Christmas time, when excessive drinking caused an increase in violence, he offered a gun amnesty, and then melted the arms down into cutlery. When it came to transport he invested in the Ciclovia programme which, every Sunday, closed 50 miles of inner-city roadways to cars, leaving them to cyclists, skaters and walkers. The project was extended into the poorer neighbourhoods and a free bike-hire scheme was launched, offering a means for the various groups in the highly segregated city to mix.

In 1998, on the back of his successes in Bogotá, Mockus stood for election as Columbia's president, which he lost. As mayor he was succeeded by Enrique Peñalosa, leader of the local Liberal party. Peñalosa inherited a city that was in the process of social transformation but also on a solid financial footing: Mockus left a budget surplus of $700 million. As a result Peñalosa was able to continue the progressive social agenda but also invest in structural change within the city – in particular reinventing the role of transit as a means of addressing inequality. As he announced: 'Urban transport is a political and not a technical issue. The technical aspects are very simple. The difficult decisions relate to who is going to benefit from the models adopted.'[13]

For Peñalosa, the modern city should be rebuilt with the poor and children in mind, and as a result it needs a radical new way of thinking about public spaces and how people travel around: 'Everything we did we tried to increase equality, to maximise integration. In this way we are also constructing democracy ... A city is a

CORBIS

Enrique Peñalosa on his bike

physical entity, a place where people go to schools or libraries that are physical buildings, they walk on sidewalks, and use public transit and roads. If the physical quality of the city is poor, the quality of life there also will be poor.[14] This was enshrined in the 2000 Territorial Ordering Plan of the Capital District that emphasised the need to work on urban renewal, the built environment, sustainable development and low-income housing.

New schools, parks and libraries were built. There were 100 new nurseries for children under five years old. Water was provided to all slum regions and wide-scale housing schemes were developed for the homeless. Yet Peñalosa also wanted the Bogotános to rethink the city itself. For many of the poor, the street is where much of life is conducted, so he proposed taking the street back from drivers, suggesting that the car was the symbol of inequality.

Between 1991 and 1995 the total number of cars in Bogotá had increased by 75 per cent; by 1998 private cars occupied 64 per cent of all road space but were used by only 19 per cent of the population. Thus Peñalosa pedestrianised large sections of the city, including a 17-kilometre stretch, the longest pedestrian street in the world, as well as a 45-kilometre greenway that was originally planned as an eight-lane motorway. He banned parking on pavements, commenting that 'motor vehicles on sidewalks were a symbol of inequality' and placing concrete bollards along the street. Then he went on the attack against the car itself. He raised the tax on petrol and forced commuters to leave their cars at home at least two days a week, later creating a car registration reader monitoring car usage during the rush hour, making sure that 40 per cent were off-street at peak times. One Thursday every year was declared a car-free day when everyone had to leave their car at home.

In place of the car, Peñalosa encouraged the bicycle, announcing that 'cars isolate people. Bicycles integrate socially'.[15] He extended the Ciclovia scheme, adding another 300 kilometres of dedicated bike lanes, protected from automobile traffic so they could be used by children without fear. In addition, the car was replaced by a complete overhaul of the transit system which was designed to serve the most needy.

The development of TransMilenio, inspired by the successes of Jaime Lerner's Curitiba BRT, was proof that transit could be used to transform a city as large as 7 million. Until 2000, the city transit system was in the hands of a cartel of private companies, and as a result there was a constant conflict between high fares and the number of buses, often in terrible condition, on the road. While the average car journey was 42.6 minutes, an average bus journey was another 50 per cent longer: 66.8 minutes. The poor who depended on this unreliable service were punished both in cost and time.

TransMilenio was a public–private initiative initially designed to cover two main city routes: Avenida Caracas and Calle 80, a length of 42 kilometres, with the aim of carrying 35,000 passengers an hour in each direction, at a cost of $0.85 per person. There were 470 buses in the initial fleet and a dedicated lane in each direction was given over to the scheme. An elevated station, similar to those at Curitiba, was planned every 700 metres or so with pay booths, registering machines and surveillance cameras. In addition to the main lines, a series of feeder buses brought travellers from the outskirts, with stops every 300 metres or so, especially in the poorer neighbourhoods. After 2006, the system grew to include nine separate routes covering more parts of the city, and another two lines were opened in 2011.

The TransMilenio transformed Bogotá. Today, it provides transit for 45,000 people per hour per direction, at an average speed of 29 kilometres per hour. As the system has grown and become popular, travel times have improved as more people leave their cars at home and jump aboard. The scheme has been as popular with the rich as the poor, and as a result is one of the great melting pots of the city rather than a badge of shame, with 76 per cent of users rating the system as good or very good. In addition, it has reduced air pollution, with a decrease of 1,000 metric tonnes of particulate emissions a year, delivering health savings of an estimated $60–70 million. There was also an 88 per cent drop in traffic fatalities.

It is for this reason that traffic and transit experts around the world are looking to Latin America for the next innovation in how transportation can make the cities of the future work. In his 1995 book *Hope, Human and Wild*, the leading environmental writer Bill McKibben presented Curitiba as an alternative for urban living. This appeal was then taken up by the British architect Lord Rogers, who visited the city and then, in his 1995 Reith lectures, pronounced it as a model we could all learn from. In 2006 the American National BRT Institute produced a report looking into whether the success of the TransMilenio could be replicated in the US, concluding that while the benefits of the scheme are manifest, the popular ignorance of those benefits and the social stigma of carlessness would make such a project difficult. In short, US cities lack mayors like Lerner and Peñalosa who are willing to make the case for the relationship between social change and transit.[16]

Public transit is not the only way to think about the relationship between the city and transportation. The impact of walking has long been ignored, and is only now being revealed as one of the key components in developing a happy city. As Enrique Peñalosa says: 'God made us walking animals – pedestrians. As a fish needs to swim, a bird to fly, a deer to run, we need to walk, not in order to survive, but to be happy.'[17]

I first became interested in cities by walking, sometimes lost and without purpose, later coming to learn the urban ways and rhythms until it became a place called home. Walking is still the way that I wish to encounter any new city on arrival. In cities like Venice walking is perhaps the only practical means of getting around. As you arrive at the main railway station, having left your car in Padua or elsewhere, there is little that prepares you for the scene you encounter stepping out of the shadows of the Modernist loggia in front of the Stazione Santa Lucia. In summer the long, low steps in front are covered with travellers facing out towards the Grand Canal and the choppy waters and bustle of the vaporetto stations. To the left, one is immediately confronted with the Baroque wonder of the city, the church of the Scalzi; straight ahead stands the noble copper dome of St Simone Piccolo.

Walking across the broad stone piazza and crossing the canal, one is instantly thrown into the human throng. There is no room for more than the rare buzz of a Vespa amongst the narrow alleys and walkways around the city; no buses, no cars, no trains. Venice reminds us of the joys of finding a city by foot, of the fact that the metropolis is best discovered at the pace of the human step, and at eye level. It is only at times like this that one feels the city as part of the crowd, rather than sealed away behind the wheel of a car. Indeed walking in the city, and making cities more walkable, has a remarkable impact on our individual sense of well-being as well as on the building of happy communities.

In the late 1960s, the English urban planner Donald Appleyard, who was at that time teaching at Berkeley University, California, conducted an experiment comparing three streets in San Francisco which were similar except for the level of traffic passing down the route. He named each street depending on the density of the traffic: Light Street saw 2,000 vehicles per day; 8,000 travelled on Medium Street; while Heavy Street suffered 16,000 vehicles on a daily basis.

Appleyard's subsequent results were surprising. He discovered that traffic had a huge impact on neighbourliness and community: an average resident of Light Street will have three more friends and at least six more acquaintances than a resident of Heavy Street. The community on Light Street was more integrated and likely to share the time of day on the front step; children were more likely to play together. As traffic increased, the sense of common ownership decreased rapidly, with little or no pavement life to be found on Heavy Street, which had a particular impact on the lives of the elderly and the very young. It is thus important to remember that every time you get into your car you are driving down someone else's street and your trip will have an impact on their lives.

In order to get people into buses, we need to create effective transit solutions; in order to get people to walk in the city, we have to create appealing public places and streets that we want to be in, that are safe, visually stimulating, popular, and open. At the moment, however, it is easy to see why one might not bother to go for a walk. When the city has been designed for cars, by planners such as Robert Moses, there is little to attract the casual stroller and as a result between 1977 and 1995 Americans walked 40 per cent less. What can we do?

There is reason to be more cheerful than expected, however, because city dwellers are in fact more likely to use the pavement than is commonly assumed. As *New York Magazine* reports: 'The structure of the city coerces us to exercise far more than people elsewhere in the US, in a way that is strongly correlated with a far better life expectancy.' We walk in the city more than we imagine we do: to the train station or bus stop; to the corner store or to the gym. The compact nature of the city allows us to consider walking as an option rather than jumping into our cars to run a local errand.[18] A native New Yorker in fact walks more than most other people, and faster; and as epidemiologist Eleanor Simonsick discovered, this quicker pace is a reflection of health status.

Living in the city can, in fact, make us fitter and healthier. In another paper by Lawrence Frank of the University of Vancouver on the relative fitness between young men in inner Atlanta and the city's suburbs, the average city dweller, compelled to walk more often, was 10lbs lighter than their suburban neighbour, who preferred to use the car for routine trips. When one considers that obesity is now the cause of nearly 10 per cent of all National Health Service expenditure in the UK,[19] the impact of encouraging people to walk more is persuasive. The reduction in body mass index caused by increased exercise also has a knock-on effect on levels of heart disease, diabetes and even cancer. And, of course, the reduction of CO_2 emissions means a cleaner and healthier neighbourhood.

The creation of more walkable streets also has a huge impact on the resident community. In a study completed in 2008 by Transport for London, it was calculated that living in a walkable neighbourhood could potentially raise property prices by £30,000 and, on a specific project looking at improvements to The Cut in Southwark, it showed that widening pavements, improving lighting and adding trees had increased the overall value of the street by significant sums. This is also true of the relationship between walkability and retail: a pedestrianised high street increases both the number of visitors and the amount people are willing to spend.

Walkability can also be one of the many benchmarks of inequality within the city. Richard Florida celebrates the fact that walkable communities are better educated and more creative neighbourhoods than others: they are 'a magnet for attracting and retaining the highly innovative businesses and highly skilled people that drive economic growth, raising housing values and generating higher incomes'.[20] By contrast, there is a perceived fear that poorer neighbourhoods – often because they have fewer parks, facilities and more degraded civic amenities like lighting and pavements – are more dangerous and crime-riddled, making them more unwalkable. If the benefits of walkability are so palpable, it seems absurd that they are the preserve of the rich. Perhaps one should redefine the right to the city as access to the benefits of open, walkable neighbourhoods.

Designing the city around walkability sounds like an impossible fantasy, in the face of the ever-spreading suburban sprawl that is centrifugally spinning the metropolis further outwards. The railway line that delivers me to work was first laid in the 1870s, and now stretches over 35 kilometres from the furthest northern reaches of the suburbs into the heart of the West End, within twenty minutes arriving at Canary Wharf in the far East End of the capital. On an average day I am just one of the 400,000 people travelling along this route, totalling over 127.5 million journeys a year. Ten years ago, when I lived in the inner city, it only took twenty-five minutes for me to walk into work in the centre of London, but now it would take at least an impossible two hours on foot. We need to think of creating walkable communities connected to the rest of the city by a robust and efficient transport infrastructure.

But how do we create places that make us want to explore rather than sit in traffic? For Robert Cervero and Kara Kockelman, the possible solutions to this can be found in the three Ds – density, design and diversity – a reminder that the design of the city around the automobile has more than just an impact on infrastucture and road-building: it also affects the social life of the inhabitants. The end result of the autopolis was that home and the office were divided by a freeway to be traversed as quickly as possible; speed was prioritised above sociability and as a result the modern city has few places worth walking to; supermarkets and malls were constructed out of town, killing off the high street, turning places of local diversity into soulless cloned thoroughfares of identical outlets; personal relationships were allowed to wither: regular interaction with the bank teller became an encounter with the ATM. These are not places that register in the memory or encourage exploration; they are non-places. But there is a chance to reclaim the streets, to make them more walkable and make them more equal. And in some cities, these opportunities are already being seized.

There are few more delightful urban pleasures than walking along the south bank of the Seine on a bright, crisp November Sunday morning. Strolling along the erstwhile Expressway, built in the 1950s to alleviate the central Parisian traffic, it feels strange and somehow luxurious to follow the flow of joggers, cyclists and idle wanderers like ourselves. Navigating from the Pont de l'Alma towards the Tuileries Gardens, it seems as if the heart of the city, a 2-mile stretch of riverside promenade taking in some of Paris's most splendid sites, has been rediscovered.

Beside the Seine: the Paris Plage, 2010

In 2010 the city mayor, Bertrand Delanoë, who had already gained some renown by converting a similar stretch of embankment into an urban beach each summer, announced that he was declaring war on 'the unacceptable hegemony of the automobile'.[21] As he explained, 70,000 cars used the Expressway every day, while cars caused two-thirds of the city's total pollution, but such a project was about more than just carbon emissions: 'It's about reducing pollution and automobile traffic, and giving Parisians more opportunities for happiness. If we succeed in doing this, I believe it will profoundly change Paris.'[22]

In August 2012 Delanoë confirmed that a 2.5-kilometre stretch along the south bank would be permanently pedestrianised between the Musée d'Orsay and the Pont de l'Alma and that plans were afoot to add parks, sports courts, restaurants and even a floating botanical gardens. Where former president Georges Pompidou once announced that 'Paris must adapt to the car',[23] the city is now being returned to the walker. If this can happen in the centre of a busy European capital like Paris, it is possible anywhere.

10

HOW MANY LIGHTBULBS DOES IT TAKE TO CHANGE A CITY?

Standing on the crest of the hill, it was strange to think that I was, officially at least, in the centre of the city. The wind was still and the temperature unseasonably hot; a heat shimmer softened the edge of everything. I looked northwards across virgin wetlands where a creek meandered lazily through the landscape, backed by a solid band of verdant woodland. There was almost no sign of human habitation until I peered up towards the horizon and saw the famous skyline of downtown Manhattan. The new World Trade Tower rose into the air behind the skyscraping castellations of the cityscape.

I was standing on the North Mound of the Fresh Kills landfill site, my view towards the city 14 miles away contrasted with what appeared to be a completely untouched landscape. The site is named after the creeks and wetlands, the 'kills', which in the 1950s were considered to be wasteland rather than a natural habitat. Yet I was on top of 150 million tonnes of garbage, the collected detritus of nearly fifty years of the city's waste that had been gathered, put on barges, shoved into trucks and dumped into what was once the largest landfill site in the world: rotting food, plastic bags and kitchen waste, packaging, discarded newspapers and broken goods – everything the city threw away.

After 9/11 it was here, on the West Mound, across from where I was standing, that 1.4 million tonnes of twisted metal, crushed cars and mountains of rubble from the collapse of the Twin Towers were transported so that government agents in white jumpsuits could comb the material for evidence, while families who had lost relatives in the attack could come and hope to recover some meagre memorial to record their loss.

Now it seemed like nature had reclaimed the landscape. There was an osprey nest by the creek and there had even been reports of a coyote. As I stood there, I watched a butterfly flit between the poppies and the meadow flowers that had clustered and grown across the mound. I was told that other water birds had returned, as well as foxes and vultures, and that rather than using petrol-powered lawn mowers to maintain the grass, a herd of goats kept the meadow at a manageable length. If I did not know it, I would have thought that I was on a heath that had been left for decades, not a project designed to restore the blighted landscape and which had only been started in 2003. The only reminder of where I was were the towers in the far distance, like the Emerald City of Oz, and a sequence of taps and pipes sticking out from the top of the mound which were used to siphon off the methane and leachate that came off the waste only a few feet down.

Fresh Kills was first opened in 1947, one of Robert Moses's grand schemes for the improvement of the city. It was meant to be a temporary landfill, used for no more than three years, but after the infrastructure and the disposal systems had been put in place, delivering 29,000 tonnes of waste a day, it was decided that this corner of Staten Island was far enough away from Manhattan for the problem to be out of sight and out of mind, and it remained a

The view from the North Mound, Fresh Kills, with Manhattan in the distance

permanent dumping ground. From then on the islanders had to endure not just the smell, and the swarm of seagulls that circled the trash mountain, but also the indignity of being the refuse tip for the rest of the five boroughs. Every year there were complaints that the Island was getting the foul end of the bargain. By the 1990s, the rubbish had formed into four vast heaps on either side of the once marshy creek where barges came in and out, every day dropping off their odorous load. In addition, the community was growing, its housing moving ever closer to the fenced edge of the depot. The site was closed in 1997 and the newest housing developments now abut its perimeter with rows of neat, white suburban homes.

What are we to do with places like Fresh Kills? It is in the city – its noxious, polluted air, the lack of green space, the mountains of trash – that the questions of climate change, waste and quality of life are most clearly delineated and most urgent. One does not need to see pictures of the garbage from Fresh Kills, or be reminded of the recycling factories of Dharavi, or measure the level of toxins in the air at a particularly busy crossroads to be reminded of the everyday hazards of urban living. It is calculated that millions die every year, even in the most dedicated of clean cities, from respiratory disease. We can now measure carbon emissions at every street corner and count the millions of tonnes of greenhouse gases that rise from the urban landscape. The city today may no longer look like the sooty industrial hell of Friedrich Engels's Manchester but this has only disguised its poisons. And yet, for all this, the city might also be the place with the greatest potential to answer the age's most pressing issue.

The story of what was done at Fresh Kills – which was eventually transformed into the verdant landscape I found myself standing upon on my trip to New York – is the story of a successful large-scale government project that should make people think about the city in different ways. The site was finally closed after political pressure had prevailed to make each of the five boroughs deal with their own waste rather than dumping the lot on Staten Island. After that it was decided that Fresh Kills was to be capped and then turned into parkland and a nature reserve. However, the process of the transition itself shows how complicated such operations can be.

The first stage of the project was overseen by the New York Department of City Planning which, in 2001, launched an international landscape-design competition. At the same time, the process of treating the ground and making sure that the waste was safely capped was placed in the hands of the Department of Sanitation, itself split into two sections – maintenance and solid waste – which did not always agree on either methods or outcomes. The NYDoS was also charged with overseeing the continuing maintenance of the gas and leachate that must be processed onsite. In 2011 this provided $12 million's worth of natural gas that was then sold on the local market; while the leachate was treated and cleaned, creating fresh water. The ground, once it had been capped with an impermeable layer of plastic, was spread with high-grade soil – in places even better soil than can be found in Central Park – and left for five years as it settled. It was then handed over to the New York Department of Parks and Recreation, which remains in control of planting and cultivating the parkland and its ecology.

The NYDoPR had to follow strict rules about soil usage and design. It also had to respond to the semi-natural environment that had been created. The impermeable cap, which made any leakage through the skin impossible, changed the way the normal landscape operated: it meant that rainwater ran off at a faster rate than elsewhere because it could not soak down to the water table. As a result the ground had to be sculpted with run-off in mind. In addition, a team from Pratt College conducted a study to establish whether tree roots could pierce the cap. There were disputes between the two sections of the Department of Sanitation over how high the grass should be allowed to grow, as well as questions about where the seeds for the wild flowers should be cultivated, leading to the creation of a seed bank on site.

The 2001 competition called for designs from five of the world's leading landscape architects and was won by James Corner Field Operations, a company run by the Manchester-born James Corner who, at the time, was a professor at Pennsylvania University with an office consisting of only three people. The Fresh Kills site was bigger than anything else built in New York's history: a space within the city limits that was three times the size of Central Park. Corner produced a masterplan in 2003 that was then shared with 'agencies, stakeholders and [the] community' as well as conducting a series of more formal environmental-impact studies and departmental reviews. The plan was bold in every way, imagining a process spanning to 2040 and placing a priority on community participation at all stages. This would have repercussions on the speed at which things could be achieved, but all parties felt that this was a worthwhile price to pay.

The site was to be split into five regions: the four mounds, south, north, east and west, and 'the confluence' in between that ran along both sides of the creek and tidal flats. By 2006 work had been completed on the caps for the North and South Mounds and by 2011 it was underway on the East Mound. While the western limit looks like a grown-over, natural landscape, it is still awaiting treatment that will begin in the next few years. The confluence will provide a centrepoint within the four mounds, a space for educational facilities, services, cafés and retail outlets for the expected visitors who will soon be arriving to enjoy a touch of nature within the boundaries of the five boroughs. The Fresh Kills Park Conservancy was founded in 2012 to oversee the management of the area and plans are already in place for wind-powered cafés, zero-carbon energy and green toilets.

Yet, as with all big government projects, Fresh Kills is susceptible to politics and budgets. The original tally was $200 million but has now been reduced to $112 million following the economic downturn. This has not derailed the project, however; rather it has been spread out over a longer timeframe with the hope that each new budget period might see a change in fortunes. For, despite the bureaucratic, interdepartmental headaches, everyone involved so far still feels that the park will be an essential part of the future of New York. It is certainly far more than an election-winning photo opportunity – but what will its real impact be on the city?

Visiting the offices of James Corner Field Operations, situated just north of the High Line, which was also designed by Corner, one is immediately struck by the atmosphere of a successful architectural practice: there is complete silence as rows of young people look intently into their Apple screens, and yet there is a sense of furious activity and concentration. Meeting Tatiana Choulik, who has been working on Fresh Kills since the beginning, highlighted the fact that the role of the landscape architect was to do more than encourage the land to return to some perceived idea of wilderness. She explained that Corner's aim is to create a certain kind of landscape that promises more than wasteland: a place, like the High Line, that offers those rare moments in the city where one is allowed to be in contact with something natural. And it is important that these places are socially inclusive, and yet are allowed to evolve. This philosophy is encapsulated in Corner's concept of 'lifescape': 'an ecological process of environmental reclamation and renewal on a vast scale, recovering not only the health and biodiversity of ecosystems across the site, but also the spirit and imagination of people who will use the new park'.[1]

As I stood on top of the North Mound, and looked across towards the outline of Manhattan, I was hugely impressed by what had been done already. I felt sure that in time people from the city would go there to enjoy the scenery and the wildlife, and – for some – it would be their first real encounter with the countryside. Yet I wondered whether this would change the way they think about how they live back home in the city. When they visit they will be walking up mounds of their own rubbish, but will it make them think about how they dispose of this refuse in the future? Only a few hundred yards away, I could see the waste plant that still processed Staten Island's garbage, and there also were the barges that took the material further away to North Carolina for disposal. Would that river traffic ever cease or would we just become better at sending our garbage further out of mind? Can we ever get away from the fact that the city is an environmental crime scene? If we are being honest with ourselves, are large-scale projects like Fresh Kills little more than gestures with few provable positive outcomes?

The debate on the sustainable city is happening now: from international government conferences like Rio+20 in June 2012 to local campaigns to encourage people to recycle or compost, the imperative to clean up our urban lives can no longer be ignored. Yet what is the most effective way to make real change happen? Expensive exercises like inter-governmental conferences may bring together the most powerful people on the planet to make promises and discuss solutions, but they are going to have little impact unless they have some influence on the everyday behaviour of individuals, and vice versa.

At the same time, mayors are trying to think about if and how to alter the fabric and infrastructure of their cities to reduce carbon emissions: creating new standards for housing; finding technologies for public transport that reduce harmful gases; devising waste-management strategies to deal with our rubbish in a more responsible way, whilst also encouraging changes in the behaviour of the ordinary citizen: persuading people to rethink the way they travel, consume and live. Pushing from the other direction are the people themselves, who are justifiably unhappy with the slow rate of change, infuriated by the blind spots of national policy, driven by the fear that we have all left it too late, and that putting profit first will always scupper any chance of a safe future.

If we can understand better and enhance the advantages of urban living, as well as agreeing on ways to improve the sustainability of life in the city, then we might just survive. It may appear counter-intuitive but the city could be our ark, rather than our coffin.

Part of this process begins with realising that living in the city actually offers a far greener way of life than is commonly imagined. Until recently many environmental thinkers and campaigners presumed that the city – the place where there were the most people, the most waste, and the most energy usage – was unnatural and ecologically dangerous. Its air was thick with pollution; it was a breeding ground for disease; the demand for water and food in places where there were no reservoirs or fields made the transportation of life's necessities a logistical suicide note. They saw the city as a centre of wanton consumption that never gave anything back.

This image of the concrete jungle was held up as a stark contrast to the homely view of the bucolic smallholding deep within nature. And the statistics seemed to support their view: cities hold over 50 per cent of the world's population, but take up less than 3 per cent of the planet's surface; they consume nearly 80 per cent of all our energy. How can living in the city possibly make you greener?

As I travelled by bus from the Fresh Kill site towards the Staten Island ferry depot that would take me across the water to

Manhattan, I had to remind myself that I was still within the heart of New York itself. My journey began in semi-rural quiet and as I headed north the houses began to cluster together. Soon a street of houses, surrounded by green yards, was replaced by homes with a front garden, only enough space for a car and a small lawn. By the time we reached the ferry port the suburban buildings had been substituted by urban streets, tightly packed with shops facing out onto busy pavements; blocks of flats and tenements rose above them into the sky. Once on the ferry, having made my way to the front of the boat, I watched with wonder as we approached Manhattan, a scene that will never cease to be impressive. In only a few kilometres I had travelled from the quiet periphery to the very heart of the urban world, and with each step my environment was becoming increasingly dense: green space squeezed out and replaced by concrete, asphalt and brick.

Yet in 2009, the journalist David Owen revealed the astonishing truth that living in New York is a more environmentally friendly lifestyle than living in the suburbs or even the countryside. He showed that, contrary to most assumptions, when people live in close proximity to each other, in a walkable environment, they actually become far more environmentally efficient. Despite the heavy energy usage and the costs of transportation within the city, it is nonetheless a remarkably smart way of gathering people together. For example, per square foot New York generates more greenhouse gases, uses more energy and produces more waste than any other place in America of a comparable size; however, New Yorkers individually are actually more energy efficient, emit less carbon and produce less waste than the average person outside the city.

In 2010 New York as a whole emitted 54.3 million tonnes of carbon. Some 75 per cent of this came from buildings, 21 per cent from transportation, 3 per cent from solid waste, 2 per cent from waste water and

0.1 per cent from streetlight and traffic signals. In total, 96 per cent came from burning fossil fuels. In New York, the energy use of an average household is 4,696 kilowatt hours per year. This is a difficult figure to understand; it sounds huge and it is certainly larger than most European cities – and definitely greater than any Chinese or Indian family – but it is small compared to sprawling Dallas, where a household uses 16,116 kilowatt hours a year. Similarly, although New York emits 1 per cent of all the greenhouse gases of the US (which taken as a single figure seems enormous), this figure is incredibly efficient when you take into account the fact that the city contains 2.7 per cent of the entire population.

One way to explain this unexpected efficiency is to return to Geoffrey West's model for the metabolism of the city. As he showed, when a city doubles in size, there is a scaling of efficiencies. This means that as more people come to live in the metropolis they share services and resources; thus as a city doubles in population size, it only needs to increase its carbon footprint by 85 per cent, including everything from heating and housing to the number of petrol stations; representing an energy saving of 15 per cent. As the metropolis grows it becomes more energy efficient, not less. Indeed, in one interview Geoffrey West went so far as to state: 'The secret to creating a more environmentally sustainable society is making our cities bigger. We need more metropolises.'[2]

Yet, once again, it also matters what kind of city that you live in. New York is a very different city from, say, Houston. While the average New Yorker emits 6.5 metric tonnes of carbon a year, the Texan produces a staggering 15.5 tonnes. Why is there such a vast difference? Firstly, in Manhattan people are forced to live close to each other and on top of each other, while in Texas there is no limit to the expansion of the city, and therefore everyone can have their own home in the suburbs with their SUVs parked outside.

Even within a city like New York or San Francisco, however, there is also a difference of environmental outcomes, depending on where you live. There is a cost in choosing between living in suburbia and enjoying the advantages of the inner city. Transport and housing takes up approximately 40 per cent of all household energy use in the US (about 8 per cent of all world carbon emissions). In both cases it is more energy efficient to live in the city than the suburbs.

Inner-city dwellers take up less space. Since the Second World War, the average American home has doubled in size, creating vast houses or apartments that are often empty yet are still being heated, with the lights left on and the televisions on standby. In contrast, apartments and homes in San Francisco have shrunk. It is also far more efficient to heat a block of flats than it is to heat a suburban house. In a study from the 1980s, it was calculated that an ordinary Bay Area apartment block used 80 per cent less fuel to heat itself than a new tract house of the same size in Davis, California, 70 miles away. This is because each apartment insulates and heats the apartments on either side. In addition, each dwelling is less exposed to the outside and therefore less likely to lose heat through windows. Finally the roof itself will create a smaller 'heat island' effect for the number of people in the building.

Secondly, stacking people close together creates the kind of community that promotes Jane Jacobs's ballet of the street. In New York, only 54 per cent of householders have a car and within Manhattan they use only 90 gallons of gasoline a year. By contrast, Houston has been built around the car, with over 1,100 miles of freeway to take the suburbanite from his idyll into the centre of the city. It is calculated that 71.7 per cent of all journeys in the metropolis are taken by single drivers on their way to the office, and as a result those drivers are likely to sit in 58 hours of traffic every year. In the clearest indication of the difference between living in the centre of the city or the suburbs, the economists Ed Glaesar and Matthew Kahn calculated the costs for heating and travel between each neighbourhood: they found that the average suburban New Yorker uses $289 more energy a year than their inner-city counterparts just to get around and heat their homes.[3]

The reason people do not use their cars in the city is obvious: in a dense city everything is on your doorstep. You are more likely to walk to the convenience store than jump into the car. In addition, the cost of running a car is becoming prohibitive. In both America and Europe there has recently been a decline in car usage by 18–29 year olds. Between 2000 and 2009, the average vehicle miles travelled by this age group dropped by 23 per cent, and the number of young people who do not have driver's licences has risen to 26 per cent.[4] With improvements in bike lanes as well as public transport, more people are leaving their cars at home, or even at the dealership, when they travel into the city. In addition, as the promotion of more walkable cities gains momentum, they are also preferring to use the pavements, thus adding to the ballet of the streets.

But this is not enough. Despite the advantages of urban living, we are still using too much energy, spewing out an unsustainable level of carbon emissions. We are producing too much waste, our cities create 'heat islands' that raise the atmospheric temperature, the materials – bricks, steel, plastic, glass – we use to build our houses and our streets are inefficient. Cities are centres of consumption and goods from around the world are transported there to obtain the best prices; at a time of scarcity, water and food are brought long distances to keep the metropolis fed and alive.

The city is already under threat from the damage we have inflicted upon the environment in previous centuries. According to Matthew Kahn, the change in climate will affect many of our major cities and will have very serious consequences: as the polar ice cap melts, coastal settlements will become the first to suffer. San Francisco, London, Rio and New York will all be affected as the water rises and swamps the lower-lying (and often the poorest) communities. For example, San Diego in Southern California will be particularly hit: by 2050 the sea level will be approximately 12–18 inches higher and the temperature will have risen by an estimated 4.5° F. Meanwhile the city will have continued to grow, bringing with it an increased demand for services such as water. However, despite rising sea levels, at the same time the Colorado River will dry up; there will also be a greater threat of wildfires in the hot, dry hinterlands. Kahn predicts that while the population of San Diego becomes increasingly elderly – as the average age of citizens grows and the young will have more of a chance to leave when the threat approaches – it will be society's most vulnerable that will be on the front line as the waters rise.

Yet it is possible to prepare for this, Kahn tells us. We can move to the burgeoning sun-belt cities where flooding is less of a risk. And we can build defences against the rising tides, which are expensive but worthwhile: the Thames Barrier, for example, which spans the river to the east of London, was erected in response to a flood in 1953 that submerged Canvey Island in Essex and killed 58 people. Since its completion in 1984, the frequent raising of the barrier in emergencies has increased: in the 1980s, it was raised only four times; this went up to thirty-five in the 1990s, and has more than doubled to seventy-five in the last decade. More worryingly, engineers now estimate that the current barrier will only last until 2060. Plans for its replacement to deal with increased flooding are underway.

But such forethought is rare. Too often, as was seen in New Orleans following Hurricane Katrina in 2005, it is only after the disaster that essential preventative measures are put into place. As Katrina also shows, it is a damning indictment of the city authorities that the lion's share of protection and preparation were focused on the preservation of the richer neighbourhoods, while the most vulnerable were left to fend for themselves. Thus, whilst an environmental disaster can have a calamitous effect on a whole community, the way the damage falls out across neighbourhoods is defined by society's choices.

So what is to be done? Kahn suggests that the market will correct itself and provide the answer: that innovation and people's sense of self-preservation will ensure that we face the dilemma of climate change and triumph, just as we have done so often before throughout history. In this reading of disaster economics, Kahn proposes that 'what does not kill us will make us stronger'.[5] But it is not a convincing argument: we cannot base the survival of the planet on the trickledown effect. We are going to have to make rather more concrete plans for the future.

Perhaps we should start again and build our cities from scratch? Masdar City is currently being built by the Abu Dhabi Future Energy Company, designed by the leading architect Norman Foster, in the desert. Foster's career has always been about pushing the boundaries of architecture, having as a young man been deeply influenced by the American designer Buckminster Fuller, whose geodesic dome (famously designed on a massive scale as a protection for the city) was a shining example of 'doing more with less'. With iconic commissions such as the HSBC Bank in Hong Kong, the Gherkin (30 St Mary Axe) in London, and the truly impressive Beijing Airport, Foster has been at the forefront of finding a technical solution to questions of sustainability, investing in new materials, working on designs that reduce energy use, and always remaining visually innovative.

Breaking the ground at Masdar

The architect's model for the zero-carbon city

At Masdar Foster takes the idea of the sustainable city to its current limits. He began his quest by studying traditional Arabic building methods to understand how societies had grown up and thrived in such a hostile environment. To this he added a lifetime's passion for the latest technologies and materials. Built upon a raised 23-foot-high base, the projected city was designed to benefit from desert breezes, creating a natural cooling system. One of the most futuristic ideas that Foster developed in his prototype was the replacement of all cars by personal rapid transport (PRT), pods that run along rails through the underground level of the city. This allowed for a tighter street grid, which once again helps to keep the ground level shady and cooler.

The whole project is intended to be as 'zero carbon' as possible, and a 45-foot Teflon-coated wind tower situated in the centre of the city will display how much energy the community is using. For as Fred Moavenzadah, head of the Masdar Institute, which was one of the first buildings to be constructed in the city and opened in 2012, points out, this is an experiment in futuristic design – the smart eco-city – but it also has a human element. Despite the fact that all photos of the site currently have few people in them, this will be home to 50,000 residents and 40,000 commuters who will leave their air-conditioned cars at the city boundaries. Once inside they will be forced to adapt to a more sustainable lifestyle: 'We are living and experiencing what we are trying to . . . educate people about . . . We're using roughly half the energy of a normal building of this size. We are producing no carbon because it's all renewable. Our water consumption is less and our waste generation is relatively low.'[6]

Masdar is an example of the new eco-cities that herald the possible future of urban living. It is ironic, however, that Masdar is only a few miles from the oil fields of Abu Dhabi that paid for the experiment. In fact, while funding the project, the Abu Dhabi

Future Energy Company is also actively searching for new oil ventures in Oman and Libya as well as south-east Asia.

China, also, has invested in engineering new eco-cities. Despite its reputation as a dirty industrial economy, developing polluted and congested cities at an alarming rate, China is also the largest investor in green technologies. In 2007 the government bought 35 million solar water heaters – more than the rest of the world combined. They will soon be leading the way in wind energy. Already China can boast ten eco-cities and eco-regions: new settlements outside Beijing and Shanghai, Chongqing, Guiyang, Ningbo, Hebei, Tongling, Liaoning, Shandong and Jiangsu.

Yet these eco-cities perhaps promise more than they can deliver. An engineer's solution looks very comprehensive in their brochures and the media is keen to report the projected figures before the projects are even off the ground but, like the images of Masdar, the numbers do not tell the human story. The eco-city without people voluntarily living more responsible lives is just an exercise in gadgetry and political gestures.

For example, there was a big celebration when the new Sino-Singapore city of Tianjin Eco was opened in spring 2012, just an hour by train from the centre of smog-bound Beijing. The new city was built in three years on top of abandoned salt pans, alongside an already existing industrial city, old Tianjin, which had gained a reputation as China's centre for innovation and hi-tech industries (enticing companies like Airbus, Motorola and Rockefeller to set up branches there). The eco-city was so well designed that, according to one report, 'the residents will not be expected to make any particular effort to be green'.[7]

Yet, as architecture critic Austin Williams points out, there is a huge divide between the publicity and the reality. Tianjin places transport at the heart of sustainability, promising that 90 per cent of all journeys will be on public transit. The city promises that carbon emissions will be reduced to 150 tonnes per $1 million of GDP. In ten years' time, the aim is for each person to use a maximum of 120 litres of water a day. Finally, 12 square metres of green space has been reserved for each citizen. This all sounds impressive until you compare it with an existing city like London. In each case, Tianjin is promising a new future that has already been achieved. In London, over 50 per cent of all trips are already on public transit; London produces only 99 tonnes of carbon for every $1 million of GDP; each Londoner already only consumes 120 litres of water a day without regulation; and there is a staggering 105 square metres of green space for every citizen.[8]

In another instance, the rise and fall of the much-heralded eco-city of Dongtan is a cautionary tale. Launched in 2008 with a huge publicity campaign and backed by both Prime Minister Tony Blair and President Hu Jintao, Dongtan was to be the project from which all other plans would draw inspiration. Located on Chongming Island, Shanghai, it was to be completed in time for the 2010 Shanghai Expo, and it was the paradigm of east-meets-west green development.

Except that it never happened: by 2009, the farmers and peasants had been removed from the land and a visitors' centre had been built. By the time of the Expo, the local party leader Chen Liangyu was in prison for bribery, most of the contracts had lapsed, and the technology companies were finding it difficult to adapt their innovations to the situation on the ground. Nevertheless, the world's media continued to lap up the computer-generated images of the perfect society. Eventually, the project fell off the partners' roster of current projects and the visitors' centre was closed. As Dongtan was mothballed, the farmers themselves who had invested their life's savings in the project – and who had agreed to be moved from their homes – were hung out to dry.

Even if we can rely on the innovation of planners, engineers and visionary architects to deliver the brand-new eco-city, built from scratch out of the dust and desert, this is not a practical future for the majority of the world. The costs are prohibitive: in the face of the global downturn repeated cuts have been made to the construction site at Masdar, as certain projects no longer make economic sense. Thus, initially the settlement was to be built on a vast platform that allowed the desert air to circulate and cool the whole city as well as create an underground layer in which to place all the infrastructure and transport including the eye-catching PRT system. But this was cancelled when the overall costs were reduced from $22 billion to $16 billion.

The biggest obstacle to greening our cities is the fact that most of us already live inside them; so how can we make the places where we live now greener and better prepared for the future? Must we rely on an engineering solution, developing greener ways of living by design? What role will our mayor and politicians play in bringing greener infrastructure to the city? And above all, what do we need to do ourselves to ensure that the way we go about our lives improves the places in which we live?

As recent climate-change summits – such as Kyoto, Copenhagen and Rio+20 – have shown, the level of trust between nations to put environmental standards before profit is very low. It will be cities therefore, rather than nations, which will be at the forefront of the climate-change challenge, driving initiatives, setting out practical policies and ensuring that they are followed through; but the individual city authorities will only get things done with the collaboration of grass-roots active citizens.

The C40 group was created in 2005 as a union of the leading cities of the world to combat the challenges of climate change, and to share ideas and policies on how best to reduce emissions, and find design solutions for the city of the future. Each city within the group has now published goals and projections for improving carbon emissions: Buenos Aires aims to reduce emissions by a third by 2030; Chicago hopes to reduce them by 80 per cent by 2050; Madrid will halve its emissions by 2050; Tokyo promises to cut them by 25 per cent by 2020. In addition to carbon emissions, the C40 group has highlighted eight key areas to prioritise – building, energy, lighting, ports, renewables, transport, waste and water – and they are asking for radical solutions.

So far, responses have been diverse; for example, San Francisco has begun planning the largest city-owned solar-power station in the world; Oslo, Norway, has pledged 10,000 intelligent street lamps that will reduce energy consumption by 70 per cent and save 1,440 tonnes of CO_2. In Emfuleni, South Africa, they are installing a city-wide water-efficiency system that reduces the pressure within the network thereby reducing costly leakages. This is proof, at least, that city governments acknowledge the issues and are starting to search for interesting solutions regardless of national policy. But there is no single solution for every city; every metropolis faces its own problems.

In 2007 Mayor Michael Bloomberg announced the PlaNYC, with the promise 'to prepare the city for one million more residents, strengthen our economy, combat climate change, and enhance the quality of life for all New Yorkers'.[9] The plan brought together twenty-five city agencies in order to set a focused agenda for the five boroughs that would cover every aspect of New York, from housing, parks, water, waste and air quality, to how to remain competitive within the global market. At its launch there were 127 proposed initiatives, and by 2009 almost two-thirds had been achieved.

Some examples of the projects illustrate the realities of dreaming the green city, retrofitting the existing urban framework rather than building from scratch. Balancing the new with the need to renovate and maintain much of the city's fabric, 64,000 housing units have been constructed or redeveloped in line with a fresh set of green building codes, which outline energy use, materials and emission limits. In addition, 87 per cent of these units can boast easy access to public transport. There was also a concerted effort to build more parks so that 250,000 more people were no less than a ten-minute walk away from a green spot. Over half a million trees were planted. There was a $2.1 billion project, Water for the Future, designed to clean up the waterways. There was also a promise to double waste recycling to 30 per cent of all garbage by 2017, and the city is currently on track to reduce carbon emissions by 30 per cent by the same year.

Transport is responsible for at least 25 per cent of all of New York's emissions. But there have been huge advances in making public transport more efficient and encouraging people to use both the subway and buses. In addition, the transfer of the traditional yellow cabs to green fuel is moving apace, with 30 per cent of the total fleet running on biofuels. A new fleet of 18,000 apple-green cabs – Boro Taxis – will be able to pick up passengers outside Manhattan.

There have also been attempts to combat congestion. Mayor Bloomberg first announced in 2007 that he would promote congestion charging and the news was welcomed by many groups, businesses and residents on the island. Reports were written, feasability tests made, proposals put forward for an $8 levy to be raised on any private vehicle, and a map was drawn up introducing a cordon across South Manhattan between 6 am and 6 pm on weekdays. However, in the following years negotiations with the city council and then the state assembly became more complicated, as objections were raised by Brooklyn, Queens and the Bronx as well as the state beyond the city. In the end it seemed that not even congested New York was willing to penalise the motorist.

But the proposal is not completely shelved. In March 2012 Sam Schwartz, former first deputy transportation commissioner of the New York City Department of Transportation, announced that he had independently been working on a plan that would integrate congestion charging and a system of tolls that would ring the city, with the less than snappy title 'A More Equitable Transportation Formula for the NY Metro Area'. His proposal would reduce traffic dramatically as well as make $1.2 billion a year for the indebted Metropolitan Transportation Authority and provide 35,000 locals with jobs. The scheme was structured around congestion – as befitting the man who invented the word 'gridlock' – rather than sustainability, but nonetheless it seems a powerful incentive for getting cars off the road. It is also designed to use existing infrastructure more efficiently, applying higher pricing where there is most congestion and where public transit is available. The plan was highly praised throughout the media because it spread the burden across Manhattanites as well as those who were travelling to the island. The proposals have not yet been adopted by City Hall, but they keep alive the hope that congestion charging could be one useful method to green the city.

One of the more unusual proposals in Schwartz's plan was the creation of special bike and pedestrian bridges to further encourage cycle use in the city. By summer 2012, bike numbers had doubled over the previous five years. Safety is an important factor in encouraging people to commute on two wheels, and statistics show that crash rates have declined by 71 per cent between 2000 and 2010. The widespread bike-lane network that has been added to the city's road system over the last decade has certainly helped, with 288 miles of lanes – 185 miles exclusively for bikes – designated throughout the five boroughs.[10]

This has not occurred without campaigners and activists such as Transport Alternatives pushing City Hall to address the problems of roads, bike lanes and safety. Founded in 1973, this group has been constant in promoting bicycling as the most sustainable way of getting around the city, but this has also led to discussions of efficient public transport, as well as promoting liveable streets for all. As their website says, it is more than just the bike: 'The most perfect street we can imagine is one in which a child can safely play and regularly has the space to do so. With streets and sidewalks 80 per cent of New York City's public space, Transportation Alternatives works with individual communities to make those spaces and local streets safe for all.'[11] The greener neighbourhood is, in their opinion, a more pleasant, human place to live.

This increase in bike usage has had an unexpected knock-on effect in the city. With so many people now riding into town, they need somewhere to put their bikes and parking bars are becoming increasingly scarce. As a consequence, some offices are now providing storage spaces, with the *New York Times* reporting 'more and more this is a selling point for the real-estate industry',[12] and 'bike rooms' are awarded extra points according to the LEED sustainability award scheme. The transport commissioner is also using old, decapitated parking-meter posts to which people can tie their bikes, to add to the additional 6,000 new racks that have been ordered.

There is an alternative, however, which does not involve having to remember where you put your bike – or worry about it being stolen. In September 2011 Mayor Bloomberg announced the launch of the Alta Bike Scheme that will make 10,000 bikes available around the city. This scheme has a long history, starting with the White Bike initiative in Amsterdam in 1965. Today there are similar projects in 165 cities including Paris – the Vélib – since 2007 and the 'Boris Bikes' that were launched in London in 2010. The

From the street, Brooklyn Grange, Queens

The view from Brooklyn Grange towards Manhattan

largest scheme in the world can be found in Hangzhou, China, where there are 61,000 bikes available. The New York 'Citibike' is heavily sponsored by Citibank and Mastercard but there have already been some complaints about the pricing structure.

The iconic skyline was less than a mile away but once again it felt strangely distant. I was standing on the roof of a six-storey building in Queens, a borough across the water from Manhattan, less than five minutes on the M subway. To one side I looked out across a busy train depot, to the other ran asphalt and low-level industrial buildings. Around the edge of the rooftop were planted a row of tall looping sunflowers that peered over the side of the building, the only indication of what was hidden here. For Brooklyn Grange is a 1-acre farm in the heart of the city, accessed by lift from the reception area of an ordinary office block.

The project began in 2010, when head farmer Ben Flanner, who had already experimented with roof farms at Eagle Street, Brooklyn, heard that an office block in Queens was considering the development of a green roof in order to improve their environmental standards. Co-opting a group of local restaurateurs and activists, the architects Bromley Caldari and the investment fund Acumen Capital Partners, Flanner persuaded the building owners that rather than a green roof, the top floor could be turned into a commercial farm. And so, over three weeks in spring 2010, 1.2 million lbs of soil was lifted on to the roof and sowing for the summer harvest began.

As I wandered through the rows of tomatoes, beets, carrots, herbs, chard and beans, I spotted a line of beehives, and later I found a small chicken coop. The tender plants had been planted close to the air-conditioning ducts so that they were preserved through winter. In the first full year, the farm produced 15,000 lbs of fruit and vegetables that were sold directly to local restaurants and farmers' markets. Demand for the produce has been so popular that the farm does not even need to deliver to Manhattan, just across the water. In a recent survey conducted both at roof level and on the street below, it was discovered that whilst on the ground the air quality was as expected from the inner city, six storeys up it was nearly pure.

According to the farm manager, Michael Meier, who had come to New York to work in advertising but, inspired by childhood memories of working on his grandparents' farm, changed careers and now spends most days at Brooklyn Grange, the project is a privately owned enterprise but with a strong community basis. Thus many of the rows have been sown by local children and there is a large table set between tomato trellises where classes can be conducted. Brooklyn Grange has been so successful that work is already in hand on another rooftop farm in Brooklyn Navy Yard.

There is something wonderful about walking through rows of vegetables and still feeling in the heart of the city. Yet it also felt so obvious; I wondered why we had not all been doing this for decades. In fact it is only recently, following successes like Brooklyn Grange, that city-zoning regulations have allowed similar projects – which encourage green development – to be launched. The new laws, called Zone Green, allow greenhouses to be erected on roofs, along with solar panels and wind turbines; they also promote gardens and local food production, and in general address the wider needs of retrofitting the city, of making greener the city we have in hand. The Mayor's Office hopes that just by withdrawing current restrictions there could be $800 million of annual energy savings.

However, whilst Zone Green is enabling change to occur in New York, it is still the case that nearly 75 per cent of the city's carbon emissions come from construction and from heating homes and offices. Everywhere you look, cranes rise into the air, and developers are breaking down old houses, setting new foundations on brownfield sites. The city is constantly in transformation; it never stops being constructed. In an average city 2–3 per cent of the materials are improved every year, it would take at least fifty years for a city to be completely updated; can we wait this long?

Can the rules that allow for the greening of roofs be used to promote more efficient building practice, both in terms of construction and maintenance? We certainly have the technology to improve the buildings in which we work and live. The very same innovation that is creating the smart city (see Chapter 8) can also be used to monitor and regulate energy usage and find efficiencies. As a result, the smart building can control lighting and heating and it uses the latest materials to reduce energy leakage. Once again, the big software firms like IBM and Siemens are investing heavily in promoting the concept of 'smart building' as a component of the smart city.

In the US the LEED national standards for sustainable building were created, in the main, for developers constructing new homes or for the rich who can afford expensive turbines and solar panels to improve the value of their homes on the real-estate market. When the project was launched it set the agenda for new thinking about building, making 'green' a selling point in housing for the first time, something that added value to the bottom line; and as a result many people saw mileage in speculating on green architecture and design.

But the LEED standards do not deliver on the promise of nurturing the green city. The real proving ground for the green city is not found in how new buildings are constructed but how the older stock and fabric can be converted in order to make it more sustainable. Currently just over 45 per cent of the surface space of New York is taken up with buildings. In 2000 tax incentives were announced to encourage businesses and landlords to retrofit their own properties. Since 2010 government buildings and employees themselves have been leading by example with the addition of solar panels and green roofs. As a result, carbon emissions dropped by 4.9 per cent, nearly 170,000 tonnes in total, between 2009 and 2010.

Following on from the 2007 PlaNYC, in May 2012 the Mayor's Office launched the 'Greener, Greater Buildings' programme setting out a six-point plan to retrofit the city's existing buildings. As Scott Burnham's work in Amsterdam on building trust demonstrated, the process of building green is as important as the materials and construction itself. The first of the six points therefore recognises the unique position of cities, by proposing a local New York City Energy Code separate from the local state code. This would let the city – with its very different needs and challenges – set its own agenda and standards.

Secondly, as the report notes, 'you can't manage what you don't measure',[12] so large offices and blocks should be tested annually. However, this procedure should be as simple as possible: the filing of an online form based on recent energy bills. It is estimated that lighting constitutes a large part of all of the city's energy, so using a system of sub-meters that can find out if offices keep their lights on at night or at unnecessary times of the day will provide the kind of data that could help a company look at its energy wastage. (Thus changing lightbulbs might not change the city, but it certainly has a part to play!)

The plan also outlines a system of energy audits every ten years to check that buildings are emitting as little carbon as possible. And finally, it emphasises the need for a concerted effort to develop the green building economy, encouraging new jobs as well as ensuring advantageous financing for green projects. The programme estimates that these innovations could create 15,800 new construction-related jobs in the city.

The 'Greener, Greater New York' plan underscores the idea that there is a connection between the creation of a green city and the development of a green society. New standards of construction and the encouraging of people to work and live in new ways have clear environmental, economic and social benefits. This rather undermines the views held by many exasperated campaigners such as Green Alliance activist Julie Hill, who writes 'we actually need ... to have some choices taken away from us'.[14] Instead, what is happening in New York shows that we need to see the advantages of making these changes and feel part of the transformation that they bring so that we choose the alternative for ourselves out of preference.

I found something like this in an unexpected place. After visiting Staten Island, I returned to Manhattan and headed to the East Village, a once run-down neighbourhood that had gained a reputation for its edgy, artistic atmosphere. It was here that, in the 1940s, Robert Moses knocked down much of the slum housing and replaced it with the projects, vast social-housing tenements that became synonymous with crime and drugs in the 1980s. Amongst the older streets that circled Tompkin Park, lined with barely gentrified brownstone houses, I was fortunate enough to be following a guided tour prepared for me by the Museum of Reclaimed Urban Space, a newly created campaign group hoping to celebrate the squats and local-community gardens of Alphabet City. The tour started at the C squat at 155 Avenue C between 9th and 10th Streets, one of the most famous reclaimed sites in the neighbourhood, which also houses a small theatre known for staging popular concerts.

Opposite the squat was a community garden, and upon entering I found an urban paradise. On such a hot day this was one of the most beautiful places I had visited in any city in the world. Trees offered dappled shade in the small plot made out of a gap in the street front where a row of houses must have once stood.

The garden itself was divided up into small rooms, each offering different delights: in one, a woman was tending her vegetables with her grandson; in another two men were sitting on a bench, shooting the breeze in the shade; there was a hut with a table, stove and kettle, obviously where the gardeners came together after a day's toil. I wandered along pathways made of broken-up bricks and found a quiet corner, to get out of the heat and to enjoy this moment of tranquillity in one of the busiest places in the world.

Heaven on earth, a communal garden on Avenue C

There are about 640 communal gardens in New York and at least sixty of them can be found in the dense neighbourhood of the East Village. Many of the gardens emerged from community activism, driven by local campaigners who saw the value of transforming abandoned and derelict properties into verdant oases. Often the plots were taken, like the squats, because no one else wanted them and the legal status was only worked out afterwards. In 2002 the district attorney Elliot Spitzer negotiated that the city should acknowledge the gardens and offer some safety of collective ownership. They are now mostly run by the GreenThumb programme, first started in the 1970s as a partnership between activists and the civic authorities, which helps with developing standards and promoting education. Today over 80 per cent of all community gardens grow food, and over 40 per cent have a link with a local school.

On my tour I visited the Green Oasis on East 8th Street – first built in 1981, when a series of raised beds were planted on top of the building's foundations that had collapsed from neglect. There, three vividly painted beehives stood within a glade of trees. On the next street, East 7th Street, I found the Ecology Centre Garden, started in 1990, even before the city sanitation department began to recycle. There I found bins for all kinds of waste, while the covered walkways had been made with recycled ketchup bottles and cans. Each park was lovingly tended by the locals, who quietly tilled their patches, or otherwise sat around, chatting and welcoming me in to share their pride. It struck me that the gardens were not just built by the community, but formed one as well.

There was a very different feeling between taking a deep breath standing in the centre of Stockholm and inhaling the air in the heart of New York. Both cities are surrounded by water, but as I gazed out across the sea in front of the Royal Palace on Stadsholmen Island the air was so clean, and the atmosphere so relaxed, it was hard to believe that I was in a thriving capital city. The waves rocked the boats in the harbour to my left, which sat in front of the National Museum, nestling in parkland. To my right was the world-beating contemporary art museum, the Moderna Museet, its white stone glistening, perched on top of the Skeppsholmen Island, which once housed the military academy and naval yards. Had I taken a ferry to one of the nearby islands, I could have swum off the rocks in clear water.

Stockholm is blessed by geography, nestled within an archipelago of islands, so that the city has developed over the centuries as a major port, first as a depot for the Hanseatic League in the thirteenth century, and later becoming a cultural and political capital. In 2009 it was estimated that it was home to 2 million citizens and covered an area of 6,519 square kilometres. In the 1960s the sea around it was so polluted that fishing and swimming in the city's waters was banned, yet today there are twenty-four official swimming beaches and salmon are often fished and sold. There are nearly 1,000 parks and green spaces, covering over 30 per cent of the city's landscape, ensuring that 95 per cent of the population are only 300 yards away from the nearest patch of grass.

It is not possible – or always desirable – to pull down all the old stock of buildings and re-route the infrastructure. Yet the disused factories and industrial buildings of the historic centre no longer make sense in the post-industrial city, and it is clear that old buildings are the least sustainable: they leak heat and energy from their joints and windows. Similarly the streets and highways (which lead commuters out to the suburbs) have been designed with gas-guzzling cars in mind. So how do we take the old idea of the city and transform it for the new age? How do we bring people together through this transformation, so that it occurs with them, rather than to them? Stockholm presents the perfect balance between preserving the heritage of the city while also showing a determination to prepare for the future.

In 2010 Stockholm was named the European Green Capital of the Year. This was partly in recognition of the efforts already made by the city, but also because of its future programme, Vision 2030, which identified six main areas for new policy: changing transport policy to make it more environmentally efficient with an emphasis on reducing carbon emissions; encouraging green cars and public transit, and providing bike lanes; reducing the use of toxic chemicals in manufacturing and construction; more efficient use of energy, water and land; improving waste management; and finally 'a healthy indoor environment': upgrading social housing and reducing noise pollution.

While the average European carbon footprint stands at 10 tonnes per capita, as opposed to 22 tonnes per capita in the US, Stockholm has already reduced its carbon emissions to 3.4 tonnes per capita and it promises to be fossil-fuel free by 2050. This reduction has been brought about by improving the city's infrastructure and promoting public transport, as well as developing a widespread bike culture, with an 'ecobike' system and the establishment of an extensive cycle infrastructure, so that on any winter's day 19 per cent of Stockholmers will be using their bicycles – a figure that rises to 33 per cent in summer.

Stockholm has also been able to improve energy efficiency in heating. The city government, alongside the energy company Fortum, has invested heavily in alternative sources of energy, including biofuels, solar power and hydropower (fossil fuels are only used when the weather is really cold); in addition 80 per cent

CORBIS

Clear water, bicycles and clean air: the benefits of a green Stockholm

of the city is now supplied by a 'district heating system', so that power stations generate heat as well as power that is then distributed around the city through insulated pipes. Such a scheme takes a long time and huge initial investment but it has major long-term benefits: since 1990 emissions of greenhouse gases in the city have dropped by 593,000 tonnes.

Alongside green initiatives and the development of infrastructure there is also a strong commitment to education. Stockholm believes in its role as a creative capital and knows that as it grows it will also become more innovative; thus the future of the city begins at school. Together with the development of transport hubs, cleaner, more open neighbourhoods and new shopping areas, there is also a pledge to invest in the Kista Science City, the Stockholm Public Library and the College of Arts, Crafts and Design at Telephonplan by retrofitting and repurposing the existing industrial buildings rather than planning the latest innovations in new suburbs far from the city centre. Thus Stockholm is determined to become greener but not at a cost to the city's economic competitiveness in the global market.

And how does this change the city? Do the citizens feel healthier and cleaner as a result of the greening of Stockholm? Talking to Swedish friends who live there, I discovered that many of the changes have happened without controversy or complaint. Rather, they have grown out of the long-standing personality of the city itself, for Stockholm has always placed a premium on community. Thus, why should citizens not share heating arrangements when sharing is not seen as a disadvantage? Projects on this level take huge governmental will and resources, but they mean very little unless the rest of the population are as engaged as their leaders in the future of their shared city.

As cities like Stockholm – in contrast with, say, New York – show, the more equal and trustful a city is, the more likely it is also to be green. It is impossible to project a sustainability programme without engaging with the people on the street, and this is almost impossible when the level of trust is low. Why would you recycle if you did not trust your neighbour? How can the city be green if there is one rule for the rich and one for the poor? This can be seen in the decisions that people make when they get into their cars. An efficient public-transport system reduces not only congestion and pollution but also health inequality, but some of the barriers for using such transit include the fear that it is inefficient, and the social stigma of 'riding the bus'. Getting cars off the street and cutting out unnecessary journeys has a social as well as environmental result: it reduces carbon footprint and improves air quality, but it also, as we saw with Appleyard's experiments on his Heavy and Light Streets, enhances communities.

* * *

I was reminded of this fact when I went to meet Colin Beavan, a writer living in Manhattan who decided to reduce his carbon emissions to zero. He recounted the travails and the joys of his year of living green in a wonderfully entertaining and honest book and documentary film of the same name, *No Impact Man*. The story is a salutary narrative that is not afraid to expose the difficulties and sacrifices necessary to get used to a more sustainable life. In the end, the freedoms and benefits were palpable.

On many occasions the results were unexpected and amusing. Early on, Beavan realised that he could no longer order takeaways because of their cardboard containers, and his misery was compounded when he could not even indulge the impulse for a slice of pizza on the street because of the plastic plate and packaging. Getting around the city became hard and Beavan was transformed into a bicycle fanatic; however on at least one occasion he could not take his daughter to a birthday party because it was raining. Discussing holiday plans with distant parents also became an ethical as well as emotional minefield.

As he began to shed all unnecessary things in life he recorded how his day-to-day existence was changing. Thus one day he calculated that because he could no longer use lifts, after taking the dog for a walk three times a day, dropping off his daughter at childcare and completing his daily chores, he had walked up 124 flights of stairs – nine more than the Empire State Building.

Yet over the months, as they turned off the heating in winter and used only candles, recycled as much as they could, composted on the fire escape, and grew their own vegetables in a communal plot, the Beavan family began to transform. In the end, Beavan admitted that the fear of change was more dangerous than the change itself. When they turned off the electricity, having invited a group of friends around to the apartment for the ceremony, each holding a candle in preparation, the moment before the circuit breaker was pulled was much worse than the first second of darkness. 'What's hardest? Everybody wants to know. Is it no packaging or the biking everywhere or the scootering or the living without a fridge or what? Actually it's none of these things. What's hardest is habit change. Plain old forcing yourself out of a rut and learning to live differently. Everything about yourself wants to fall back into the rut, at least for a while. By "for a while", by the way, I mean a month. That's how long they say it takes to change a habit.'[15]

Beavan's experience shows that creating the sustainable city begins with the family and then grows outwards. Yet this does not mean that the city should just turn off the switch and descend into night. Rather, their experiment allowed Beavan and his wife to understand what was necessary and what was not: 'there were two parts of the equation: one is figuring out what is the good life – how many and what kind of resources we need to make us happy. The other is figuring out how to deliver the same level of (reduced) resources, by western standards, to everyone in a sustainable way.'[16]

This sounds so simple, but how do we go about making it work at a global level without us all having to go through a season without electricity to jolt ourselves into action? There are, thankfully, a number of surprisingly small and common-sense changes we can make to our everyday lives that can make a difference. For example, the UN Environmental Programme offers a number of simple solutions to the question of 'thermal comfort', such as putting on a jumper instead of the heating over the winter and rolling the blinds down rather than turning on the air conditioning in the summer. The programme also highlights the fact that many shops feel obliged to keep their doors open, thus letting out a great deal of energy – sometimes 50 per cent of all heating costs (indeed some use a machine that blows a jet of hot air across the doorway to stop leakage); but why do they not simply close the door?

Since his experiment, Beavan has been attacked by some commentators. The leading environmental correspondent for the *New Yorker*, Elizabeth Kolbert, dismissed his efforts as an 'eco-stunt'. She argued that, because Beavan was not in control of the heating system in his building, and because he was able to use the electricity from the Writer's House in which he wrote his blog, this proves that it is actually impossible to live inside the city without having some kind of impact.

These are fruitless objections that miss the point. The whole city cannot follow Beavan in his experiment but it is interesting to see how far one can go if one tries, and perhaps it will encourage others to cut back. Beavan reminds us of our individual responsibility as citizens – the people who live in cities – to look for ways that we can change our own behaviour to deliver a greener metropolis.

Beavan's darkened flat in Greenwich Village stands in stark contrast to the massive works currently underway at Fresh Kills, but they are both necessary in order to prepare the city for the coming environmental challenges.

11

A PLACE CALLED HOME

At the end of 2011, my family and I moved to suburbia. According to my mother this felt as if we, the prodigal family, had finally made it back home; I am not so certain. I grew up in a place like this, far from the centre; and now, here I am again, making the same journey to the periphery in search of an extra bedroom and a bit of garden. I have followed a well-worn rite of passage that comes to many comfortably secure people living in the city in the western world at the beginning of the twenty-first century.

We have moved to what many people call the 'inner suburbs' of London, the ring of development that encircled the city during the first decades of the twentieth century. Here, we are no longer within easy distance of the centre, but looking down our perfectly regular street northwards I see urban sprawl all the way to the horizon. Our house was built in 1907 when pasture was turned over to tarmacadam and respectable housing, built with a hint of Elizabethan historicism, aimed at middle-ranking professionals who could get into St Pancras Station within fifteen minutes on the commuter train.

When we bought it, the house had been kept in its original state, but like many others in the street we have adapted it to our modern

Home in north London

tastes. We have changed colour schemes and added our own furniture into the standardised room plan that can be found in every abode along the street; our pictures now hang from the walls, making it our own through decoration. We knocked down the wall that divided the kitchen and the dining room in order to make one large room with a view of the garden, so that this room becomes the heart of the house, where once it was a service area. We still have not decided what to do with the privy, an outdoor toilet.

The house was built at the dying moments of London's pre-eminence as the world's capital city, the twilight of empire reflected in an increased passion for domestication. The home was raised up as a last redoubt against the horrors of the city, as the antithesis of the office, a barrier against the tide of the world, as described by the Metroland advertisements:

> London is at your very doorstep, if your needs must keep in touch with London, but it is always pure country at the corner of the lane beyond your garden fence ... Metroland is a strip of England at its fairest, a gracious district formed by nature for the homes of a healthy, happy race.[1]

But my street now looks nothing like the Arcadian brochures produced by the Metroland Company that had young Edwardian ladies cutting flowers, or groups of young, shiny couples heading to the tennis club. And if London is changing this is only a small reflection of what is going on in cities around the world.

According to the American urbanist Alan Ehrenhalt, I am heading against the current, and we are currently experiencing the Great Inversion, a reverse white flight from the periphery to the centre of the city. This will have a huge impact on the life of American cities in the next decades, with the reinvention of downtown, while the poor are being driven out of the centre to the outskirts, the *banlieus*, far from metropolitan opportunities.

This return to the centre in some cities and the benefits of increased densification stands in contrast to the galloping suburban sprawl of cities like Houston. Which is the best way forward? It is increasingly hard to find a connection between our everyday lives and the enormous shifts that are happening to cities around the globe. How can I relate my own life, with its daily decisions and mundane trials, to what is going on with the rest of the planet's cities? Where do I fit in, and what can I do about it?

It is easy to feel lost as one faces the sheer scale of the urban world. For much of the last 300 years we have assumed that when we talk about the city, we are talking about a social form that derives – like Rem Koolhaas's Roman Operating System – from the ancient European template. But the balance of world urban populations is shifting. It is not only cities getting larger, but where they are, that will define their future shape.

In 1950 there were only eighty-three cities that had a population exceeding 1 million; today there are over 460. Sixty years ago, there was only one mega-city, defined as an urban area containing more than 10 million people. In those days New York had a total population of 12 million, London just under 9 million and Tokyo, the third-largest city, accounted for 7 million. The development of new mega-cities was a sharp, millennial shift: in 1985, there were nine in all; this rose to nineteen in 2004, and today is estimated at twenty-five. By 2025 the number will have climbed to thirty-six. It is significant where these cities have grown and how fast. Here is the top ten:

Tokyo	34.5 m	0.6 per cent growth per year
Guangzhou	25.8 m	3.8 per cent
Jakarta	25.3 m	3.2 per cent
Seoul	25.3 m	1.25 per cent
Shanghai	25.3 m	4.0 per cent
Mexico City	23.2 m	1.7 per cent
Delhi	23.0 m	3.0 per cent
New York	21.5 m	0.35 per cent
São Paulo	20.8 m	1.3 per cent
Mumbai	20.8 m	2.0 per cent.[2]

The size, as well as the speed at which these cities are growing, will have a huge impact on how the urban world develops. As I saw in Mumbai, in the next decades as urbanisation continues at such a rapid pace, many world cities will become world slums. We know that it is estimated that two people are arriving into cities every second, 180,000 every day, yet as the figures above show, these new citizens are not just making their journeys to the established metropolises of Tokyo and New York. Rather, it is estimated that the urban population in Africa and Asia will double by 2030; for example, the population of Kinshasa, the capital of the Democratic Republic of the Congo, currently stands at about 8.75 million; by 2025 this will have risen to 15.04 million. China will continue to urbanise, and in the next twenty years over 350 million will settle in new cities, more than the entire population of the US. India, a nation that its liberating founder Mahatma Gandhi claimed had its soul in the village, will, by 2030, be a country of sixty-eight cities of over 1 million, thirteen cities with over 4 million and six mega-cities with a population each of over 10 million, with the capital at New Delhi reaching 46 million, twice as large as the total population of Australia.

What will these mega-cities feel like? In many ways, they have already arrived and one only needs to visit Mexico City or Nairobi to experience the impact of so many bodies crammed into one place together. Getting around Mumbai was a constant battle. Bodies, cars, taxis, autorickshaws, the unusual sight of an ox-drawn cart and the back-breaking effort of pulling a hand trolley laden with packing boxes, overstuffed sacks and timber. Riding the train at rush hour was a test of urban grit and savvy as on average nearly 4,700 people routinely pile into a space meant for less than a quarter of that number. People hang from the doors, learning the skills of jumping off as the engine enters the station before the next human wave attempts to fill the final crannies of the compartment. As the writer Suketu Mehta so rightly observes, Mumbai is a city where one is always adjusting, bunching up and making a little more room for the next person. Amongst this traffic, going by foot seemed the best of all possible methods of getting around.

Hanging on to the train's door jamb, it was easy to think that at that moment the world was too full. Mega-cities can be seen both as a sign of increasing efficiency in our management of lives and proof that we are over-populated. In 1789 the Reverend Thomas Malthus warned that mankind was doomed if it ever reached 1 billion, because 'the power of population is infinitely greater than the power in the earth to produce subsistence for man'.[3] In 1968 Paul Ehrlich came up with the same cry for help in his influential book, *Population Bomb*, whose first editions started with the prediction: 'The battle to feed all of humanity is over. In the 1970s hundreds of millions of people will starve to death in spite of any crash programs embarked upon now.'[4] Even James Lovelock, the father of Gaia, warned in 2009 that we faced 'death on a grand scale from famine and lack of water [unless there is] a reduction to 1 billion people or less'.[5]

However, cities might just be the only solution we have in the face of such prophesies. In 1994 the American journalist P. J. O'Rourke calculated that if the world's population were gathered together in a place with the same density of Manhattan, 'everyone on earth can live in former Yugoslavia'.[6] This constitutes less than 0.08 per cent of the planet's surface. Today, the world's population might need slightly more wriggle room, but no more than Nicaragua. Therefore, living together in crowded spaces is clearly not the problem; how we live, and how we are allowed to live together, is what matters most.

Cities are often the places that we blame for overcrowding when they are the places where the bustle is most visible. However, it is the city that offers one of the answers to the supposed demographic time bomb. Urbanisation itself, the movement from the countryside to the city, will act as the single most important factor in halting the current unsustainable rates of population growth in the next century. According to most estimates the global population will continue to rise until 2050, reaching somewhere near 9 billion, the same year that the world becomes 70 per cent urban. This means that we will be growing at about 1 billion every 14–20 years. The global population will continue to rise, peaking at about 10.1 billion in 2100. It will then start to decline.

There are many factors included within these predictions: the current economic crisis has already had an impact, as people are having fewer babies during the recession. The urbanisation of women is also dramatically affecting fertility rates. In the developed world this is reflected in the rise of professional women who have remained unmarried or without children until much later in their lives.

In 2011 it was revealed that the highly successful TV programme *Sex and the City* was not far off the mark. While 34.8 per cent of women over fifteen had never been married in New York State, within the city itself this figure rose to 41.7 per cent. It was also calculated that there were 149,219 more single women in the city than single men. Female New Yorkers also tend to get married much later, and will plan to have fewer children.

Cities are becoming more female – almost everywhere in the world, the proportion of women to men is changing. In her groundbreaking 2010 article in the *Atlantic*, 'The End of Men', Hannah Roisin showed how the economic downturn of 2008 transformed the workplace and now more women work in America than men. While there continues to be protest for the lack of women in the boardroom, now 'women dominate today's colleges and professional schools – for every two men who will receive BA this year, three women will do the same. Of the fifteen job categories projected to grow the most in the next decade in the US, all but two are occupied primarily by women'.[7] The rise of women in the city is perhaps one of the least-discussed aspects of the urban future, and its impact cannot just be found in the developed world.

Elsewhere across the planet, the same imperatives of access to work, contraception and better healthcare are allowing women to make choices that were not available to them in the village. Coming to the city offers the new female immigrant previously unthinkable opportunities. In 2007 the UN Population Fund produced a special report stating that 'the best recipe for a life without poverty is still to grow up in the city'.[8]

The advantages start early, with access to education. In developing countries, school attendance for girls between the ages of 10–14 is 18.4 per cent higher in the city than in the countryside. This percentage rises to 37.5 per cent between the ages of 15–19. For young women, child marriage is also a barrier to empowerment and is more prevalent in the countryside where, for example, 71 per cent of all young women in Bangladesh are wed by the time they are eighteen years old, as opposed to 31 per cent in the city. In a survey conducted in the slums of Addis Ababa, a quarter of all young migrants aged 10–19 were escaping a forced marriage. Women in the city, even in the slums where healthcare and conditions are precarious, are having fewer children. As a result, fertility rates are lower in the city than in the village. In addition, more children are staying alive. Where in the 1950s it was necessary to have somewhere between five or six children born to replace both parents, twenty years later this dropped to 3.9; by 2000 it was 2.8 and by 2008, 2.6 (in the developed world it is closer to 2.1).

Spending time in airports can give you a strange perspective on the world. Looking at a map of the major flight paths criss-crossing the globe appears like a spider's web, displaying the network of major centres. Airports are solid examples of the connections between cities. Have you ever stood in front of a departure board and thought, 'Where shall I go today?'

Standing in Terminal 3 of Dubai International Airport at four o'clock in the morning was one of the most bizarre moments of all my travels while writing this book. I was outside a stall displaying all the newspapers of the world, while an endless bustling crowd circled and swirled around me. This was a place without time; there were so many people whose body clocks were working in different time zones that it did not seem to matter that dawn was an hour away. From this position, just reading the headlines, I could find out what was happening in every city from Cape Town to Los Angeles. As this was Dubai, I could also pay for the paper with any currency, as long as I was happy to accept dirham as change.

Terminal 3, Dubai Airport

I can also buy the latest bestseller in any number of languages, as well as the finest French wine from a concession that displays Château Pétrus in its window. There are shops heaped with luxury labels from electronics to perfume. International high-end fashion hangs on railings beneath glossy images of supermodels, waiting to be bagged up and carried to who-knows-where. Expensive golf clubs are racked beside posters of impossibly verdant greens in the middle of the desert.

The terminal itself was constructed as a single long space, and completed in 2011. Below a broad curved ceiling, it is the third-largest building in the world. As I wander in a daze past familiar chain cafés and fast-food restaurants, there is a palpable babble of languages being spoken around me, and I can imagine that thousands of people are coming together for a matter of moments and then departing to all points of the globe, never to meet again.

The airport is an instant city, continuously in tumultuous overdrive. Part of me is disoriented as I walk through the terminal, waiting for my connecting flight back home. I am uncertain that I understand this place as it is so different from any other public space that we normally encounter in a city. It feels like the agglomeration of every city, and yet has no real identity of its own. There is no sense of history, nationality or personality: a consumption-scape that leaves no impression upon the memory. Yet the airport only makes sense as a place because of the network of other airports to which it is linked. In terms of scale, Dubai Airport is a mega-city, the fourth-largest hub for international passengers in the world, dealing with over 50 million travellers in 2011 alone. Yet it is also the reminder that the airport itself is a place of perpetual movement, a super-connected place that gives it a completely different power of scale altogether.

If the idea of the mega-city seems daunting, the arrival of the interconnected mega-region – the vast conglomerations of major cities – will be a further challenge to the urban future. In the coming decades we will see not just the escalation of cities over 10 million people but the development of connected megapolises to create massive economic powerhouses that dwarf our common understanding of the city. This will likely change the way that we think about urban infrastructure, how the metropolis works. We will no longer judge the city just on its internal strengths but, like Dubai Airport, on the power of its connections.

In 2007 Richard Florida and his team at the Martin Prosperity Institute decided to look at a global map of the world at night in order to discover not just where the great mega-cities of the world were, but also to see how they connected with other major conurbations. Comparing this data with other statistics such as GDP and population, they were able to work out that there were forty mega-regions in the world. In addition, they calculated that these regions were the fastest-growing areas of the globe – accounting for 1.5 billion people or 23 per cent of total population – as well as the most productive, accounting for 66 per cent of the world's output and 86 per cent of all innovation. The mega-region, in effect, is the end result of Geoffrey West's experiment in urban metabolism – the superlinear benefits of size.[9]

Some of these mega-regions had been identified for some time. The relationship between Washington, New York and Boston was first named in 1961 by the French geographer Jean Gottmann who came up with the word 'megapolis' to indicate a city growing so large that it was reaching outwards beyond sprawl. Gottmann meant it as a warning to overdevelopment, stretching out of control. Today the America 2050 organisation reports that there are eleven mega-regions across the US: the Arizona Sun Corridor, which includes Phoenix and Tucson; the Cascadia, which stretches from Seattle to Vancouver; the sun-belt cities of Florida from Miami to

Jacksonville; the Front Range, which stretches along the southern Rockies from Denver to Wyoming; the cities of the Great Lakes that include Chicago, Toronto, Detroit, all the way to Buffalo; the Gulf Coast; the northern corridor from New York to Boston; the Bay Area in California; the Piedmont Atlantic from Atlanta to Carolina; the southern Californian conurbation from San Diego to Las Vegas; and the Texas Triangle of Dallas, Fort Worth, Houston.

What is noticeable about these new mega-regions is that in most cases they are not defined by states; more than that they are not even restricted by national boundaries. It seems that being part of a mega-region has more influence on the economic prosperity of a place than the national government. This perhaps stretches plausibility when looking at Europe where the powers-that-be have decided to emphasise the nature of the economic union by defining two main mega-regions. The naming of the power regions does not help the economist's case: the Blue Banana – which begins in Liverpool in England – connects with London, Brussels, Paris, Frankfurt, Munich, Zurich and ends in Milan, northern Italy. This is in contrast with the sun-belt Golden Banana, which stretches along the Mediterranean from northern Spain to northern Italy.

Perhaps the most innovative development of a mega-region can be found on the planning desk of the Danish architect Bjarke Ingels, one of the most exciting thinkers about city design. In a short career Ingels has already started to make people think differently about the urban space they live in. His team has gained acclaim for what he calls the practice of 'hedonistic sustainability', designing buildings that are sustainable not because of what has been taken away in order to make them greener but because the architecture encourages enjoyment and increases quality of life. This is expressed in 8House in Southern Orestad, a suburb of Copenhagen, which offered housing, retail and offices in a vertical, twisting, layered village. Proximity increases efficiency, and everything is designed with the carbon footprint in mind: it is possible to bicycle around the whole complex without having to get off.

A similar sense of fun can be found in Ingels's designs for the Superkilen, a 33,000-square-metre playground in vibrant colours that provides a unique space for Copenhagen's children. Ingels realised that the neighbourhood of the proposed site contained fifty different ethnic groups and as a result the park gathers together the signs, colours, even the manhole covers from around the world. In some ways resembling something from *Yellow Submarine*, the half-mile-long park is a 'surrealist collection of global urban diversity that in fact reflects the true nature of the local neighbourhood'.[10] Ingels has also proposed a vast waste-to-energy incinerator plant in the centre of Copenhagen that doubles as a mountainous ski slope, and that also releases a smoke ring every time the plant emits 200 kilograms of carbon into the atmosphere.

At the Venice Biennale in 2010, Ingels launched his ideas to unite the Danish capital of Copenhagen and the southern Swedish city of Malmö. Currrently the two cities are connected by the Oresund Bridge, a four-lane superhighway that spans nearly 8 kilometres across the strait of water, which then links to the artificial island of Peberholm, after which the journey is completed through a 4-kilometre tunnel. The bridge was designed by George Rotne and opened in 2000. Ingels suggested that a Loop City should be created, connecting the two cities at two points around the Oresund Straits, developing a single urban link that crosses boundaries. The impact for Copenhagen would be like a release valve on the problems of population growth, spreading out the industrial corridor and increasing mobility as well as addressing climate-change issues. The design also included innovative architecture such as a living bridge, where houses and offices were built into the body of the piers.[11] As a new mega-region, reaching across boundaries as well as water, Ingels's vision is a vivid example of how our cities – and their limits – are growing out of our current definitions and assumptions.

The mega-regions of the future, however, need to be planned; they will not happen organically. The designs of smart infrastructure to link together urban centres – such as Ingels's living bridge – have to be bold, thought out in advance, and will undoubtedly be expensive. Such projects can also inflame political divisions, where parties can make capital out of proposing or opposing schemes. Thus while business interests might back a particular scheme – such as a new airport, more roads, or an industrial park – it can then often be attacked by protesters or local residents.

In the UK, the campaigning fervour of Nimby activists has been brought to bear in protest against most developments in recent years. However, the proposal of adding high-speed rail to the transport infrastructure is one of the hotly contested debates of the moment. The new train link, HS2, will connect England's second city to the capital, cutting travel times to forty minutes. This will have a big impact on both cities: in the next twenty years London's population is expected to grow by 1.3 million; there will also be an estimated 730,000 new jobs in the capital, mainly in the service sectors. Where are these people going to live? With a high-speed link to Birmingham, some of those jobs could be spread out to the Midlands; alternatively Birmingham might be able to support some of the population growth with its own economy. The alternative is that London grows and Birmingham will find it difficult to compete.

This is more than a debate between 'mega-regions' advocates and Nimbys. For its advocates, HS2 is an obvious sound investment, an infrastructure project that equates to Roosevelt's New Deal initiative of the 1930s. The ecological campaigners Friends of the Earth support the scheme because it will reduce carbon emissions. Yet HS2 will cost £33 billion, will not be completed until 2026 and, protesters say, will destroy countryside, villages and offer little provable economic value. The debate highlights another consequence of the rise of mega-cities and mega-regions. In the mind of politicians and planners, the economic power of the cities has become more important than the homes and livelihoods of the rest of the nation. The mega-regions are super-charged regions of creativity and productivity but they come at a price: the cost of expensive infrastructure projects but also the concerns of those who are affected or even excluded from their benefits.

This begs the question: do cities need countries any more? There are increasing signs of trends that cities are becoming independent of their surroundings, that London, Paris and Tokyo have more in common with each other than they do with Britain, France or Japan. When people ask me where I come from I am more likely to say 'London' than 'Britain'. Are we now citizens rather than patriots?

My city has become a world city: it is engaged with a global market but it has also absorbed people from around the planet. Today over 40 per cent of people in London were born into ethnic groups outside white British; there are over 300 languages spoken. I experience this multi-culture on a daily basis. In 1923 an 'Empire Exhibition' was held in neighbouring Wembley to display the wonders of the British Imperial reach. Now Wembley is the most diverse community in Europe. Where once London was the capital of the world, it is now the world within a city.

My neighbourhood itself has a strong Irish community that moved here in the nineteenth century to work on the local railways; at the end of my street is the Catholic church, which is always full on Sundays. Across the road from the church is a mosque that is becoming so popular that the local council is concerned about parking congestion. We also have a Hindi Cultural Centre. A few streets away an Afghan community has developed and runs a series of shops along the high street. Early every morning, by the builders' depot, groups of Eastern European labourers congregate in all weathers, hoping to pick up some work in the city's bustling construction sites. Thus, the vastness of the globalised market interweaves with the intricate threads of the local.

We live in an age of hyper-mobility and this is most clearly seen on our own streets. You are no longer defined solely by where you are born, and you are more likely to travel – sometimes long distances – in order to find a job. Once this would have entailed a carriage ride from the provinces to the capital; today it is a long-haul flight across oceans and national borders. Thus the rise of mega-cities, mega-regions and the world city will not happen 'over there' but around you. But the world city is a different place from one we have experienced so far: it forces new levels of social toleration and mixture. As a result the city is more than just a crucible where cultures come together and mix; it is a place where something completely new is formed.

In the past few decades Los Angeles has been reinvented as a Latino city. In the 2010 census, 47.7 per cent of the city's population was Latino or Hispanic, as opposed to 27 per cent white non-Hispanics, 8.7 per cent black and 13.7 per cent Asian. As leading urban sociologist Saskia Sassen points out, the city disguises great differences within this group: LA is often called the second city of Mexico, but also has a larger Salvadorian population than San Salvador itself. These groups are intermixing: 14 per cent of all Mexican Angelenos are married to members of other ethnic groups (this percentage increases to 50 per cent in New York and Miami). The Latino community is becoming a city within a city, but at the same time LA is becoming increasingly Latinised, thus redefining what it means to be a southern Californian.

In his book *Magical Urbanism*, Mike Davis looks at how the geography of LA has been transformed by the Latino community, creating an enclave within the metropolitan centre, focused in the old central manufacturing district, while the valleys, beaches and surrounding hills remain 'Anglo-majority' neighbourhoods. In addition, the Latino community has also become concentrated in particular areas of the economy: services, catering, light manufacturing, home construction. These neighbourhoods are transformed: the shops and the streets are different, the music pumping from the windows, the fast food being sold from sidewalk vendors. In the suburb of Southgate you can even see the difference in the colours the houses are painted. The community also encourages alternative urban spaces and *placitas* or small plazas have been retrofitted into the city plan. As Davis observes:

> All of Latin America is now a dynamo turning the lights back on in the dark spaces of North American cities. While there is lots of abstract talk in planning and architectural schools about the need to 'reurbanise' American cities, there is little recognition that Latino and Asian immigrants are already doing this on an epic scale.[12]

Today, Marseilles, the French port on the Mediterranean, is the first European city to become a majority Muslim community, as a result of the significant immigration of people from the Magreb. It has long been a joke that Marseilles is in fact the first African stop-off on the famous Paris to Dakar road race. Yet walking through the city, this otherness is not the only thing one appreciates.

Along the Vieux Port during the summer of 2012, there was a sense that Marseilles was searching for a new identity on a number of different levels. It had already been named the 2013 European City of Culture and preparations were apace on getting things ready. The historical neighbourhood, once famously seedy and exciting, was being turned into the largest pedestrianised area in Europe. Historic buildings, the glories of civic pride, were being spruced and cleaned. Marseilles was transforming itself from a thriving port that had seen better days, into a heritage site, forgetting the intervening decades of history.

Yet only a street away, going from the centre up to the Place Notre-Dame-du-Mont, one quickly found a different space. At the foot of the hill there was a series of Moroccan shops selling piles of olives, scoops of brightly coloured spices. Further up the road was a fabric store filled to the roof with bolts of highly tinted cloth from central Africa. As the evening was drawing in a barbecue was being set up outside a small café promising specialities from the Cap Verte.

Being in the centre was obviously no way of seeing the complete panoply of the city. Rather it was still at the peripheries, amongst the *banlieus*, where the new Marseilles was evolving. Nonetheless, even here one got the impression that a new city was growing out of the fabric of the old, that the new arrivals were adapting and using the traditional social spaces to find a compromise with the European way of doing things. In those corners of the city Marseilles was not just French, or just Africa, but something in between.

It is exactly this energetic mixing of cultures that ignites the genius of the metropolis. As we become increasingly mobile, the city will become globally connected and as the network gets stronger, so it starts to develop its own identity. This is what urban theorist Saskia Sassen means when she talks about 'the global city'. Globalisation has unified the urban experience: those who live inside the city have more in common than those outside. There is a set of norms, a code of conduct to living in the city, a passport that allows one to move from city to city, east to west, without having to change. For Sassen, the global city is a by-product of the globalised economy: our sense of citizenship determined by our place within the worldwide market that influences our behaviour, hopes and fears. The great cities of the world – London, New York and Tokyo – have become 'one transterritorial marketplace'.[13]

There are, therefore, consequences of this worldwide network of cities; for the metropolis is not just a mixture of cultures but a vector of markets. Take the relationship between a house foreclosure in Florida and ramifications of the toxic credit default swap – an incomprehensible financial instrument created to hedge the subprime mortgage market – in banks around the world. A family arranged a loan to buy their own home, to become part of their community. Yet this promise of repayment and the payment schedule were bundled together with similar promises from other families, businesses and institutions, and then sold off once again in packages that supposedly balanced out the riskier bets with more safe investments. After 2008, when families suddenly found that they could no longer honour their agreements, a shock wave juddered through the worldwide financial system. No one who had been involved in this network of transactions was safe.

The global network is highly interdependent, and even without the calamity of the international banking crisis, another example shows us how the activities in one city can have an impact on another. Many of the leading high-street retailers in London and New York have their underwear and cotton goods manufactured in Chittagong, Bangladesh. The factories moved there in the 1960s when it became too expensive to have the goods made in the traditional factories of Bradford in the north-west of Britain. Yet, since 2010, Bangladeshi garment workers have been campaigning for a minimum wage.

Earlier that year the government had raised the limit from $25 to $45 per month, but the workers claimed the factory owners had not implemented the policy. These factories supply outlets such as Walmart, Tesco, H&M, Zara, Carrefour, Gap, Metro, JCPenney, Marks & Spencer, Kohl's, Levi Strauss and Tommy Hilfiger. In more than one case, the companies are now looking for new factories in China and elsewhere with lower costs and fewer industrial disturbances. The garment industry provides $10 billion annually to Bangladesh and the government is determined to keep its workforce competitive. This has resulted in violent clashes, strikes and vicious disputes as the workers defend their rights, even if it jeopardises their own competitiveness with other markets.[14]

We have now reached the end of an era when the world was divided between the 'developed' and the 'developing' world. The impact of the 2008 credit crunch on the world's cities offers a very sobering overview of the global economy. In terms of the world's leading cities, the rate of urban growth of New York, Tokyo, London (0.35 per cent; 0.6 per cent; 0.8 per cent respectively) is almost flatlining; 'developed' could easily be mistaken for stagnant. Elsewhere, as we have seen, in the rust-belt cities like Detroit, as well as in the former Soviet nations of Eastern Europe, some cities are, in fact, in decline. By contrast, the rate of development of cities such as Karachi, Pakistan (4.9 per cent), Luanda, Angola (4.7 per cent) or Beijing (4.5 per cent), shows that parts of the world are urbanising at an impressive velocity.

For the foreseeable future cities like my home, London, and New York will maintain their economic predominance; elsewhere, the remainder of the leaders' pack will be shuffled. In the 2012 Wealth Report produced by estate agents Knight Frank and Citibank, the top ten cities that matter today, and in ten years' time, show the rapid movement towards the east:

2012	2022
London	London
New York	New York
Hong Kong	Beijing
Paris	Shanghai
Singapore	Singapore
Miami	Hong Kong
Geneva	Paris
Shanghai	São Paulo
Beijing	Geneva
Berlin	Berlin.[15]

London is in the fortunate position of being able to charge the best prices for the luxuries that it offers. As a financial and legal capital it attracts many of the major institutions as well as high-net-wealth individuals who enjoy the benefits of a light-touch fiscal policy and regulations as well as the level of expertise within the city financial services. But the rich do not come to London simply because of the advantageous non-domicile tax policy; the city also delivers on top-quality culture, fashion and liveability. It is a place where the rich want to visit, invest and consume. The city has thus benefited economically from an increase in the share of the world's financial markets (from 2 per cent in 1998 to 3.7 per cent in 2008) as well as through promoting an open, welcoming culture.

Yet this position is not secure. According to the 2012 *Honor Chapman Report* produced by a group of leading land-management firms, London needs to remain competitive over the next decade. The report warns that the city needs to attract new industries to reinforce global leadership. Other concerns include a low standard of education within the city itself, making a home-grown knowledge economy more difficult to launch; the high price of property and the failures of an ambitious housing policy; the problems with infrastructure such as rail and airports; the increasing gulf between the political needs of the city and the UK at large; and the failure to establish itself as a leader in sustainability.[16]

In particular, London is forced to consider its competitiveness not only against historic rivals such as Amsterdam, Paris or New York but also against a new group of emerging economies that seem supercharged in comparison, especially a rapidly transforming urban China. At the start of 2012 it was estimated that 691 million people lived in the cities of mainland China, nearly double the figure – 389 million – of the mid-1980s. In other words, one out of every twenty-five people in the world today moved to a Chinese city in the last thirty years. And this will continue. By 2030 China will be 70 per cent urban, having started off as 26 per cent urban in 1990. These huge numbers of people are spread out over 800 cities, with the expectation of 15–20 million new arrivals settling down every year. In terms of housing, the state needs to provide a new Greater Chicago annually to respond to demand.

The Chinese were building impressive cities long before the first gates were constructed in Europe. Evidence of the first cities can be found in the Shang Dynasty dating to about 1600 BCE in places like Banpo. From that moment the character for 'wall' – *cheng* – was the same as for city. The early Chinese cities were also highly symbolically designed. Chengzhou, which was created as a holy refuge by the Duke of Zhou in 1136 BCE, was designed to follow intricate cosmological rules, so that the order of the heavens could be reflected in the same equilibrium on earth. The design was so successful that the Duke's ideas, called the Zhouli, influenced urban planning throughout the empire for the following centuries.

As was seen from Marco Polo's description of Beijing nearly 2,500 years later, the Chinese city has always been strictly regimented. In addition to a celestial order, other readings of the universe – I Ching, feng shui and geomancy – were used to devise the Imperial City, to reflect the rigid human hierarchy. This remained a constant until the arrival of European merchants in the nineteenth century, when the economic demands of international trade forced the city to absorb foreign plans.

Foreign communities developed in Shanghai after the first Opium War in the 1840s, making the port a multicultural entrepot. This had an impact on the port as well as the fabric of the city, as ex-pats brought their own ways and customs with them. The Bund, a wide road running along the Huangpu river, became a showcase for the finest in European architecture. The French Concession, a section of land given to the French government in 1849, became renowned for its shops as well as its distinctive domestic architecture, which seemed to transport a hotchpotch of styles from colonial plantation to Art Deco, ranged along avenues lined with British plane trees.

During the Mao era, Shanghai remained a formidable trading city, as well as a hotbed of radical ideas. Nevertheless, the revolution made little impact upon the fabric of the city. Between 1949 and the late 1970s, Shanghai generated over $350 billion yuan in taxes for the central government, but 99 per cent of this was redistributed to smaller cities in the heartland. It was not until 1980 that a new era of super-development rocketed into being. That year the central government decided that four secondary cities – Shenzen, Zhuhai, Shantou and Xiamen – should be opened up to foreign investment. Four years later fourteen other major metropolises – including Shanghai – were added to the list of 'open cities'.

Between the 1970s and the 2000s the nature of the urban Chinese economy was transformed: where once 70 per cent of the population worked in the public sector, this was reduced to 25 per cent; by contrast the private sector exploded, rising from 4.7 per cent of the workforce to 20.8 per cent. Foreign investment started to pour in; according to one estimate, $10 billion a year since 1992. Shanghai's economy itself galloped, growing at 15 per cent a year. In 2011 the city's GDP peaked at 1.92 trillion yuan. But this success brought with it huge demands. Between 2000 and 2010, the population rose by 13 per cent, to over 23 million. Included within this are 9 million long-term migrants who are working despite the Hukou system.

This urbanisation has had an impact on China's creativity, which is a further threat to established centres like London. The new mega-regions that encircle Beijing, Shanghai and Hong Kong house 25 per cent of the nation's population, but produce 68 per cent of China's economic output. While it is often assumed that this rise is due solely to manufacturing, China's cultural creative industry is in fact growing faster than the annual GDP. In 2007 GDP in Beijing, Shanghai and Shenzhen grew by 12.3 per cent, 13.3 per cent and 15 per cent respectively, while the creative industry of these three cities increased by 19.4 per cent, 22.8 per cent and 25.9 per cent. Part of this is a result of a government-driven attempt to develop 'creative clusters', cultural quarters within existing cities, just like Tech City.

This, in turn, produces a positive feedback loop, the creativity encouraging more innovation, resulting in a vibrant art scene that is becoming increasingly popular as well as a ready market. Between 1996 and 2001 the number of registered patents from these cities – one way of auditing the creativity of a metropolis – rose by 400 per cent. In 2008 Beijing was producing as many patents as Seattle, home of Microsoft, while Shanghai has become as creative as Toronto. Just as in Amsterdam in the seventeenth century, China's new industrial power is inspiring a real cultural revolution. Some observers, such as Richard Florida, have commented that it might take up to twenty years before China produces its first Steve Jobs or Bill Gates. But twenty years is not actually that far away; it suggests that the seeds have already been planted.

Shanghai offers a mixed picture of what the future of urbanism might look like. It is just one example of the explosion of urban China and how an authoritarian government is attempting to manage its economic transformation through the city. While the growth of Shanghai, Beijing and Wuhan are well known, it is also going on in places we rarely hear about. In 1970 there were 200 cities in China; today there are over 700, over 160 with a population of more than 1 million; in the US there are only nine, and four in the UK. Will the sheer force of numbers change the way the city works?

The rebirth of Shanghai since the 1980s has been a sustained period of 'creative destruction' – the city has not just grown beyond its traditional boundaries, it has been razed to the ground and rebuilt at the same time. In the 1990s more people in Shanghai were displaced, their homes destroyed and rebuilt, than over thirty years in the whole of the US; between 1992 and 2004 this amounted to 925 million square feet. It was also claimed that half of the world's cranes can be found in the Pudong District, which has become the new city centre.

It was in the Pudong District, in the former rice fields to the east of the Huangpu river, that the authorities first dreamed of a modern city in the 1980s; it was even renamed 'the head of the dragon' by President Deng Xiaoping himself. From this discarded agricultural land a new city was to be born, divided into the Jinqiao Export Processing Zone, the Waigaoqiao Free Trade Zone and, most important of all, the Lujiazui Financial and Trade District as well as a deep-water port leading to the Yangzte river to take the goods manufactured in the factories of the city to the rest of the world.

Of these districts, Lujiazui would be the centrepiece of the metropolis, a 'golden zone' dedicated to capital. It was decided therefore that just as the marketplace was being opened up to foreign investors, so the district itself should be put into the hands of foreign designers. At first a team of French planners led by Joseph Belmont, who was instrumental in the Grands Projets of Mitterrand in the 1980s, were consulted, while the plans of local designers were ignored by Shanghai mayor Zhu Rongji. Yet the authorities did not want to hand over plans to a single office; rather they wished to maintain control of the reins while also attracting international attention and expertise.

Belmont then delivered a list of eight super-architects who were invited to participate in a consultancy: Renzo Piano, Jean Nouvel, Norman Foster, Kazua Shinohara and four others: Richard Rogers, Toyo Ito, Dominique Perrault and Massimiliano Fuksas who, in May 1992, were the only ones flown over to the site – which was already being prepared by demolition experts – and asked to submit proposals. But rather than adopting one single plan, the authorities took the best of each design and mixed them – in effect, celebrating the symbols of the mega-city without deciding on an urban philosophy to bring all the parts together.

Lujiazui is not exactly a city but a forest of icons to business, heralded by the completion of the Pearl of the Orient, the broadcasting tower that stands on a promontory of the river. Appearing like the Eiffel Tower adapted for the TV cartoon *Futurama*, and designed by a team from the local Shanghai East China Institute of Architectural Design, the Pearl was the first skyscraper that broke the skyline in 1993, standing 1,535 feet tall. Since then, the district has become a laboratory for urban experimentation, not just in towering architecture but also infrastructure that is sorely tested as it copes with the rapidly growing numbers of cars in the city. In addition the underground subway system currently has a capacity of 1.4 million people a day, but plans are afoot to increase this by 500 per cent.

Shanghai also boasts the fastest train system in the world, built to connect the centre with the ever-expanding periphery.

Shanghai is an example – like Dubai – of building a global city from scratch. There is nothing organic or unplanned about any of this. Take, for example, Century Avenue, which begins at the Pearl TV tower and then runs 3 miles to the east. At its outset, the Hong Kong architect Tao Ho had warned that the planners should be careful not to be seduced by the notion of modern urbanism as purely a collection of tall buildings; and yet the Shanghai designers did just that. As a result, rather than an impressive, bustling urban centre, the main thoroughfare of the city is a combination of a Texan expressway with the hubristic hauteur of a Parisian rue de Rivoli.

The results are plain to see. Despite the warnings, the city authorities wanted their route to be 'one metre wider than the Champs-Elyśees'[17] and a showcase of impressive skyscrapers. But the plans never developed the packed density of Manhattan, the thrilling juxtaposition of lively streets and business district: the sense that here the whole world was coming together to do a deal. Instead, the buildings are ordered and divided by broad public spaces where no one is in a hurry and which are virtually empty throughout the day. The buildings do not scale into the air because of the intense competition for space within the district but because each developer wants an instant icon. The Avenue itself is 330 feet across, and includes an eight-lane road, four bicycle lanes and pavements so wide that gardens and public art have been added to give some sense of a human scale.

Century Avenue is the opposite of Jane Jacobs's Hudson Street, and perhaps it will never gain the complexity required truly to become a city; many even question whether instead it is a suburban industrial park planted within an urban centre. One might also wonder whether this was a different type of urbanism, a new

Chinese model, and its strangeness is only the result of looking at it through western eyes. But what of the people?

As real estate became increasingly expensive within Shanghai, the housing market boomed alongside the business market. From the 1990s many people were moved out of their traditional houses in the urban centre to make way for office blocks and as a result were rehoused in new tenements and flats. Rather than living in houses, people are now living on top of each other, so that nearly 50 per cent of the total population live in space that covers only 5 per cent of the land in the city. Yet as the populations continued to grow, even these towers did not respond to the rising demand. In 1980 there were 121 buildings at a height of over eight storeys; by 2005 this number had increased to 10,045. This new style of vertical living also had an impact on the way people interacted, as the life on the street needed to be replaced by new public spaces.

Since 1999, Shanghai has grown at the astonishing rate of 20 million square metres every year, and part of this has included a spread outwards as the city sprawled in all directions. One of these schemes, launched in 2006, was to build a whole new city and nine new towns on Shanghai's outskirts, with a combined population of 5.4 million. These new settlements are to be connected to the centre through a high-speed rail link. In addition, a further sixty new towns with a population of 50,000 each are to be planned and built within the next decade.

As they formulated the One City, Nine Towns project, the planners wanted to confirm Shanghai's new status as a global city within the designs themselves. And as a result the plans for each of the nine towns were handed over to a foreign designer, commissioned to bring their own native urbanism to the project. Therefore Thames Town in Songjiang New City, 40 kilometres from the centre, is a model English Tudor village, with cobbled streets and red telephone boxes. The

CORBIS

Thames Town from the air, a fantasy of Britishness

architects, Atkins Design, claimed that the borough crammed '500 years of British architecture into a five-year construction project'.[18] The Disney theme continues and is brought to stark relief in the German town, Anting, close to Shanghai International Automobile City, where the Volkswagon factory and Formula 1 track can be found, and was designed by Albert Speer, the son of Hitler's favourite architect. The Swedish town, Luodian, is close to the Volvo factory, and is based on a very idiosyncratic interpretation of the Nordic style, even appropriating the iconic mermaid statue from Copenhagen. There are also Spanish, Dutch, Italian and American-themed settlements.

Yet the massive development of housing highlights some of the problems of Shanghai's urban miracle. While the shape of One City, Nine Towns has been painstakingly plotted by the designers, it has been built by speculators and there have been a number of noticeable failures. In Anting, few of the houses face east–west, as is

Chinese tradition. There is still no regular train service to Thames Town and so the settlement is usually empty, except at the weekend when people come to take photos. Often the foreign planners failed to communicate adequately with the local developers, and low skills and poor-quality materials mean that many of the buildings are showing stress even before the project is completed. The Dutch architects even walked away in exasperation.

Is this the future? While we watch the economic rise of China in awe, there are perhaps other scales that we need to measure. For there seems to be no sense of how one should behave in these hybrid, hyper-modern citadels. Shanghai seems to be a mega-city in its building schemes, massive infrastructure and population, but has it become complex enough to herald a new way of urban living? The Chinese have a word, *suzhu*, to promote all the good qualities expected of the new citizen. But how do we define this 'quality' needed to thrive in the metropolis?

This rapid transformation of urban life is something that the west has not seen since the nineteenth century with the exponential growth of industrial cities such as Manchester and Chicago. In my suburban street in London, I am living in the dying glow of this historic moment. Despite a constant churn of new building and improved infrastructure, it is unlikely London or New York will ever expand and change as they once did. But sometimes it takes time for a community to adapt to the changes around it.

Looking out of my window at the houses across the road, they would probably not seem out of place in Thames Town. They are neatly constructed, appropriating the historic signatures of Tudor architecture but with twentieth-century materials. When they were first developed they were built to attract the new middle classes who desired space and a domestic haven a short train's commuting distance from the office. The outward designs signalled the first golden age of

England – the land of Elizabeth I, Shakespeare and Sir Francis Drake – in the hope of reviving the nation's self-confidence in the face of a disconcertingly changing world. In contrast, Shanghai does not raid the past to applaud its own continuity, culture and significance; rather it takes the world and makes it both modern and local.

Yet it cannot appropriate the ballet of the streets. The houses along my street, despite their architectural uniformity, are a home for the world, and as families move in and out, some residents die and new tenants arrive, we have slowly developed a way of living together – a code of conduct that includes weak ties, neighbourliness and the cultivation of a certain amount of trust. We notice when a family has builders and scaffolding goes up around the outside of the house. We hold parcels for each other if the postman comes and someone is out. My children go and play with the children of other families. In June 2012 some neighbours organised a Jubilee party, the road was blocked at both ends and a long table placed down the centre where tea was served for everybody. It is these small things that we do for each other that keeps the city alive. These new communities – the appropriations of the One City, Nine Towns scheme, just as much as the burgeoning megacities and mega-regions – have to find their own dance that fits the rhythms of the time and particular genius of place. In exactly the same manner, I have to listen to the changing steps of the performance outside my own front door and adjust accordingly.

This is the heart of the relationship between the place called home and the wider global changes that are transforming the city: they are not two different worlds, beyond touch, but are intricately connected. Today what happens in faraway places has an impact on our streets. The ways that cities work make us part of a larger network, and this should encourage us to be citizens rather than to resign from participation.

Epilogue
AFTER HUDSON STREET

Halfway down the High Line, I found a bench shaded from the main route where I could sit for a moment and watch the other visitors go by. This is one of the joys of the city: people watching; seeing families together, children running ahead while the adults chat away; couples talking as if there is no one else around; people going up to the flowers and plants checking on their own knowledge of urban horticulture. These are brief moments when there is no one nearby, the flow of bodies reduced to a trickle when one can imagine that one is almost alone. At times like this it is difficult to remember that cities can be hard, dangerous places.

Leaving the High Line at the southern exit on Gansevoort Street and returning to city level, I was thrown back into the throng. But it was a short walk towards Chelsea, where I had come to make a pilgrimage to 555 Hudson Street, the home of Jane Jacobs and where she wrote *The Death and Life of Great American Cities*. I did not really know what I was expecting but I was not disappointed.

Hudson Street was larger than I had imagined; there was little traffic that afternoon but this was clearly a busy route. The White Horse Bar was still there, suitably shabby, a memorial to a particular kind of bohemian night. The bar-room itself had changed little from the photographs that showed Jacobs herself seated at the bar. There were tables and seats outside on the pavement, filled with people, talking and drinking, enjoying the heat. There was a café at the other end of the block, and a small hole-in-the-wall Mexican counter. The street was ramshackle: different-coloured awnings fronted the row of shops, there were bicycles tied up to lamp posts, two garden benches stood outside one shop where neighbours were encouraged to enjoy the shade, a table and chairs sat by the window of a dog parlour. A launderette was next door to a sushi shop, near a real-estate office.

Number 555 itself was inconspicuous. There was no plaque or sign as one might find in London, celebrating the former inhabitant. Instead the large front window advertised Glassybaby – 'Flowers wilt, chocolates melt, Glassybaby forever' – with a row of hand-blown glass

555 Hudson Street

candleholders running along the mantel. The door itself was even more anonymous, with three brass numbers screwed above the pane, slightly lopsided. This was exactly the kind of place I imagined Jacobs would have lived; the inspiration behind her celebration of the ordinary, regular and yet idiosyncratic. It was a reminder once again that even the greatest cities were built from such places, and that these were the spaces from where we should measure the city's success. The life of the street was the reason why cities are good for us.

In 2004 Jane Jacobs wrote what would become her last book, *Dark Ages Ahead*. By this time she had left New York and moved to Toronto. She had abandoned the US in 1968 because she did not want her two boys to be conscripted into the Vietnam War. In Canada, she continued to campaign for her belief in the life of the city, and was a central figure in the protests that halted plans for the Spadina Expressway, as well as fighting for the renovation of the St Lawrence neighbourhood in Toronto. She also involved herself in the heated Quebec sovereignty issue, arguing that cities should become increasingly separate from countries.

Her final book, however, was an unexpectedly gloomy view of the future, a call to save ourselves before it was too late. In it, she predicted the breakdown of the communities that made up the city. In her argument, the sources of these problems did not necessarily come from the city itself but rather the decline of the family in the face of the neo-liberal market; the death of scholarship in our universities as students pursued credentials rather than learning; the elevation of economics as the predominant 'science' so that every idea had to be productive; the takeover of government by big corporations; and finally, what she saw as a culture of short-term satisfaction. While all these factors did not come from the city, the results were most apparent in the decline of the fabric and the failure of the urban infrastrucure. The city itself was becoming a dangerous place because of the failures of planners, researchers and politicians to notice the signs of decay.

This prognosis was most clearly explained in the example of the Chicago heatwave of 1995, when over one week more than 730 died from heat exhaustion, dehydration and kidney failure, despite warnings from meteorologists and the media that dangerous weather was on its way. During those blistering hot days, the hospitals found it impossible to cope. In a vain attempt to help, an owner of a fleet of refrigeration trucks offered his vehicles to store the dead, but he soon found that they were filled with the bodies of the poor, infirm and elderly, and he could carry no more. Afterwards the autopsies told a grim tale: the majority of the dead were old people who had run out of water, or had been stuck in flats without air conditioning, abandoned by their neighbours.

In response to the crisis, a team from the US Center for Disease Control and Prevention scoured the city for the causes of such a high number of deaths, in the hope that they could prevent the disaster in another place at another time. The results were predictable: the people who died had failed to find help or refuge. In effect, the report, as Jacobs pointed out, had blamed the dead for their failure to leave their flats or to ensure that they had enough water and that the air conditioning was working. Yet Jacobs offers an alternative scenario, telling the story of Eric Klinenberg, who did his own research on the heatwave, independently of the official scientists; rather than focusing on the faults of individuals, he looked at the districts that were worst hit by the disaster. For example, there were forty deaths per 100,000 people in the North Lawndale neighbourhood, while in South Lawndale there were only four deaths per 100,000. Why was this?

Klinenberg's research examined the differences between the two communities, revealing findings that put an emphasis on neighbourhood failures rather than individual folly. North Lawndale was a community in decline; it had nowhere for old people to go: no stores, gathering places or parks. As a result there was no functioning community to look out for the most vulnerable in times of trouble. The failures of the district had been a long-term problem and could be charted systematically: it had lost many residents to the suburbs and these numbers had not been replaced by newcomers. The local shops found the market slowing up and had also moved on. As the eyes on the street became fewer, so too did the sense of community. Klinenberg showed that it was not the individuals who should be blamed but the community as a whole. Why had this neighbourhood been allowed to wither and fade away? Who was watching? Who was looking the other way?

Yet if we are honest, we can find similar neighbourhoods closer to home, in every city. They are not the slums, but they are struggling. The crime rate is higher than it used to be. The fabric of the streets is looking slightly too shabby, the shops are closing, and perhaps the library is empty. Too often we wait until the community burns in a riot, or falls into disaster before we act. But are we too late? Have Jacobs's predictions of the impending Dark Age come to pass already?

I don't think so.

Yet one might have been forgiven for thinking the worst when watching the impact of Hurricane Sandy upon New York in November 2012. The super storm occurred as I was reading through these pages for the final time and it underscored some of the more pessimistic feelings that many have towards the city, and indeed the future. The natural disaster battered the Five Boroughs and the aftermath was an unnerving reminder of the fragility of the city.

As the water rose and started to fill Lower Manhattan, it was proof that not even Wall Street was beyond the reach of nature; as the lights went out – and stayed out for days afterwards – there was a strange awareness of the possibility of this kind of disaster happening more often, anywhere in the world.

The stories that came out of that single night of terrible weather highlight the many different faces of New York. In addition to the blackout, the infrastructure of the city broke down: the subway system was flooded and filled with silt and debris. The images from Staten Island showed whole neighbourhoods being flattened by the floods as cars were picked up by the rising waters and dumped, like flotsam. Meanwhile in Breezy Point, Queens, an exploding generator caused a fire across a number of blocks and destroyed more than a hundred homes. And then there were the human stories: the patients of NYU Langone Medical Center, Manhattan, who were evacuated *en masse* as the winds picked up after the hospital's back-up generator failed; the young policeman in Staten Island who drowned trying to save his family; Glenda Moore, a black woman trapped in her SUV in South Beach who lost her two children when they were ripped from her arms by the flood waters. When she went in search of help, nearby residents refused to open their doors to her.

If this is the future of the city then surely dark days are ahead? Perhaps, but this is also why so many urban thinkers are talking about the importance of resilience. Not even a city mayor such as Michael Bloomberg can stand amidst the wreckage of Sandy and tell us that everything is fine and that a disaster of this magnitude will never happen again. We have to accept that events like Hurricane Sandy cannot be designed out of the city's future; there will be natural disasters and human catastrophes. However, the true measure of a healthy and just city must be seen in how the metropolis survives and builds itself back up again.

As government agencies like FEMA, the City's transport

engineers and small businesses ready themselves to open up again, and on-the-ground activists like Occupy Sandy do their best to bring the city back to life, we need to ask, how will the city recover? Will it regain its feet and learn the lessons of these terrible events? Might it even become a better place? Will Sandy change the way we think about the reality of climate change? This is the true test of the resilient city; that it is, in the words of the economist Nassim Nicholas Taleb, 'unfragile'; that it can withstand the tumult and build itself back up again and, most importantly, that it loses none of its freedoms as it faces an uncertain future.

Thinking about a better city is often dismissed as utopian dreaming, and there is a long history of planners, politicians and architects who have imagined such a dazzling mirage. Thomas Moore's *Utopia* itself was a sly joke on a place that did not exist, in contrast to 'eutopia', the ideal metropolis. And this ideal has taken many forms: it has found political legs respectively in Plato's Republic, Karl Marx's communism and Henri Lefevbre's Right to the City, which all sought in different ways to construct the best society out of the human power structures that make up the city. Planners like Patrick Geddes, Le Corbusier and Ebeneezer Howard also hoped to find paradise in the creation of its physical form. For economists, the city is the ideal marketplace where trade can flourish: for some this means the complete liberty and freedom of exchange without restrictions; for others it requires laws and regulation. Meanwhile, for thinkers such as Scott Burnham, the city can be a place that – if we get it right – has the capacity to encourage and nurture trust. As we have seen, there have been many historic examples of cities that were built to change our behaviour – to suppress revolution, to make us more rational, to encourage us to kiss – and often this has had unexpected results. Even today we can find architects, planners and politicians who think that they have the design solution to making the city a place that might make us greener, fitter, smarter – perhaps even happier.

The ways that we come together have changed over the centuries, and this has had a huge impact on how we interact and behave with each other. Walking through New York, heading southwards along Hudson Street, it is hard to forget that Manhattan is a nineteenth-century city, created on a grid first set out in 1811. Looking up to the skyline, one can still see water towers on top of the brick buildings that were created after Elisha Otis's technological innovation, the safety elevator, which allowed architects to scale over five storeys high for the first time. We can see similar creative and engineering innovation in Sir Joseph Bazalgette's London, Baron Haussmann's Paris, Boston after the fire of 1872, the San Francisco that was built from the rubble of the 1906 earthquake. These were cities born of an engineer's dream. Today, we have as much right as those Victorian masters to think the city anew. Yet we must not repeat their mistakes.

As the Victorians saw the city as a problem that could be reconstituted by buildings and infrastructure – railways, lifts and sewers – today we see our own city in a different view: it is a complex, connected place constructed around people. In addition, unlike the historic metropolis, this city is not a problem that can be rationalised and ordered. Rather we must understand its intricate nature and work with this counterintuitive rhythm rather than against it. The acknowledgement that we live life on the edge of chaos should not stop us from dreaming of a better city. By understanding the city more we can make it a better place. We must trust that the metropolis brings out the best aspects of ourselves: trusting, open individuals working within something that is bigger than each of us.

As I walked from Hudson Street, I acknowledged that it was

Jacobs who taught me that it is the people that matter, the way that they are allowed to interact, intermingle and connect. In addition, that the street is the essential, energetic measure of the life of the city. As Jacobs reminded us, if we can make sense of the street, we can then hope to reconstruct the life of the city in a way that is for the benefit of all.

Finally, I reached Washington Square, the heart of the Chelsea neighbourhood, where Jane Jacobs helped in her first campaign against Robert Moses's systematic reduction of the city to the logic of the automobile. There, I watched the world seemingly come together. There were a couple of jazz players, energetically thumping their instruments; couples were lying on the grass, oblivious to the people around them. There was a group of young students giving away bottles of chilled water. Another group had erected a tent near the arch and showed the new Citibank bike scheme to anyone who was interested to sign up. There were some office workers, perhaps from the nearby university buildings, who were quietly chewing on their lunch. There were a couple of sleepers on the benches opposite, but no one disturbed them. There also seemed to be people from around the globe, a reminder that this was a world city.

From a place like this we can dream of the ideal city without losing perspective or becoming utopian. Thinking of the city at this local level makes change seem possible, a place where the individual can make a difference. It is from here that one can campaign for a local community garden, as can be found in East Village; it is at this scale that we have seen the most successful attempts to revive the neighbourhoods of Detroit; it is making a difference at this local level that drove Colin Beavan to stand for the Green Party of America and start his campaign in Brooklyn. And from this base, great things can emerge, as proven by the work of Betterblock.org:

the right message spreading rapidly, networks combining, neighbourhoods becoming cities, the street talking to city hall.

Nevertheless, it is wrong not to acknowledge that the city can also be the opposite of Utopia, and history has shown us that dreaming of the ideal metropolis can sometimes result in terrible hardship. Cities are extraordinary economic engines of wealth and innovation, but this same mechanism can cause terrible inequality and poverty. Throughout history, cities have risen and fallen and one need only look at the ruins of Uruk or the desperate situation of Dharavi and wonder what part bad luck, fate or poor governance played in such devastation. Yet we should be very careful about coming up with easy answers. The answer to the slum cannot be found in exposing it to the marketplace, but searching for a solution from within the community.

While living and acting locally, we cannot become myopically parochial: the world is changing beyond the neighbourhood at an alarming pace. Most importantly, we must acknowledge that 'the west' does not offer the only road map for the city of the twenty-first century. Today, planners, politicians and urban thinkers can no longer seek answers for local problems from America and Europe. As we have seen in Songdo and Masdar, the latest technological innovations are not being tested in Europe or America. It is Singapore and Shanghai that lead the world as the business centres of the future. South America – the cities of Santiago de Chile, Curitiba, Rio de Janeiro, Bogotá and Medellín – is developing the most pertinent political models of how to run a city. Meanwhile, Beijing, Mumbai, Nairobi, Dhaka and Islamabad – and many other cities in Asia and Africa – are facing the brunt of the largest human migration that the world has ever seen. This enormous movement of bodies raises issues of healthcare, housing, sustainability and opportunities, but also tips the balance of world power away from its traditional centres. By the end of the century this transformation might have revolutionised our understanding of what is a city.

Yet, despite this anxiety of change, there are three key areas that we can, and must, address in order to make the dream of the new city a possibility: sustainability, trust and inequality. What is surprising, however, is that these three factors are inextricably linked: you cannot have a green city without trust and more equality; you cannot have equality without trust; there is no city at all without trust. Trust is a process that comes out of the smallest of gestures, the everyday performance of neighbourliness. If we can start here, then it is possible to dream of what else can be achieved.

This is the city I want to live in. This is a future worth hoping for.

NOTES

PREFACE: ON THE HIGH LINE

1. Hallo, W., 'Antediluvian Cities', *Journal of Cuneiform Studies*, Volume 23, no. 3, 1971, p. 57.
2. Rousseau, J.-J., www.memo.fr/en/dossier
3. Rae, D., *Urbanism and its End*, Yale University Press, 2003, p.225.

CHAPTER 1: WHAT IS A CITY?

1. Jacobs, J., *The Economy of Cities*, Pelican, 1972, p. 42.
2. Polo, M., *The Travels of Marco Polo*, www.gutenberg.org, Book 2, Chapter 11
3. Jacobs, J., *The Death and Life of Great American Cities*, Modern Library, 1993, pp. 66–70.
4. Batty, M., *Complexity in City Systems: Understanding, Evolution and Design*, UCL Working Paper 117, March 2007, p. 2.
5. Weaver, W., 'Science and Complexity', *American Scientist* 36, 1948.
6. Ibid.
7. Jacobs, J., 1993, p. 50.
8. Koolhaas, R. et al, *Mutations*, ACTAR, 2000, p. 11.
9. Granovetter, M., 'The Strength of Weak Ties: A Network Theory Revisited', *Sociological Theory*, Volume 1, 1983, p. 2.
10. Lehrer, J., 'A Physicist Solves the City', *New York Times*, 17 December 2010.
11. Ibid.
12. Bettencourt, L. and West, G., 'A Unified Theory of Urban Living', *Nature*, 21 October 2010.
13. Lehrer, J., 17 December 2010.

CHAPTER 2: INSIDE THE BEEHIVE

1. www.bbc.co.uk/news/uk-10321233
2. Preston, C., *The Bee*, Reaktion Books, 2006, p. 55.
3. Shakespeare, *Henry V*, Act 1 Scene 2, pp. 188–92.
4. Preston, C., 2006, p. 57.
5. Hollis, L., *The Phoenix: The Men Who Made Modern London*, Weidenfeld & Nicolson, 2007, p. 339.
6. Jacobs, J., 1993, p. 40.
7. Seeley, T. D., *Beehive Democracy*, Princeton University Press, 2010, p. 5.
8. Hobbes, T., *Leviathan*, Kindle Edition, Chapter 13, paragraph 9.
9. Ai Weiwei, 'The City: Beijing', *Newsweek*, 28 August 2011.
10. Hack, K., Margolin, J.-L. et al, *Singapore from Temasek to the 21st Century: Reinventing the Global City*, NUS Press, 2010, p. 337.
11. Wood, A. T., *Asian Democracy in World History*, Routledge, 2004, p. 82.
12. Clark, G. and Moonen, T., 'The Business of Cities: City Indexes in 2011', www.thebusinessofcities.com, pp. 12–3.
13. Hack, K., Margolin, J.-L. et al, 2010, p. 325.
14. 'Singapore Faces Life without Lee', *New York Times*, 15 May 2011.
15. Ibid.
16. www.ida.gov.sg/Aboutus/20100611163838.aspx
17. Hack, K., Margolin, J.-L. et al, 2010, p. 375.
18. Ifill, G., *The Breakthrough: Politics and Race in the Age of Obama*, Doubleday, 2009, p. 143.
19. www.nytimes.com/2012/04/14/nyregion/mayor-cory-booker-says-he-felt-terror-in-fire-rescue.html?ref=corybooker
20. www.big.dk/projects/tat/
21. Dailey, K., 'Cory Booker's Snowspiration', *Newsweek*, 27 January 2011.
22. Coleman, E., *From Public Management to Open Governance: A New Future or the More Things Change the More They Stay the Same*, dissertation, University of Warwick, April 2011, p. 37.
23. Ibid., p. 36.
24. Ibid., p. 38.

CHAPTER 3: BUILDING BETWEEN BUILDINGS

1. Squires, N., 'Scientists Investigate Stendhal Syndrome', *Daily Telegraph*, 28 July

2010, www.telegraph.co.uk/news/worldnews/europe/italy/7914746/Scientists-investigate-Stendhal-Syndrome-fainting-caused-by-great-art.html

2. Barney, S. A. et al, *The Etymologies of Isidore of Seville*, CUP, 2006, Book XV.
3. Mairet, P., *Pioneer of Sociology: The Life and Letters of Patrick Geddes*, Lund Humphries, 1957, p. 184.
4. Ibid., p. 185.
5. Hollis, L., *The Stones of London: A History in Twelve Buildings*, Weidenfeld & Nicolson, 2011, p. 310.
6. Le Corbusier, *Essential Le Corbusier: L'Esprit Nouveau Articles*, Architectural Press, 1998, p. 8.
7. Ibid., p. 45.
8. Hall, P., *Cities of Tomorrow*, Blackwell, 2002, p. 222.
9. Le Corbusier, 1998, p. xxv.
10. Ibid., p. 227.
11. Jencks, C., *Le Corbusier and the Tragic View of Architecture*, Allen Lane, 1973, p. 74.
12. Flint, A., *Wrestling with Moses: How Jane Jacobs Took on New York's Master Builder and Transformed the American City*, Random House, 2011, p. 37.
13. Ibid., p. 43.
14. Rybczynski, W., *Makeshift Metropolis: Ideas About Cities*, Scribner, 2011, p. 55.
15. Flint, A., 2011, p. 87.
16. Ibid., p. 145.
17. Rybczynski, W., 2011, p. 59.
18. Jacobs, J., 1993, p. 5.
19. Whyte, W., *City: Rediscovering the Centre,* Doublday, 1988, p. 3.
20. Ibid., p. 7.
21. Ibid., p. 57.
22. Ibid., p. 9.
23. Tellinga, J., from talk, 12 November 2010, International New Town Conference, www.newtowninstitute.org
24. Gehl, J. and Koch, J., *Life Between Buildings: Using Public Space*, Island Press, 2011, p. 29.
25. Gehl, J. and Gemzoe, L., *New City Spaces*, Danish Architectural Press, 2003, p. 54.
26. Ibid., p. 58.
27. 'The Origin of the Power of Ten', www.pps.org/reference/poweroften
28. *Tactical Urbanism*, Volume 1, pp. 1–2.

CHAPTER 4: A CREATIVE PLACE

1. www.wired.co.uk/news/archive/2010–11/04/david-cameron-silicon-roundabout
2. travel.nytimes.com/2007/09/23/travel/23bilbao.html
3. www.guggenheimbilbao.es/uploads/area_prensa/notas/en/PR_Results_2010.PDF
4. www.nytimes.com/2007/02/01/arts/design/01isla.html
5. Bettencourt, L., Lobo, J. et al, *Growth Innovation, Scaling and the Pace of Life in Cities*, PNAS, 16 April 2007, p. 7, 303.
6. Schama, S., *The Embarrassment of Riches*, HarperCollins, 2004, p. 347
7. Ibid., p. 303.
8. UN, *Creative Economy*, UN, 2010, p. 38.
9. Florida, R., *Who's Your City?*, Basic Books, 2008, p. 99.
10. Moretti, E., *The New Geography of Jobs*, Houghton Mifflin, 2012, Introduction.
11. Florida, R., 2008, p. 3.
12. Ibid., p. 71.
13. www.londonlovesbusiness.com/comment/the-debate-is-tech-city-working
14. www.theatlanticcities.com/neighborhoods/2011/12/stuck-or-content/770
15. Sassen, S., *Urban Age Project*, LSE, 2011, p. 56.
16. www.techhub.com/about.html
17. www.guardian.co.uk/business/2011/nov/27/tech-city-digital-startups-shoreditch
18. Nathan, M., 2012, pp. 109–10.

CHAPTER 5: REBOOTING THE COMMUNITY

1. Novak, M. and Highfield, R., *Super Cooperators: Beyond the Survival of the Fittest*, Canongate, 2011, introduction.
2. www.economist.com/node/21541709
3. Jaffe, E., 21 March 2012, www.theatlanticcities.com/jobs-and-economy/2012/03/why-people-cities-walk-fast/1550
4. Jacobs, J., 1993, pp. 77–8.
5. Griffith, P., Norman, W., O'Sullivan, C. and Ali, R., *Charm Offensive: Cultivating Civility in 21st-Century Britain*, Young Foundation, 2011, p. 25.
6. Ibid.
7. Lindsay, G., 'Demolishing Density in Detroit', *Fast Company*, 5 March 2010.

8. www.cardiff.ac.uk/socsi/undergraduate/introsoc/simmel.html
9. Smith, D., *The Chicago School: A Liberal Critique of Capitalism*, Macmillan Education, 1988, p. 123.
10. Sorkin, M., *Twenty Minutes in Manhattan*, Reaktion Books, 2009, p. 89.
11. CEQR Technical Manual, March 2010.
12. Wilson, J. Q. and Kelling, G. L., 'Broken Windows', *Atlantic Monthly*, 1982, from www.manhattan-institute.org
13. Bratton, W. and Tumin, Z., *Collaborate or Perish: Reaching Across Boundaries in a Networked World*, Crown Business, 2012, Chapter 1.
14. Nagy, A. R. and Podolny, J., 'William Bratton and the NYPD', Yale School of Management, Yale Case 07-015, 12 February 2008, p. 14.
15. www.economist.com/node/12630201
16. Putnam, R., *Bowling Alone: The Collapse and Revival of American Community*, Simon & Schuster, 2001, p. 115.
17. Ibid., p. 19.
18. Minton, A., *Ground Control: Fear and Happiness in the 21st-Century City*, Penguin, 2009, p. 21.
19. Griffiths, R., *The Great Sharing Economy*, Cooperatives UK, Penguin, 2012, p. 1.
20. Ibid., pp. 4–11.
21. www.shareable.net/blog/policies-for-a-shareable-city
22. www.shareable.net/blog/policies-for-a-shareable-city-11-urban-agriculture
23. www.theuglyindian.com

CHAPTER 6: TRUST IN THE CITY

1. www.tampabay.com/news/humaninterest/article1221799
2. Ibid.
3. Ibid.
4. www.guardian.co.uk/world/2012/mar/23/obama-trayvon-martin-tragedy
5. Jacobs, J., 1993, p. 73.
6. Fukuyama, F., *Trust: The Social Virtues and the Creation of Prosperity*, Penguin, 1996, p. 7.
7. Putnam, R., 2001, p. 137.
8. Uslaner, E., *The Moral Foundations of Trust*, CUP, 2002, p. 33.
9. www.ipsos-mori.com/researchpublications/researcharchive/15/Trust-in-Professions.aspx
10. www.gallup.com/poll/122915/trust-state-government-sinks-new-low.aspx

11. www.gallup.com/poll/149906/Supreme-Court-Approval-Rating-Dips.aspx
12. www.gallup.com/poll/122897/Americans-Trust-Legislative-Branch-Record-Low.aspx
13. news.bbc.co.uk/1/hi/uk/8159141.stm
14. Norris, C., McCahill, M. and Wood, D., *The Growth of CCTV: A Global Perspective*, Surveillance and Society, www.surveillance-and-society.org/cctv.htm
15. NYCLU, Fall 2006, p. 2.
16. Graham, S., *Cities Under Siege: The New Military Urbanism*, Verso, 2011, p. xv
17. Graham, S., 'Olympics 2012 security: welcome to lockdown London', www.guardian.co.uk/sport/2012/mar/12/london-olympics-security-lockdown-london
18. news.bbc.co.uk/1/hi/england/leicestershire/4294693.stm
19. www.guardian.co.uk/education/2006/jun/20/highereducationprofile.academicexperts
20. Graham, S., 2011, p. 263.
21. arstechnica.com/gadgets/news/2011/08/53-of-mobile-users-happy-to-hand-over-location-data-for-coupons.ars
22. www.theinternetofthings.eu/content/new-years-contest-panopticon-metaphor-internet-things---why-not-if-it-were-opposite
23. Goodyear, S., 'Do Gated Communities Threaten Society?', 11 April 2012, www.theatlanticcities.com/neighborhoods/2012/04/do-gated-communities-threaten-society/1737
24. Wilkinson, R. and Pickett, K., *The Spirit Level: Why Equality is Better for Everyone*, Penguin, 2010, p. 62.
25. Dorling, D., *So You Think You Know About Britain*, 2011, p. 73.
26. Milanovic, B., *The Haves and the Have-Nots*, Basic Books, 2012, p. 72.
27. www.nytimes.com/interactive/2011/10/30/nyregion/where-the-one-percent-fit-in-the-hierarchy-of-income.html?ref=incomeinequality
28. UN-Habitat, *State of the World Cities 2011–12*, UN-Habitat, 2011, p. 74.
29. Ferrari Ballas, M., 'Transportation Barriers of the Women of Pudahuel', Santiago Planning Forum, 13/14, 2009, p. 124.
30. Berg, N., 'Why China's Urbanisation Isn't Creating a Middle Class', 29 February 2012, www.theatlanticcities.com/jobs-and-economy/2012/02/why-chinas-urbanization-isnt-creating-middle-class/1357
31. Lefebvre, H. (ed. Elden, S. and Kofman, E.), *Key Works*, Continuum, 2003, p. 7.
32. Harvey, D., introduction to Lefebvre, H., 1991, p. 158.

33. Lefebvre, H., trans. Nicholson-Smith, D., *The Production of Space*, Blackwell, 1991, p. 494
34. pmarcuse.wordpress.com/2012/03/25/blog-10-the-changes-in-occupy-and-the-right-to-the-city
35. Harvey's lecture can be found at www.youtube.com/watch?v=DkKX-t6lTTD4
36. Mullins, C., *Festival on the River: The Story of the Southbank*, Penguin, 2010, p. 48.
37. Burnham, S., *Trust Design*, Part Four, 'Public Trust' Supplement to Volume 30, 2011, p. 7, www.w.premsela.org
38. scottburnham.com/projects

CHAPTER 7: WALKING IN DHARAVI

1. www.bbc.co.uk/news/world-south-asia-11854177
2. Roy, A., 'Capitalism: A Ghost Story', *Outlook India*, 26 March 2012, www.outlookindia.com/article.aspx?280234
3. Kasarda, J. and Lindsay, G., *Aerotropolis: The Way We'll Live Next*, Penguin, 2011, p. 6.
4. Hollis, L., 2011, pp. 268–9.
5. Riis, J., 1889, Chapter 6, www.bartleby.com/208
6. UN-Habitat, *The Challenge of the Slums*, UN-Habitat, 2003, p. 10.
7. Perlman, J., *Favela: Decades of Living on the Edge in Rio de Janeiro*, OUP, 2010, p. 321.
8. Harber, A., *Diepsloot*, Jonathan Ball, 2012, p. 12.
9. Ibid., p. 62.
10. Neuwirth, R., *Stealth of Nations*, Pantheon Books, 2011, p. 18.
11. Ibid., p. 19.
12. Saunders, D., *Arrival City*, Vintage, 2011, Preface.
13. Arputham, J., *Developing New Approaches for People-centred Development*, Environment and Urbanisation, 2008, p. 320.
14. Ibid., pp. 332–3.
15. Ibid.
16. Ibid.
17. articles.latimes.com/2008/sep/08/
18. Echanove, M. and Srivastava, R., *The Slum Outside*, URBZ.net, 20 April 2011, p. 1.
19. de Soto, H., *The Mystery of Capital: Why Capitalism Triumphs in the West and Fails Everywhere Else*, Bantam Press, 2000, pp. 301–2.

20. Burra, S., *Community-based, Built and Managed Toilet Blocks in Indian Cities*, Environment and Urbanisation, 2003, p. 20.
21. Mehta, S., *The Urban Age*, LSE, 2011, p. 107.
22. Neuwirth, R., *Shadow Cities*, Routledge, 2004, pp. 133–4.
23. www.iisd.org/50comm/commdb/desc/d16.htm
24. Brand, S., *Whole Earth Discipline: An Ecopragmatist Manifesto*, Atlantic Books, 2010, p. 26.
25. www.forbes.com/2010/06/15/forbes-india-jockin-arputham-poverty-alleviation-opinions-ideas-10-arputham_2.html
26. www.domusweb.it/en/architecture/urbz-crowdsourcing-the-city
27. www.airoots.org
28. www.airoots.org/2009/09/the-tool-house-expanded

CHAPTER 8: MAXIMUM CITY

1. Engels, F., *The Condition of the Working Class in England*, www.marxists.org/archive/marx/works/1845/condition-working-class/ch04.htm
2. Jordan Smith, D., 'Cellphones, Social Inequality and Contemporary Culture in Nigeria', *Canadian Journal of African Studies*, no. 3, 2006, p. 500.
3. Aker, J. and Mbiti, B., 'Mobile Phones and Economic Development in Africa', Centre for Global Development Paper 211, June 2010, p. 2.
4. Ibid., p. 3.
5. Florida, R., 7 December 2011, www.theatlanticcities.com/technology/2011/12/how-twitter-proves-place-matters/663
6. www.guardian.co.uk/uk/2011/dec/07/bbm-rioters-communication-method-choice
7. www.democracynow.org/2011/2/8/asmaa_mahfouz_the_youtube_video_that
8. Nunns, A. and Idle, D., *Tweets from Tahrir*, OR Books, 2011, p. 208.
9. Ibid., p. 210.
10. Ibid.
11. UN Commission on Human Rights, *Report from OHCHR Fact-finding Mission to Kenya, 6–28 February 2008*, 19 March 2008, p. 16.
12. vimeo.com/9182869
13. david.tryse.net/googleearth/
14. www.youtube.com/watch?v=6eIPM6D-LOg&feature=player_embedded#
15. Ratti, C., 'Smart, Smarter, Smartest Cities', MIT TV, 19 April 2011, techtv.mit.edu/collections/senseable/videos/12257-smart-smarter-smartest-cities

16. Townsend, A., 'Blended Reality: What Would Jane Jacobs Think of Facebook', 12 June 2007, www.planetizen.com/node/28807
17. Southerton, D. G., *Chemulpo to Songdo IBD: Korea's International Gateway*, 2009, p. 103.
18. Post, N., 'Liveable Cities Get Smarter', *Engineering News Record*, 12 December 2011, p. 34.
19. Arthur, C., *The Thinking City*, BBC Focus, January 2012, p. 56.
20. Townsend, A., Maguire, R. et al, *A Planet of Civic Laboratories*, Institute for the Future, 2011.
21. IBM Institute for Business Value, *How Smart is Your City?*, 2009, p. 3.
22. Ibid., p. 12.
23. Ibid., p. 13.
24. Ratti, C., 'Raising the Cloud', raisethecloud.org/#project

CHAPTER 9: MOVING AROUND

1. Hammer, J., 'The World's Worst Traffic Jam', *Atlantic*, July/August 2012, www.theatlantic.com/magazine/archive/2012/07/world-8217-s-worst-traffic-jam/9006/#.T_wqIdE_-qE.email
2. www.tsp.gatech.edu/sweden/compute/cpu.htm
3. Adamatzky, A. et al, 'Are motorways rational from slime mould's point of view?' *ArXiv*, 13 March 2012, p. 1.
4. Peter, P. F., *Time, Innovation and Mobilities*, Routledge, 2006, p. 154.
5. Mayor, J. and Coleman, B., *The Social and Emotional Benefits of Good Street Design*, Brighton and Hove City Council/Civitras, August 2011, p. 27.
6. www.chinasignpost.com/2011/01/dying-for-a-spot-chinas-car-ownership-growth-is-driving-a-national-parking-space-shortage
7. Owen, D., *Green Metropolis*, Riverhead, 2010, p. 48.
8. Transport for London, *Travel in London: Key Trends and Developments*, report no. 1, TfL, 2009, pp. 2–3.
9. Walker, J., *Human Transit: How Clearer Thinking about Public Transit can Enrich our Communities*, Island Press, 2011, Introduction.
10. McKibben, B., *Hope, Human and Wild*, Milkweed Editions, 2007, p. 64.
11. Rhinehart, N., 'Public Spaces in Bogotá: An Introduction', *University of Miami Inter-America Law Review*, Winter 2009, p. 200.
12. Ibid., p. 201.
13. www.pps.org/articles/epenalosa-2
14. www.planetizen.com/node/17468

15. Rhinehart, N., 2009, p. 203.
16. Cain, A., 'Applicability of Bogotá's Transmilenio BRT System to the United States', National Bus Rapid Transit Institute, May 2006, pp. 41–2.
17. www.pps.org/articles/epenalosa-2
18. Thompson, C., 'Why New Yorkers Last Longer', 13 August 2007, nymag.com/news/features/35815/index1.html
19. www.walkonomics.com/blog/2011/04/getting-our-obese-cities-walking-again
20. Florida, R., 'America's Most Walkable Cities', 10 December 2010, www.theatlantic.com/business/archive/2010/12/americas-most-walkable-cities/67988/
21. www.telegraph.co.uk/news/worldnews/europe/france/7590210/Express-way-roads-along-Seine-to-be-closed-after-40-years.html
22. www.preservenet.com/freeways/FreewaysPompidou.html
23. www.guardian.co.uk/world/2012/aug/02/paris-seine-riverside-express-way-pedestrian

CHAPTER 10: HOW MANY LIGHTBULBS DOES IT TAKE TO CHANGE A CITY?

1. Corner, J., 'Lifescape – Fresh Kills Parkland', www.nyc.gov/freshkills park
2. Lehrer, J., 2010.
3. Glaeser, E. and Kahn, M., *The Greenness of Cities*, National Bureau of Economic Research, August 2008, p. 30.
4. Florida, R., 'Why Young Americans…', 10 April 2012, www.theatlanticcities.com/commute/2012/04/why-young-americans-are-driving-so-much-less-than-their-parents/1712
5. Kahn, M., 2010, Chapter 1.
6. Vidal, J., 'Masdar City – a Glimpse of the Future in the Desert', 26 April 2011, www.guardian.co.uk/environment/2011/apr/26/masdar-city-desert-future
7. Moore, M., 'Chinese move to the eco-city of the future', 18 March 2012, www.telegraph.co.uk/news/worldnews/asia/china/9151487/Chinese-move-to-their-eco-city-of-the-future.html
8. Williams, A. and Donald, A., *The Lure of the City: From Slums to Suburbs*, Pluto Press, 2011, p. 137.
9. www.nyc.gov/html/planyc2030/html/about/about.shtml
10. www.nyc.gov/html/dot/html/bicyclists/bikestats.shtml#crashdata

11. transalt.org/about
12. www.nytimes.com/2011/11/16/realestate/commercial/for-those-who-pedal-to-work-a-room-to-store-their-bikes.html
13. 'Greener, Greater New York', April 2011, p. 3.
14. Williams, A. and Donald, A., 2011, p. 141.
15. Beavan, C., *No Impact Man*, Piatkus, 2011, p. 183.
16. Ibid., p. 190.

CHAPTER 11: A PLACE CALLED HOME

1. Jackson, A., *London's Metroland*, Capital Transport Publishing, 2006, p. 59.
2. www.citypopulation.de/world/Agglomerations.html
3. Williams, A. and Donald, A., 2011, p. 59.
4. Ehrlich, P., *Population Bomb*, Ballentine Books, 1968, p. 1.
5. Pearce, F., *Peoplequake: Mass Migration, Ageing Nations and the Coming Population Crash*, Eden Project Books, 2010, Introduction.
6. Williams, A. and Donald, A., 2011, p. 63.
7. Ibid., p. 39.
8. UNFPA Youth Supplement, 2007, p. 7.
9. Florida, R., Gulden, T. and Mellender, C., *The Rise of the Mega-Region*, Martin Prosperity Institute, October 2007, p. 2.
10. superflex.net/tools/superkilen
11. vimeo.com/14679640
12. Davis, M., *Magical Urbanism: Latinos Reinvent the US City*, Verso, 2001, p. 67.
13. Sassen, S., 2001, p. 333.
14. www.thedailystar.net/newDesign/news-details.php?nid=238966
15. Wealth Report, KnightFrank/Citiprivatebank.com, 2012, p. 17.
16. Clark, G. and Moonen, T., *The Honor Chapman Report: London 1991–2012: The Building of a World City*, April 2012, pp. 28–36.
17. Arkarasprasertkul, N., *Politicisation and the Rhetoric of Shanghai Urbanism*, www.scholar.harvard.edu/non/publications, 2008, p. 44.
18. Campanella, T., *The Concrete Dragon: China's Urban Revolution and What it Means For the World*, Princeton Architectural Press, 2008, Introduction.

BIBLIOGRAPHY

The Stockholm Environment Programme, Stockholm City Council, 2008

The Stockholm Environment Programme 2012–2015, Stockholm City Council, 2012

PlaNYC, City of New York, 2007

PlaNYC, *A Greener, Greater, New York*, City of New York, April 2011

Inventory of New York City Greenhouse Gas Emissions, City of New York, September 2011

'Singapore Faces Life without Lee', *New York Times*, 15 May 2011

Adamatzky, A. et al, 'Are motorways rational from slime mould's point of view?', *ArXiv*, 13 March 2012, Vol 1

Ai, W., 'The City: Beijing', *Newsweek*, 28 August 2011

Aker, J. and Mbiti, I., 'Mobile Phones and Economic Development in Africa', Centre for Global Development Paper 211, June 2010

Alexiou, K., Johnson, J. and Zamenpoulos, T., *Embracing Complexity in Design*, Routledge, 2010

Amin, A. and Graham, S., *The Ordinary City*, Transactions of the Institute of British Geographers, 1997

Appleyard, D., *Liveable Streets: Protected Neighbourhoods*, Annals of American Academy of Political and Social Science, September 1980

Appleyard, D., *Liveable Streets*, Routledge, 2012

Arkarasprasertkul, N., *Politicisation and the Rhetoric of Shanghai Urbanism*, www.scholar.harvard.edu/non/publications, 2008

Arputham, J., *Developing New Approaches for People-centred Development*, Environment and Urbanisation, 2008

Arthur, C., *The Thinking City*, BBC Focus, January 2012

Barney, S. A. et al, *The Etymologies of Isidore of Seville*, CUP, 2006

Barros, J. and Sobeiera, F., *City of Slums: Self Organisation Across Scales*, CASA Working Paper 55, June 2002

Batty, M., *Cities and Complexity: Understanding Cities with Cellular Automata, Agent-based Models and Fractals*, MIT Press, 2005

Batty, M., *Complexity in City Systems: Understanding, Evolution and Design*, UCL Working Paper 117, March 2007

Beavan, C., *No Impact Man*, Piatkus, 2011

Bergdoll, B. and Martin, R., *Foreclosed: Rehousing the American Dream*, MoMA, 2012

Bettencourt, L. and West, G., 'A Unified Theory of Urban Living', *Nature*, 21 October 2010

Bettencourt, L., Lobo, J. et al, *Growth Innovation, Scaling and the Pace of Life in Cities*, PNAS, 16 April 2007

Bound, K. and Thornton, I., *Our Frugal Future*, NESTA, July 2012

Brand, S., *Whole Earth Discipline: An Ecopragmatist Manifesto*, Atlantic Books, 2010

Bratton, W. and Tumin, Z., *Collaborate or Perish: Reaching Across Boundaries in a Networked World*, Crown Business, 2012

Brugman, J., *Welcome to the Urban Revolution: How cities are changing the world*, Bloomsbury Press, 2010

Bucher, U. and Finka, M., *The Electronic City*, BWV, 2008

Burdett, R. and Rode, P., *Cities: Towards a Green Economy*, UNEP, 2011

Burnham, S., *Trust Design*, Part Four, 'Public Trust' supplement to Volume 30, 2011, www.premsela.org

Burra, S., *Towards a Pro-poor Framework for Slum Upgrading in Mumbai, India*, Environment and Urbanisation, 2005

Burra, S., *Community-based, Built and Managed Toilet Blocks in Indian Cities*, Environment and Urbanisation, 2003

Burrell, J., *Livelihoods and the Mobile Phone in Rural Uganda*, Grameen Foundation, USA, January 2008

Burrows, E. G. and Wallace, M., *Gotham: A History of New York City to 1898*, OUP, 1999

Cacioppo, J. and Patrick, W., *Loneliness: Human Nature and the Need for Social Connection*, W. W. Norton, 2009

Cain, A., 'Applicability of Bogotá's Transmilenio BRT System to the United States', National Bus Rapid Transit Institute, May 2006

Calabrese, F., Smordeda, Z., Blondel, V. and Ratti, C., 'Interplay Between

Telecommunications and Face-to-Face Interactions: A Study Using Mobile Phone Data', *PLoS ONE*, July 2011

Campanella, T., *The Concrete Dragon: China's Urban Revolution and What it Means for the World*, Princeton Architectural Press, 2008

Canetti, E., *Crowds and Power*, Penguin, 1992

Chang, L. T., *Factory Girls*, Picador, 2010

Clark, G. and Moonen, T., 'The Business of Cities: City Indexes in 2011', www.thebusinessofcities.com

Clark, G. and Moonen, T., *The Honor Chapman Report: London 1991–2012: The Building of a World City*, April 2012

Coleman, E., *From Public Management to Open Governance: A New Future or the More Things Change the More They Stay the Same*, dissertation, University of Warwick, April 2011

Dailey, K., 'Cory Booker's Snowspiration', 27 January 2011

Dalton, R. J., 'The Social Transformation of Trust in Government', *International Review of Sociology*, January 2005

Daly, I., 'Data Cycle', *Wired UK*, April 2011

Davis, M., *Ecology of Fear: Los Angeles and the Imagination of Disaster*, Picador, 1999

Davis, M., *Magical Urbanism: Latinos Reinvent the US City*, Verso, 2001

Davis, M., *Planet of Slums*, Verso, 2007

De Hartog, H., *Shanghai New Towns: Searching for Community and Identity in a Sprawling Metropolis*, 010 Publishers, 2010

Desai, V., 'Dharavi, the Biggest Slum in Asia', *Habitat International*, Volume 12, no. 2, 1988

de Soto, H., *The Mystery of Capital: Why Capitalism Triumphs in the West and Fails Everywhere Else*, Bantam Press, 2000

Dittrich, C., *Bangalore: Globalisation and Fragmentation in India's High Tech Capital*, ASIEN, April 2007

Dorigo, M. and Gambardella, L. M., *Ant Colonies for the Travelling Salesman Problem*, Biosystems, 1997

Dorling, D., *Injustice*, Polity Press, 2009

Dorling, D., *So You Think You Know About Britain*, Constable, 2011

Dorling, D., *The No-Nonsense Guide to Inequality*, New Internationalist, 2012

Downs, L. B., *Diego Rivera: the Detroit Industry Murals*, Detroit Institute of Arts/W.W. Norton, 1999

Echanove, M. and Srivastava, R., *The Slum Outside*, URBZ.net, 20 April 2011

Echanove, M. and Srivastava, R., 'The Village Inside', from Goldsmith, S. and Elizabeth, L., *The Urban Wisdon of Jane Jacobs*, Routledge, 2012

Echanove, M. and Srivastava, R., 'The High Rise and the Slum: Speculative Urban Development in Mumbai', from Weber, R. and Crane, R., *The Oxford Handbook of Urban Planning*, OUP, 2012

Echeverry, J.-C., Ibanez, A.-M., Moya, A. and Hillon, L.-C., 'The Economics of Transmilenio: a Mass-Transit System for Bogotá', *Economia*, Spring 2005

Ehrenhalt, A., *The Great Inversion and the Future of the American City*, Knopf, 2012

Ehrlich, P., *Population Bomb*, Ballentine Books, 1968

Engels, F., *The Condition of the Working Class in England*, 1845, www.marxists.org/archive/marx/works/1845/condition-working-class/ch04.htm

Evans, K. F., *Maintaining Community in the Information Age: The Importance of Trust, Place and Situated Knowledge*, Palgrave Macmillan, 2004

Fainstein, S., *The Just City*, Cornell University Press, 2010

Ferrari Ballas, M., 'Transportation Barriers of the Women of Pudahuel', Santiago Planning Forum, 13/14, 2009

Fischer, C., *To Dwell Among Friends: Personal Networks in Town and Country*, University of Chicago Press, 1982

Flint, A., *Wrestling with Moses: How Jane Jacobs Took on New York's Master Builder and Transformed the American City*, Random House, 2011

Florida, R., *The Rise of the Creative Classes*, Random House, 2002

Florida, R., *Cities and the Creative Class*, Routledge, 2004

Florida, R., *Who's Your City?*, Basic Books, 2008

Florida, R. and Scott Jackson, M., 'Sonic City: The Evolving Economic Geography of the Music Industry', *Journal of Planning, Education and Research*, 2009

Florida, R., Gulden, T. and Mellender, C., *The Rise of the Mega-Region*, Martin Prosperity Institute, October 2007

Franklin, J., *Politics, Trust and Networks: Social Capital in Critical Perspective*, London South Bank University, 2004

Fukuyama, F., *Trust: The Social Virtues and the Creation of Prosperity*, Penguin, 1996

Gandhi, S., 'Housing Mumbai's Poor', *Economic & Political Weekly*, 22 September 2007

Gehl, J. and Koch, J., *Life Between Buildings: Using Public Space*, Island Press, 2011

Gehl, J. and Gemzoe, L., *New City Spaces*, Danish Architectural Press, 2003

Gillespie, A., *Whose Black Politics? Cases in Post-Racial Black Leadership*, Routledge, 2010

Gittleman, M. et al, *Community Garden Survey*, NYC, 2009/10, www.greenthumbnyc.org

GLA (ed. Lorna Spence), *A Profile of Londoners by Country of Birth*, GLA, February 2008

GLA Transport Committee, *The Future of Road Congestion in London*, GLA, June, 2011

Glaeser, E., Resseger, M. and Tobio, K., *Urban Inequality*, Taubman Centre for State and Local Government, 2008–10

Glaeser, E., *The Triumph of the City: How Our Greatest Invention Makes Us Richer, Smarter, Greener, Healthier and Happier*, Macmillan, 2011

Glaeser, E. and Kahn, M., *The Greenness of Cities*, National Bureau of Economic Research, August 2008

Goldsmith, S. and Elizabeth, L., *What We See: Advancing the Observations of Jane Jacobs*, New Village Press, 2010

Goodman, J., Laube, M. and Schwenk, J., 'Curitiba's Bus System is Model for Rapid Transit', *Race, Poverty & the Environment*, Winter 2005–6

Graham, S., *Cities Under Siege: The New Military Urbanism*, Verso, 2011

Graham, S., 'Olympics 2012 security: welcome to lockdown London', *Guardian*, 12 March 2012

Graham, S. and Marvin, S., *Splintering Urbanism: Networked Structures and Technological Mobilities*, Routledge, 2001

Granovetter, M., 'The Strength of Weak Ties: A Network Theory Revisited', *Sociological Theory*, Volume 1, 1983

Green, J., 'Digital Urban Renewal', *Ovum*, April 2011

Grice, K. and Drakakis-Smith, D., 'The Role of the State in Shaping Development: Two Decades of Growth in Singapore', *Transaction of the Institute of British Geographers*, Volume 10, no. 3, 1985

Griffith, P., Norman, W., O'Sullivan, C. and Ali, R., *Charm Offensive: Cultivating Civility in 21st-Century Britain*, Young Foundation, 2011

Griffiths, R., *The Great Sharing Economy*, Cooperatives UK, 2012

Hack, K., Margolin, J.-L. et al, *Singapore from Temasek to the 21st Century: Reinventing the Global City*, NUS Press, 2010

Hall, P., *Cities of Tomorrow*, Blackwell, 2002

Hallo, W., 'Antediluvian Cities', *Journal of Cuneiform Studies*, Volume 23, no. 3, 1971

Harber, A., *Diepsloot*, Jonathan Ball, 2012

Harvey, D., *Rebel Cities: From the Right to the City to the Urban Revolution*, Verso, 2012

Hauptmann, D. and Neidich, W., *Cognitive Architecture*, 010 Publishers, 2010

Haynes, J., *Thanks for Coming!*, Faber & Faber, 1984

Helliwell, J. F. and Barrington-Leigh, C. P., 'How Much is Social Capital Worth?', working paper 16025, National Bureau of Economic Research, 2010

Hobbes, T., *Leviathan*, 1651, Kindle edition

Hollis, L., *The Phoenix: The Men Who Made Modern London*, Weidenfeld & Nicolson, 2008

Hollis, L., *The Stones of London: A History in Twelve Buildings*, Weidenfeld & Nicolson, 2011

Hollis, M., *Trust Within Reason*, CUP, 1998

Hoskins, G., *Trust: Money, Markets and Society*, Seagull Books, 2011

IBM Institute for Business Value, *How Smart is Your City?*, 2009

IBM Institute for Business Value, *A Vision of Smarter Cities*, 2009

Ifill, G., *The Breakthrough: Politics and Race in the Age of Obama*, Doubleday, 2009

Isidore of Seville (ed. Barney, S., Lewis W. J., Beach, A. and Berghord, O.), *The Etymologies of Isidore of Seville*, CUP, 2006

Jacobs, J., *The Death and Life of Great American Cities*, Modern Library, 1993

Jacobs, J., *The Economy of Cities*, Pelican, 1972

Jacobs, J., *Dark Ages Ahead*, Vintage, 2006

Jackson, A., *London's Metroland*, Capital Transport Publishing, 2006

Jaffe, A. B., 'Technological Opportunity and Spillovers of R & D', *American Economic Review*, December 1986

Jencks, C., *Le Corbusier and the Tragic View of Architecture*, Allen Lane, 1973

Jencks, C., *The Architecture of the Jumping Universe*, Academy Editions, 1995

Johnson, N., *Two's Company, Three's Complexity*, OneWorld, 2007

Johnson, S., *Emergence: The Connected Lives of Ants, Brains, Cities and Software*, Penguin, 2002

Johnson, S., *Where Good Ideas Come From: The Natural History of Innovation*, Penguin, 2010

Jordan Smith, D., 'Cell Phones, Social Inequality and Contemporary Culture in Nigeria', *Canadian Journal of African Studies*, no. 3, 2006

Kasarda, J. and Lindsay, G., *Aerotropolis: The Way We'll Live Next*, Penguin, 2011

Kingsley, P., 'Tech City: The Magic Roundabout', www.guardian.co.uk/business/2011/nov/27/tech-city-digital-startups-shoreditch

Knowles, R., 'The Solar Envelope: Its Meaning for Energy and Buildings', *Energy and Buildings*, 35, 2003

Kohn, M., *Trust: Self-Interest and the Common Good*, OUP, 2008

Kolbert, E., 'Green Like Me', *New Yorker*, 31 August 2009

Kolesnikov-Jessop, S., 'Singapore Exports Its Government Expertise in Urban Planning', *New York Times*, 27 April 2010

Komninos, N., *Intelligent Cities and Globalisation of Innovation Network*, Routledge, 2008

Koolhaas, R. et al, *Mutations*, ACTAR, 2000

Krane, J., *Dubai: The Story of the World's Fastest City*, Atlantic Books, 2010

Krugman, P., *The Self-Organising Economy*, Blackwell, 1996

Kuhn, M., *Climatopolis*, Basic Books, 2010

Lammer, S. and Hebling, D., 'Self Control of Traffic Lights and Vehicle Flow in Urban Road Networks', *Journal of Statistical Mechanics*, 2008

Landry, C., *Creativity and the City: Thinking Through the Steps*, 2005, www.charles-landry.com

Landry, C., *Lineage of the Creative City*, 2006, www.charleslandry.com

Landry, C., *The Creative City*, Earthscan, 2000

Landry, C., *The Art of City Making*, Earthscan, 2006

Le Corbusier, *Essential Le Corbusier: L'Esprit Nouveau Articles*, Architectural Press, 1998

Lefebvre, H. (ed. Elden, S. and Kofman, E.), *Key Works*, Continuum, 2003

Lefebvre, H., trans. Nicholson-Smith, D., *The Production of Space*, Blackwell, 1991

Lehrer, J., 'A Physicist Solves the City', *New York Times*, 17 December 2010

Lehrer, J., *Imagine: How Creativity Works*, Canongate, 2012

Lindsay, G., 'Demolishing Density in Detroit', *Fast Company*, 5 March 2010

Lindsay G., *Instant Cities*, www.greglindsay.org

Lydon, M., Bartman, D., Woudstra, R. and Khawarzad, A., *Tactical Urbanism*, Volume 1, Next Generation of New Urbanists, 2011

Lydon, M., Bartman, D., Woudstra, R. and Khawarzad, A., *Tactical Urbanism*, Volume 2, Next Generation of New Urbanists, 2012

McKibben, B., *Hope, Human and Wild*, Milkweed Editions, 2007

McKinsey Reports, *East London: World Class Centre for Digital Enterprise*, McKinsey, March 2011

Mairet, P., *Pioneer of Sociology: The Life and Letters of Patrick Geddes*, Lund Humphries, 1957

Mak, G., trans. Blom, P., *Amsterdam*, Harvill, 1999

Mandeville, B., *The Fable of the Bees*, 1715, oll.libertyfund.org

Marshall, G. and Batty, M., 'Geddes's Grand Theory: Life, Evolution, Social Union, and "The Grand Transition"', UCL Working Papers Series, 162, September 2010

Martin, R., Meisterlin, L. and Kenoff, A., *The Buell Hypothesis*, buellcenter.org/buell-hypothesis.php

Mayinger, F., *Mobility and Traffic in the 21st Century*, Springer, 2001

Mayor, J. and Coleman, B., *The Social and Emotional Benefits of Good Street Design*, Brighton and Hove City Council/Civitas, August 2011

Mehta, S., *The Urban Age*, LSE, 2011

Middleton, N., Gunnell, D. et al, 'Urban-Rural Differences in Suicide Rates in Young Adults: England and Wales: 1981–1998', *Social Science and Medicine*, 57, 2003

Milanovic, B., *The Haves and the Have-Nots*, Basic Books, 2012

Miller, P., *Smart Swarm*, Collins, 2012

Minton, A., *Ground Control: Fear and Happiness in the 21st-Century City*, Penguin, 2009

Misztal, B., *Trust in Modern Society*, Polity Press, 1996

Modorov, E., *The Net Delusion: How Not to Liberate the World*, Penguin, 2011

Moretti, E., *The New Geography of Jobs*, Houghton Mifflin, 2012

Morris, I., *Why the West Rules for Now: the Patterns of History and What They Reveal about the Future*, Profile Books, 2010

Mullins, C., *Festival on the River: The Story of the Southbank*, Penguin, 2010

Nagy, A. R. and Podolny, J., 'William Bratton and the NYPD', Yale School of Management, Yale Case 07–015, 12 February 2008

Nathan, M., Vandore, E. and Whitehead, R., *A Tale of Tech City: The Future of Inner East London's Digital Economy*, The Centre for London, July 2012

Neuwirth, R., *Shadow Cities*, Routledge, 2004

Neuwirth, R., *Stealth of Nations*, Pantheon Books, 2011

New York Civil Liberties Union, *Who's Watching? Video Camera Surveillance in New York City and the Need for Public Oversight*, New York Civil Liberties Union, Fall 2006

New York, *Dept of Design and Construction Active Design Guidelines*, NYC, 2010

Norris, C., McCahill, M. and Wood, D., *The Growth of CCTV: A Global Perspective*, Surveillance and Society, www.surveillance-and-society.org/cctv.htm

Novak, M. and Highfield, R., *SuperCooperators: Beyond the Survival of the Fittest*, Canongate, 2011

Nunns, A. and Idle, N., *Tweets from Tahrir*, OR Books, 2011

Oldenburg, C., *The Great Good Place*, Da Capo, 1999

O'Neill, O., *A Question of Trust*, CUP, 2002

Ostrom, E., *Governing the Commons: The Evolution of Institutions for Collective Action*, CUP 1990

Owen, D., *Green Metropolis*, Riverhead, 2010

Owen, D., 'The Efficiency Dilemma', *New Yorker*, 20 December 2010

Patel, S. and Arputham, J., 'An Offer of Partnership or a Promise of Conflict in Dharavi, Mumbai', *Environment and Urbanisation*, 2007

Patel, S. and Arputham, J., 'Plans for Dharavi', *Environment and Urbanisation*, 2008

Patel, S., Burra, S. and D'Cruz, C., 'Slum/Shack Dwellers International (SDI) – Foundations to Treetops', *Environment and Urbanisation*, 2001

Patel, S., Arputham, J., Burra, S. and Savchuk, K., 'Getting the Information Base for Dharavi's Redevelopment', *Environment and Urbanisation*, 2009

Patel, S. and Mitlin, D., 'Gender Issues and Slum/Shack Dweller Foundation', IIED, Gender and Urban Federations, 2007

Pearce, F., *Peoplequake: Mass Migration, Ageing Nations and the Coming Population Crash*, Eden Project Books, 2010

Pereira, F., Vaccari, A., Glardin, F., Chiu, C. and Ratti, C., 'Crowd Sensing in the Web: Analysing the Citizen Experience in the Urban Space', senseable.mit.edu/papers/publications.html

Perlman, J., *Favela: Decades of Living on the Edge in Rio de Janeiro*, OUP, 2012

Peter, P. F., *Time, Innovation and Mobilities*, Routledge, 2006

Polo, M., *The Travels of Marco Polo*, www.gutenberg.org

Posshehl, G. L., 'Revolution in the Urban Revolution: The Emergence of Indus Urbanisation', *Annual Review of Anthropology*, Volume 19, 1990

Post, N., 'Liveable Cities Get Smarter', *Engineering News Record*, 12 December 2011

Preston, C., *The Bee*, Reaktion Books, 2006

Pricewaterhouse Coopers, *Cities of Opportunity*, http://www.pwc.com/us/en/cities-of-opportunity/index.jhtml

Project for Public Spaces, *How to Turn a Place Around: A Handbook for Creating Successful Public Spaces*, Project for Public Spaces, 2000

Putnam, R., *Bowling Alone: The Collapse and Revival of American Community*, Simon & Schuster, 2001

Rae, D., *Urbanism and its End*, Yale University Press, 2003

Ramirez, J. A., *The Beehive Metaphor: From Gaudi to Le Corbusier*, Reaktion Books, 2000

Rasmussen, S., *London: the Unique City*, MIT Press, 1988

Ratti, C. and Townsend, A., 'The Social Nexus', *American Scientist*, September 2011

Rees, M., *Warren Weaver: A Biographical Memoir*, National Academy of Science, 1987

Reid, S. and Shore, F., *Valuing Urban Realm*, TfL, September 2008

Resch, B., Britter, R. and Ratti, C., *Live Urbanism: Towards Senseable Cities and Beyond*, senseable.mit.edu/papers/publications.html

Rhinehart, N., 'Public Spaces in Bogotá: An Introduction', *University of Miami Inter-America Law Review*, Winter 2009

Riis, J., *The Making of an American*, Macmillan Company, 1902

Riis, J., *How the Other Half Live*, www.authentichistory.com

Rogers, R. and Power, A., *Cities for a Small Country*, Faber & Faber, 2000

Roisin, H., 'The End of Men', *Atlantic*, July 2010

Roy, A., 'Capitalism: A Ghost Story', *Outlook India*, 26 March 2012

RTTC-NY, *People Without Homes and Homes Without People: A Count of Vacant Condos in Select NYC Neighborhoods*, 2010

Rybczynski, W., *Makeshift Metropolis: Ideas About Cities*, Scribner, 2010

Saini, A., *Geek Nation*, Hodder & Stoughton, 2010

Sassen, S., *The Global City*, Princeton University Press, second edition 2001

Sassen, S., 'Cityness in the Urban Age', *Urban Age Bulletin*, Autumn 2005

Sassen, S., *Cities in a World Economy*, Pine Forge Press, 2005

Satterthwaite, D., 'From Professionally Driven to People-Driven Property Reduction', *Environment & Urbanisation*, Volume 13, no. 2, October 2001

Saunders, D., *Arrival City*, Vintage, 2011

Schama, S., *The Embarrassment of Riches*, HarperCollins, 2004

Scocca, T., *Beijing Welcomes You: Unveiling the Capital City of the Future*, Riverhead, 2011

Seeley, T. D., *Beehive Democracy*, Princeton University Press, 2010

Senior, J., 'Alone Together', *New York Magazine*, 23 November 2008

Sennett, R., *The Conscience of the Eye: The Design and Social Life of Cities*, W. W. Norton, 2002

Sennett, R., *The Fall of Public Man*, Faber & Faber, 2003

Sennett, R., *Togetherness*, Allen Lane, 2012

Shoup, D., *The High Price of Free Parking*, Planners Press, 2011

Sloan Wilson, D., *The Neighborhood Project: Using Evolution to Improve My City One Block at a Time*, Little, Brown, 2011

Smith, D., *The Chicago School: A Liberal Critique of Capitalism*, Macmillan Education, 1988

Smith, K., Brown, B. B. et al, 'Walkability and Body Mass Index: Density, Design and New Diversity Measures', *American Journal of Preventative Medicine*, 35 (3), 2008

Sorkin, M., *Twenty Minutes in Manhattan*, Reaktion Books, 2009

Sorkin, M., *All Over the Map*, Verso, 2011

Southerton, D. G., *Chemulpo to Songdo IBD: Korea's International Gateway*, 978–0–615–29978–5, 2009

Squires, N., 'Scientists Investigate Stendhal Syndrome', *Daily Telegraph*, 28 July 2010

Stremlau, J., 'Dateline Bangalore: Third World Technopolis', *Foreign Policy*, Spring 1996

Sudjic, D., *The Edifice Complex*, Penguin, 2005

Townsend, A., Maguire, R. et al, *A Planet of Civic Laboratories*, Institute for the Future, 2011

Transport for London, *Travel in London: Key Trends and Developments*, report no. 1, TfL, 2009

UN Commission on Human Rights, *Report from OHCHR Fact-finding Mission to Kenya, 6–28 February 2008*, 19 March 2008

UN, *Creative Economy*, UN, December 2010

UN-Habitat, *The Challenge of the Slums*, UN-Habitat, 2003

UN-Habitat, *State of the World Cities 2011–12*, UN-Habitat, 2011

UNPFA, *State of the World Population 2007*, UNPFA, 2007

Urban Age Project, LSE, Deutsche Bank's Alfred Herrhausen Society, *The Endless City*, Phaidon, 2011

Urban Age Project, LSE, Deutsche Bank's Alfred Herrhausen Society, *Living in the Endless City*, Phaidon, 2011

Uslander, E., *The Moral Foundations of Trust*, CUP, 2002

Vanderbilt, T., *Traffic: Why We Drive the Way We Do (and What It Says About Us)*, Allen Lane, 2008

Waldron, R., *Home Ownership in the Dublin City Region: The Bubble and Its Aftermath*, docs.google.com/viewer?a=v&q=cache:3GR-6hrbkOYJ

Walker, J., *Human Transit: How Clearer Thinking about Public Transit Can Enrich Our Communities*, Island Press, 2011

Walljasper, J., *All That We Share: A Field Guide to the Commons*, The New Press, 2010

Weber, R. and Craine, R., *The Oxford Handbook of Urban Planning*, OUP, 2012

Weaver, W., 'Science and Complexity', *American Scientist* 36, 1948

Welter, V. M., *Biopolis: Patrick Geddes and the City of Life*, MIT Press, 2002

Whyte, W. H., *City: Rediscovering the Centre*, Doubleday, 1988

Whyte, W. H. (ed. Goldberger, P.), *The Essential William H. Whyte*, Fordham University Press, 2000

Wilkinson, R. and Pickett, K., *The Spirit Level: Why Equality is Better for Everyone*, Penguin, 2010

Williams, A. and Donald, A., *The Lure of the City: From Slums to Suburbs*, Pluto Press, 2011

Wilson, J. Q. and Kelling, G. L., 'Broken Windows', *Atlantic Monthly*, 1982, from www.manhattan-institute.org

Wirth, L., 'Urbanism as a Way of Life', *American Journal of Sociology*, 1938

Wood, A. T., *Asian Democracy in World History*, Routledge, 2004

Yuan, J., Zheng, Y., Xie, X. and Sun, G., 'T-Drive: Enhancing Driving Directions with Taxi Drivers' Intelligence', SIGSPATIAL, 2010

Zukin, S., *Loft Living: Culture and Capital in Urban Change*, Rutgers University Press, 1989

Zukin, S., *The Naked City*, OUP, 2010

ACKNOWLEDGEMENTS

There are many people to thank for this book. This has been a project that has connected me to many different people in many different places – more of an adventure than a writing exercise. Most importantly, thanks to the K. Blundell Trust whose generosity allowed me to travel and see some of the cities in the book for myself. Thanks also go to: Fran Tonkiss, Mike Batty, Jeremy Black, Michael Sorkin, Rahul and Matias at URBZ, Elizabeth Varley, Scott Burnham, Emer Coleman, Rick Burdett; Patrick Walsh, Claire Conville, Jake Bosanquet-Smith and Alex Christofi; Helen Garnons-Williams and Erica Jarnes; George Gibson and Jacqueline Johnson.

This book is dedicated to Louis and Theadora because the city will one day belong to you and you must see it as an adventure, not a place of danger.

INDEX

A NOTE ON THE AUTHOR

Leo Hollis was born in London in 1972. He went to school at Stonyhurst College and read History at UEA. He works in publishing and is the author of two books on the history of London: *The Phoenix: The Men Who Made Modern London* and *The Stones of London: A History Through Twelve Buildings*. He writes regularly for the *New Statesman*, *TLS* and *Daily Telegraph*.

www.citiesaregoodforyou.com
@leohollis